ICONS &
IDENTITIES

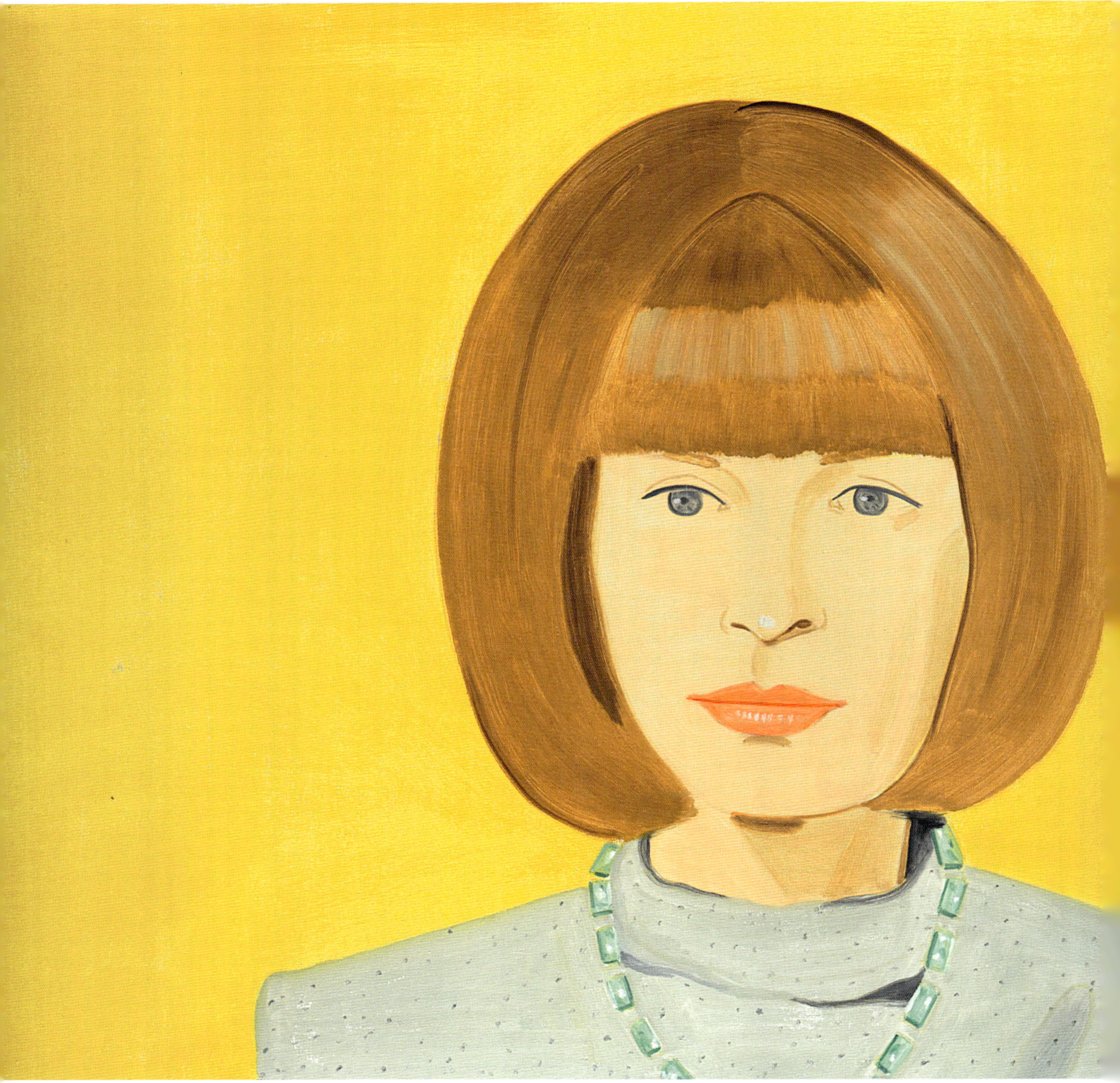

ICONS & IDENTITIES

Edited by Rab MacGibbon and Tanya Bentley

NATIONAL PORTRAIT GALLERY, LONDON

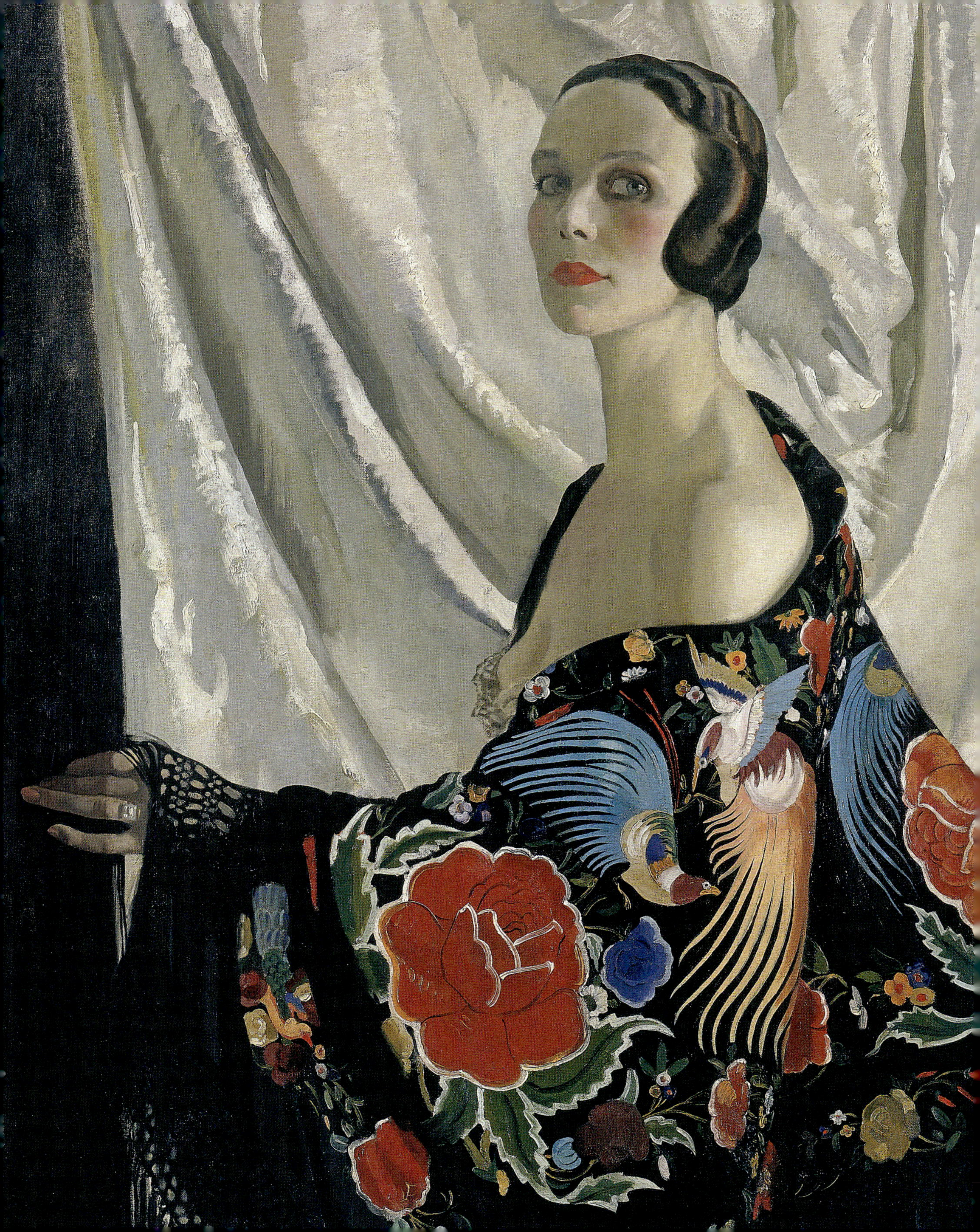

Contents

Director's Foreword

The National Portrait Gallery is one of only a rare few institutions in the world solely dedicated to portraiture. Founded in 1856, it is the oldest national gallery of portraits, and houses some of the most accomplished depictions of eminent people produced over the last 500 years. The genre of portraiture is varied and constantly evolving, as can be seen in the selection of works in this book. *Icons and Identities* features some of the most well-known faces in British and international history, from Queen Elizabeth I to Nelson Mandela (see p.47 and p.57), as well as the most acclaimed portraitists, from Sir Antony van Dyck to David Hockney and Lucian Freud (see p.67, pp.118–19 and pp.127–8). The book prompts questions that we at the National Portrait Gallery consider daily: what is it that makes someone an 'icon', and how have the outstanding contributions of such icons to society shaped our world today? In turn, how are aspects of a person's identity, often multifaceted, shown in their portrait, and does the final image present them as icon or not?

Icons and Identities moves away from a more traditional chronological approach and instead provides an overview of some of the key themes at the core of portraiture's fascination. The thematic groupings allow for thought-provoking conversations between sitters and artists across time and space. In 'Fame', Britain's best-loved poets from the sixteenth and twentieth centuries, William Shakespeare – the Gallery's very first acquisition in 1856, and a cornerstone portrait for us in reputedly being the only image of him painted from life – and Dylan Thomas sit side by side (see pp.24–5), a nod to Shakespeare's profound influence on Thomas from when he was just a young boy. In 'Identity', the visual pairing of the eighteenth-century soldier, diplomat and fencer the Chevalier d'Éon and the twentieth-century writer Radclyffe Hall (see pp.82–3) illustrates how societal gender norms were defied across the centuries in Britain. In 'Power', the portraits of Louise Jopling by Sir John Everett Millais and Malala Yousafzai by Shirin Neshat (see pp.62–3) share a defiant gaze, while the sitters also share ambitions for bettering female education.

This publication accompanies the Gallery's international touring exhibition *Icons and Identities*, a once-in-a-generation opportunity to see a selection of it's most cherished portraits together internationally, while in London the Gallery is temporarily closed as it undergoes a major transformation. We are delighted to be able to share the Gallery's Collection in such an unprecedented way for new audiences to enjoy. We would like to thank the directors and staff of our initial partner museums, in particular Byoungchan Min at the National Museum of Korea and Kris Callens at the Fries Museum in the Netherlands. Their collaboration, enthusiasm and commitment to the exhibition were instrumental to its realisation.

I am grateful to colleagues Rab MacGibbon and Tanya Bentley for curating the exhibition, and for the insightful essay, in which Rab expands on the complexities of the portrait genre and gives a fresh account of the Gallery's institutional history. Thanks also go to Melanie Pilbrow, Head of International Programmes, and Imogen Haines, International Projects Manager, for expertly organising the exhibition tour.

Nicholas Cullinan
Director, National Portrait Gallery, London

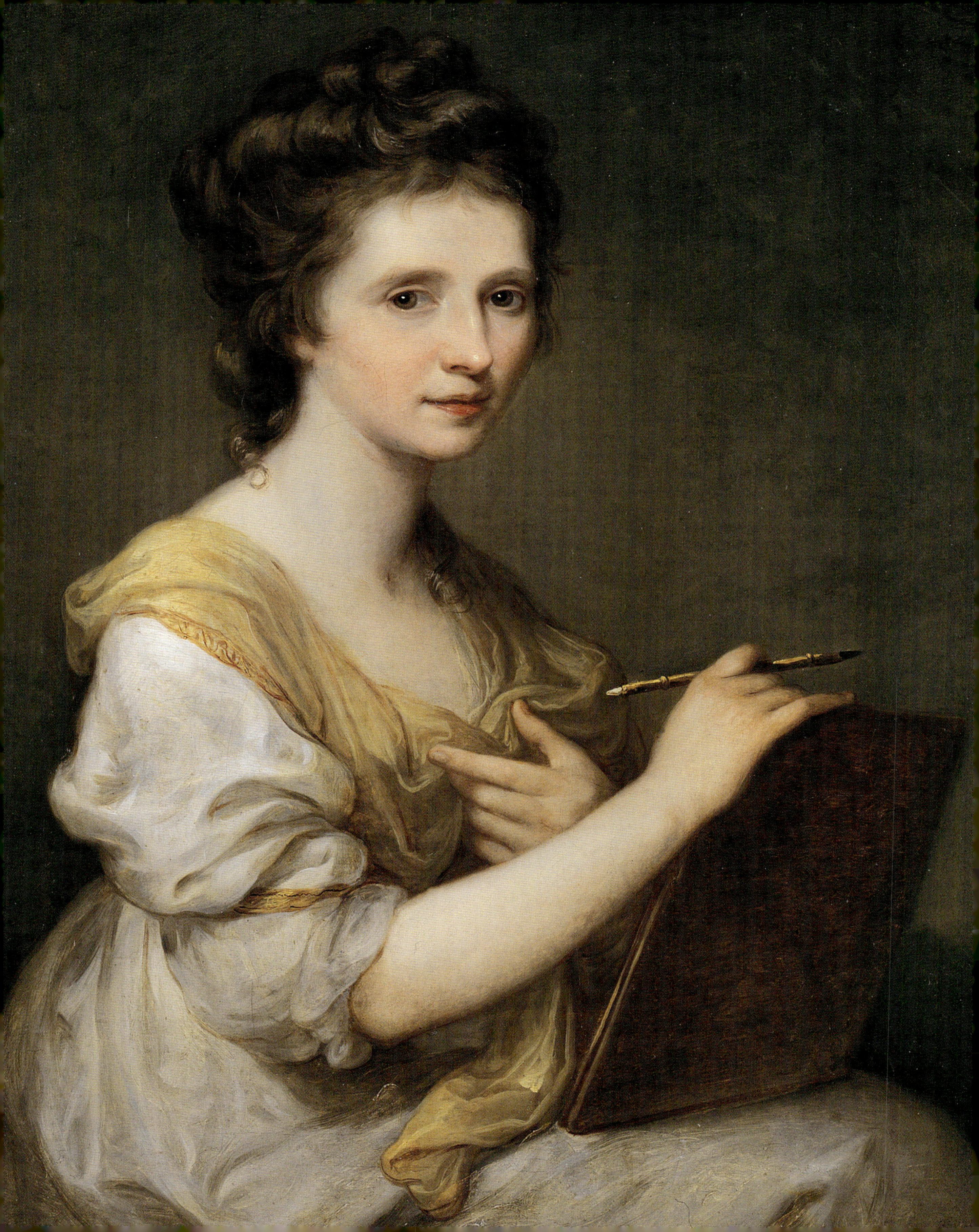

Icons and Identities

Rab MacGibbon

CATCHING THE EYE

Many of us have experienced a strange sensation while visiting an art gallery. Passing in front of a portrait, we feel that the painted eyes are somehow following us. Rationally we know that the fabricated face cannot possibly be sentient, but the uncanny sense remains that our gaze is being reciprocated. Far from being foolish, this psychological role reversal between viewer and art object is a key to unlocking the enduring and wide-ranging fascination of portraits.

From birth, humans learn to respond critically to human faces. We quickly become adept at interpreting expressions and body language. At the earliest stage and at its most basic level lies the question: is this person a source of comfort or a potential threat? Even as our perception grows in sophistication, our brains can never entirely overcome our instincts. The need for social interaction is so fundamental to our nature that it can sometimes override, or at the very least complicate, our perception of a portrait as a constructed representation rather than a living person. Viewing a portrait therefore involves a visual and mental dance between looking at an image and engaging with it as a proxy for the person represented. We can appreciate the artistic techniques involved in its creation – such as the artist's manipulation of their medium, the form, colour, composition – and we can contemplate the mysterious sense of an encounter with the portrait's subject. It can involve a form of imaginative time travel, proving a sense of communion with a sitter who has been dead for centuries. Reading the visual clues, we can speculate about the sitter's emotions, character and their life beyond the image.

DETAIL **Angelica Kauffmann, c.1770–5**

Portraits invite us to ask a host of questions: why has the sitter been represented this way? Is the image a reliable record of their appearance? Where was it intended to be seen and by whom? And what does it suggest about the society in which it was made? This combination of our instinctive responses to a fellow human and reflections on the questions that portraits raise make them at once the most immediately engaging and accessible art genre and also the most multifaceted and rewarding for further exploration.

Icons and Identities draws upon the exceptional collections of the National Portrait Gallery, London, to investigate and celebrate the variety and complexity of the genre. It draws together 'icons' – the most famous faces from British history, from Queen Elizabeth I and Sir Isaac Newton (see p.47 and p.33) to Audrey Hepburn and The Beatles (see p.108 and pp.36–7) – alongside less well-known sitters, who provide a fascinating insight into the representation of identity in portraits. Identity comprises elements that make a person unique, as well as aspects that connect them to a wider group. An individual's identity is subject to change, and different facets may be foregrounded at different times, be they nationality, religion, profession, gender, ethnicity, sexuality or others. The rich variety of methods utilised by artists to convey a sense of the sitter's identity, or identities, is a thread that runs throughout this selection of portraits. This exploration of portraiture presents the works in non-chronological groups that seek to open up new dialogues between works that may initially appear disparate.

The portraits under discussion draw from the Western tradition of art, which has historically valued the illusionistic representation of physical appearance. Portraits have been further enriched by symbolic and emblematic cues, such as clothing, inscriptions bearing the sitter's name and ancestry, or a wider pictorial narrative to convey a sense of the individual. Significant portrait traditions have flourished in many non-Western societies. Other cultures have developed creative means of expressing personal identity that are not dependent on conveying physical likeness.

The act of representation, and questions about who is represented and in what manner, have always been contested. Portraits have held opposite meanings to different people and at different times. Portraits of rulers have been used to legitimise and reinforce their authority, and those same portraits have been attacked to symbolise the ruler's fall. Acts of iconoclasm affirm the power of portraits both as a proxy for the person represented and the wider meanings that they embody.

A GALLERY OF FACES

The dual nature of portraits lies at the heart of the National Portrait Gallery. It is both a gallery of art and a museum of people. While an assessment of a portrait's artistic merits is important, the key focus has always been the significance of the portrait's subject. Founded in 1856, it is the oldest national gallery of portraits, and houses the world's most extensive portrait collection. It was established by Parliament under the guidance of the politician Philip Stanhope, the historian Thomas Babington Macaulay and the biographer and essayist Thomas Carlyle, who wrote: 'Often I have found a portrait superior in real instruction to half-a-dozen written biographies ... I have found that a portrait was a small lighted candle by which the biographies could for the first time be read, and some human interpretation be made of them.'[1]

The Gallery was founded with a strong social ethos to educate the public about national history and to facilitate 'face-to-face' encounters with inspirational people. It is significant that the first portrait to enter the Collection was not of a monarch or aristocrat but the playwright William Shakespeare (see p.24). His achievements were not the result of inherited wealth and status but his own extraordinary talent and effort. Another key principle of the Gallery was maintaining political, religious and moral impartiality. The founding Trustees established the acquisition rule that they would not consider 'great faults and errors, even though admitted on all sides, as any sufficient ground for exclusion, provided these faults and errors were not the only causes of the celebrity in question'.[2]

The mention of 'celebrity' here highlights the changing meaning of words over time. Today celebrity is often regarded as referring to a superficial and ephemeral form of fame that is perhaps unworthy of commemoration. This was not the meaning of the word in 1857, but the idea of avoiding portraits of people with little lasting significance was present in the rule that, with the exception of the monarch and their consort, portraits would only be admitted into the Collection ten years after the sitter's death. The fields of endeavour among those whose portraits were deemed appropriate for inclusion were initially specified as relating to the civil, ecclesiastical or literary history of the country. These areas inevitably reflect the Victorian context of the Gallery's foundation, with no mention of science, business, arts, sport or other areas that are today considered central to public life.

Over the subsequent century and a half, the Gallery greatly expanded the diversity of sitters and fields of endeavour represented in the Collection. There has also been a significant shift towards reflecting contemporary life with the admittance of portraits of living sitters from 1969 onwards. Today the impartiality claimed by our founders is questioned and debated, and greater analysis is undertaken into the values and inequalities that have underpinned society at different times in our history.

The inevitable development of the Gallery's priorities and concerns have resulted in the Collection serving as an ever-evolving reflection of the nation's character and values. In recent decades the Gallery has become a more active agent in this process of collective self-reflection through its pioneering programme of commissions, which has acquired portraits as diverse and outstanding as the architect Dame Zaha Hadid by Michael Craig-Martin (see p.112) and the human rights activist Malala Yousafzai by Shirin Neshat (see p.62).

PORTRAYING THE NATION

The displays at the National Portrait Gallery's home in London are presented chronologically to help tell the national story of the past 500 years. The earliest painted portrait in the Collection shows the first Tudor monarch, King Henry VII (fig. 1). Painted as part of an unsuccessful marriage negotiation, the inscription records that the portrait was created in 1505. Earlier figures from British history, such as the fourteenth-century writer Geoffrey Chaucer, are represented by portraits made at a later

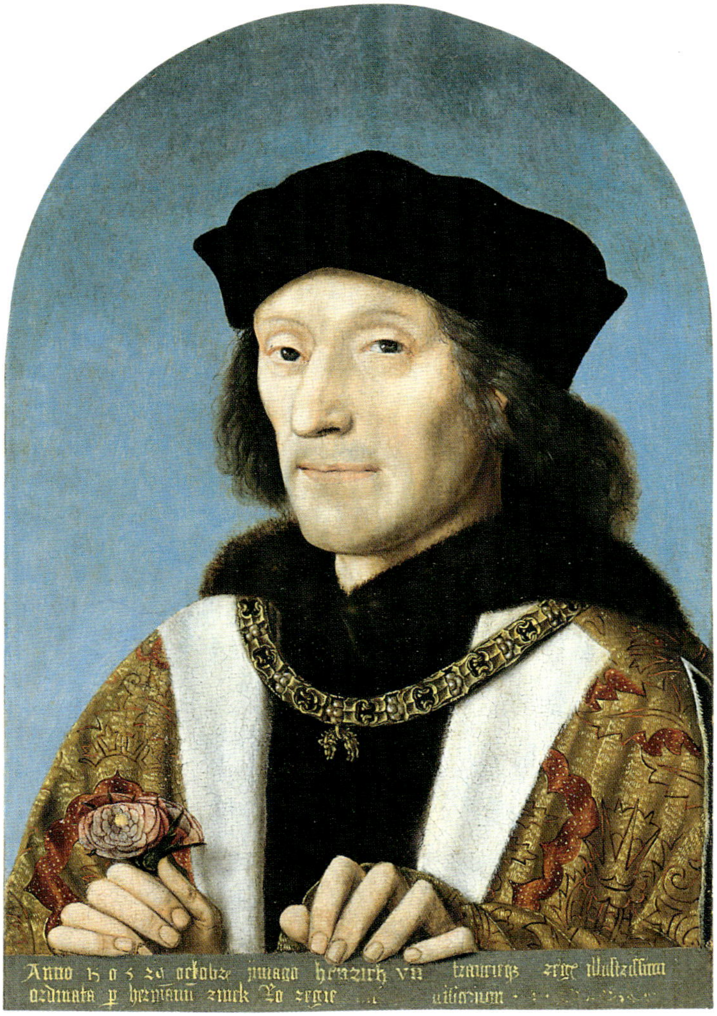

Fig. 1 **King Henry VII (1457–1509)**
Unknown Netherlandish artist, 1505
Oil on panel, 425 × 305mm
NPG 416

date. A small number of notable portraits were made in Britain prior to 1500, but it was only around this date that a more developed portrait culture emerged. The change was influenced by Renaissance humanist ideas from continental Europe, where a renewed emphasis on individual identity meant that recognisable images of specific individuals became highly prized.

During the sixteenth and seventeenth centuries portraiture was predominantly the reserve of the most wealthy and powerful members of society. Monarchs required portraits that asserted their authority, and aristocratic patrons wished to leave a favourable record of themselves and their families to posterity. With occasional exceptions, such as Nicholas Hilliard (see p.47), the market for portraits was dominated by a succession of exceptionally skilled Continental artists. The most successful of these artists made an indelible impact on how later generations have perceived their eras. The court of King Henry VIII is today viewed through the lens of Hans Holbein's portraits, just as our perception of King Charles I and his courtiers is informed by the art of Sir Anthony van Dyck (see p.67 and pp.118–19). Van Dyck had a profound influence on portraiture in Britain. His was a talent to which portrait artists aspired, and the influence of his style and compositions can be traced throughout subsequent centuries.

The eighteenth century witnessed an expansion of patronage beyond the nobility into the emerging middle classes as Britain developed a consumer society. New levels of wealth were generated by agricultural and industrial modernisation, and from the exploitation of enslaved people in an expanding empire. The racist ideologies of the colonial era mean that relatively few portraits of black sitters exist from this period. Building on the achievements of William Hogarth, British artists became more self-confident in their national and professional identity. Sir Joshua Reynolds (see p.122) was the driving force behind the establishment of the Royal Academy of Arts, and became its founding president in 1768. The Academy summer exhibitions gave artists an unparalleled opportunity to showcase their skill, enhance their prestige and attract clients. Artists such as Angelica Kauffmann (see p.120), Thomas Gainsborough (see p.87), and Sir Thomas Lawrence (see p.51) competed for the most favourable display of their work in the crowded exhibition space (fig. 2).

Social and technological developments during the nineteenth century further democratised the means by which people could make, view and own portraits. The development of photography provided portrait practitioners with a quick, efficient and increasingly affordable way of creating a likeness. Claims that photography provided an entirely objective and reliable record of a sitter's features were exaggerated both by its advocates and detractors. Fears that it would lead to the death of painting were also overstated. Photography instead extended the possibilities of portraiture, and there followed a period of creative cross-fertilisation between traditional and new media that continues to this day.

The expanded pace of social and economic change during the twentieth century, including the brutal impact of two world wars, influenced artists to challenge old certainties and conventions. Outstanding portraitists working broadly within the tradition, such as John Singer Sargent (see p.103), were joined by artists who wished to disrupt and make anew. The exploration of abstraction opened up portraiture to a host of art movements and concepts that have enlivened, deepened and enhanced the genre. Frank Dobson's bronze statue of Sir Osbert Sitwell (see p.105) exemplifies the radical simplification of form and use of reflective surfaces within modernism. Patrick Heron's portraits (see p.111) reveal the profound influence of cubism on twentieth-century art, and Angus McBean's photographs (see p.108–9) are infused with the spirit of surrealism.

In the later twentieth century, pop artists Andy Warhol and David Hockney responded to a consumerist, celebrity-obsessed society (see p.113 and p.127), while in the process becoming celebrities themselves. Photography enabled an ever-increasing saturation of imagery in our daily lives, and photographers such as David Bailey (see p.41) were crucial to establishing and broadening the fame of their sitters. Society was affected by great shifts, including the anti-colonial movements that brought an end to the British Empire, the migration of formerly colonised peoples to the UK, and the growth of popular movements demanding social equality, including civil rights, feminism and LGBT+ rights. The Collection includes international figures who have impacted on British history, such as Nelson Mandela, the first fully democratically elected president of South Africa and an icon of post-colonial social justice (see p.57).

The contemporary collections at the National Portrait Gallery reflect the pluralistic, globalised world of the twenty-first century. Digital media has further expanded the possibilities of portraiture, as seen in the portrait of Dame Zaha Hadid by Michael Craig-Martin (see p.112). Artists can experiment and express their own identity and vision freed from the expectations imposed by the artist-patron relationship in earlier times, as seen in the portrait of Anna Wintour by Alex Katz (see p.58–9). Types of sitter familiar to earlier audiences, such as monarchs and political leaders, continue to be collected by the Gallery, but so too are those in distinctly modern areas of public recognition, like the pop star Ed Sheeran by Colin Davidson (see p.30). Through its weaving together of art and biography, the Collection continues to represent the people who have helped shape British society and to engage a wide audience with compelling issues of personal and national identity.

OUTSIDE THE FRAME

Icons and Identities moves away from the chronological approach that is usually followed in displays at the National Portrait Gallery. Chronology foregrounds the social and historical context of a portrait and tends to focus more attention on the portrait as a proxy for the person represented. By grouping works in trans-historical themes, *Icons and Identities* prioritises a consideration of each portrait first and foremost as a work of art. It encourages us to think about who we are and what we value, and to draw out characteristics and features that allow us to explore what people share in common across time and space.

While acknowledging the importance of the biography of sitters, the groupings are intended to question historical assumptions and labels, and create a space in which

Fig. 2 **'The Exhibition of the Royal Academy, 1787'**
Pietro Antonio Martini, after Johann Heinrich Ramberg, Published 1st July 1787
Etching, 374 × 525mm
Rijksmuseum, Amsterdam

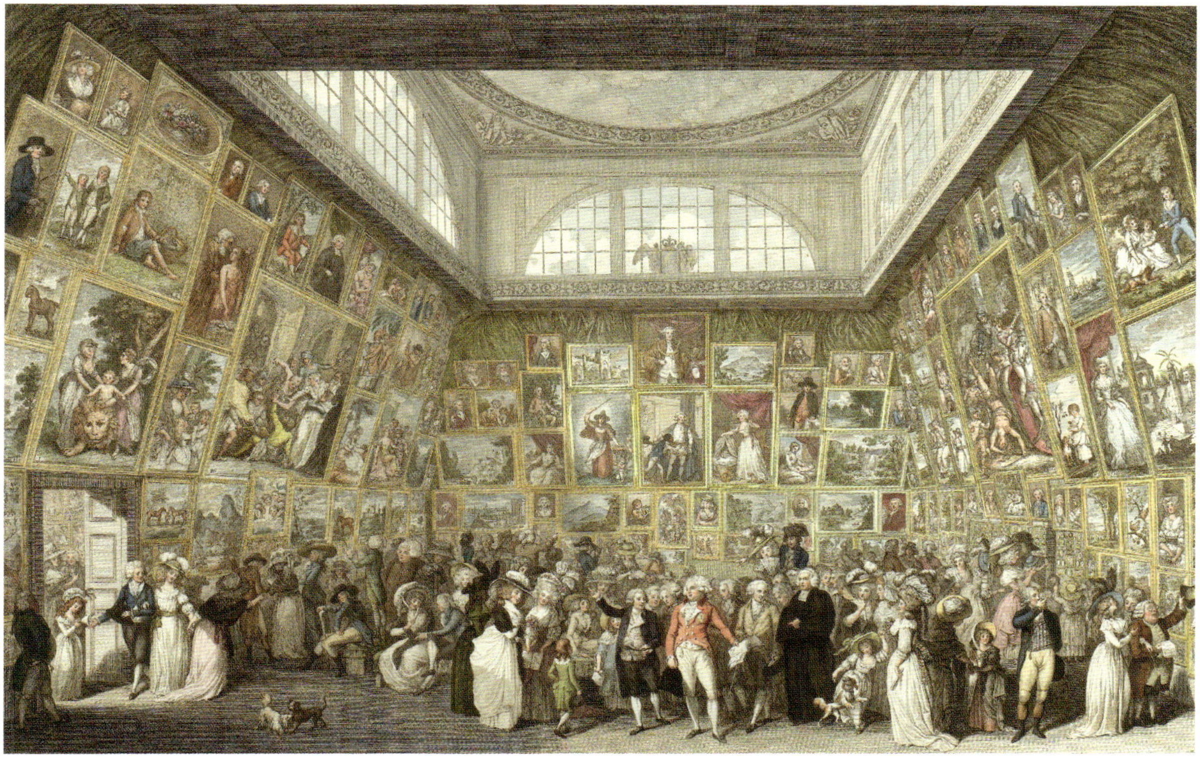

works can be looked at in new ways and interpretations can be reassessed. We are reminded that all portraits are 'contemporary' in that they were made by artists in the heat of the moment. Whether they're working in the 1500s or the 2000s, artists face similar challenges about how to balance their independent creative goals with making a representation of a sitter that will be closely inspected and judged, often by the sitter themselves.

The intention of *Icons and Identities* is to encourage new thinking about the artistic and social purposes that portraits served, and fresh insights into portraiture's variety of form and function. While recognising the iconic status of many of the sitters and the important historical contexts of many of the portraits, the groupings are designed to provoke connections and dialogues across six interrelated themes that are at the core of portraiture's fascination. 'Fame' explores the relationship between image and public renown; 'Power' looks at the use of portraiture in promoting different forms of authority; 'Love and Loss' reflects on the intimate connection between portraiture, affection and absence; 'Identity' focuses on the various ways in which portraiture represents diverse identities; 'Innovation' investigates the new ways of seeing and creating pioneered by significant portrait artists; and 'Self-Portrait' provides an insight into what occurs when artists turn their critical gaze on themselves. As befitting the richness and diversity of the genre, many of the works could have been equally eloquent in a different thematic grouping. This is not a closed interpretation but a catalyst for further reflection.

FAME

As we have seen, the founders of the National Portrait Gallery envisaged a temple of fame. The celebrity of the sitter was paramount, trumping the merits of the portrait or

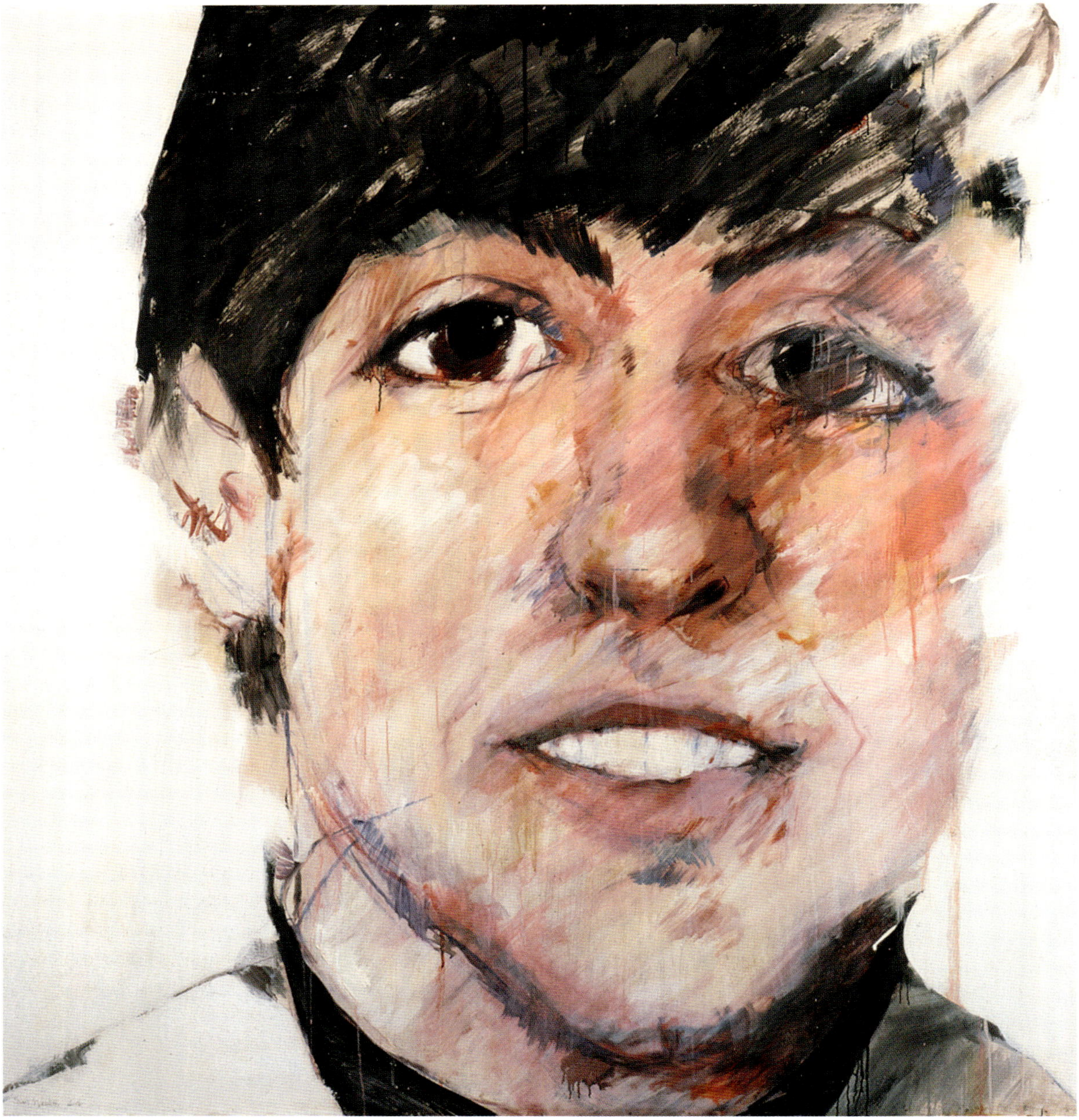

the renown of the artist. In a perhaps surprising instance of Victorian moral impartiality, they even conceded that the fact of a sitter's fame would override any concerns about whether they considered the fame to be worthy. An early test of the policy was a portrait of the seventeenth-century royal mistress Nell Gwyn (see p.26), which was displayed regardless of disapproving comments in the press. Today similar judgements are at play when commentators dismiss some famous people as 'celebrities', with the implication that their fame is not truly deserved. There is certainly a range of types of public renown, and in our culture celebrity tends to be associated with a superficial and fleeting public prominence, while fame has connotations of significant achievements that are worthy of recognition and remembrance. The status of icon is reserved for those with enduring fame, who may come to be regarded as

OPPOSITE Fig. 3 **Sir Paul McCartney (b.1942) ('Mike's Brother')**
Sam Walsh, 1964
Oil on masonite, 1625 × 1550mm
NPG 6172

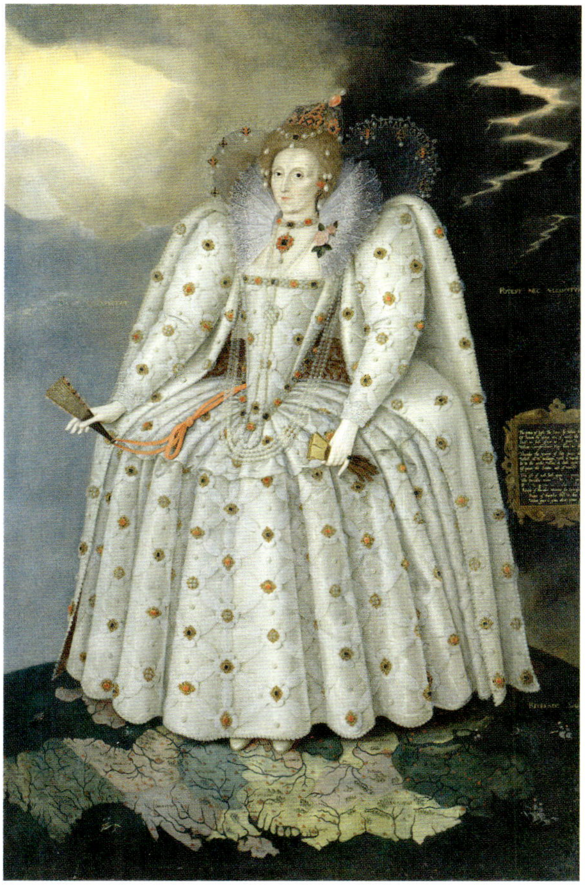

RIGHT Fig. 4 **Queen Elizabeth I (1533–1603) (the 'Ditchley portrait')**
Marcus Gheeraerts the Younger, *c.*1592
Oil on canvas, 2413 × 1524mm
NPG 2561

representative of a larger whole; take, for example, Isaac Newton (see p.33) and his association with scientific genius, or William Shakespeare (see p.24), considered pre-eminent as a literary 'national treasure'.

The very existence of the Gallery is a testament to the close relationship between portraiture and fame. Its collections show how artists have recorded the appearance of famous people for posterity. It also shows how they have worked as active agents in the creation of fame by making images that could be promoted, circulated and collected by the public. The Gallery reflects changing relationships between sitters and fame, including figures such as Mary Seacole, whose lifetime renown was subsequently obscured by racist and sexist social structures. The artist Sam Walsh made a wry comment about the nature of fame in his large and expressively painted portrait of Paul McCartney (fig. 3). Walsh was a friend of McCartney's brother, and although the painting is based on a publicity photograph taken at the height of 'Beatlemania', he undercuts the sitter's international fame with the affectionately disparaging title *Mike's Brother*.

POWER

Portraits have long played an important role in signifying the authority of people in power. More than simply representing the person, portraits affirm their power by reinforcing the social hierarchy between the subject of the portrait and those who look at it. For most of British history, black and ethnic minorities were excluded from positions of power, and their achievements were often overlooked or concealed by white hierarchies. For this reason, relatively few pre-twentieth-century British portraits of people of colour exist in the Gallery's Collection.

Royal portraiture in particular developed a range of conventional poses, props and symbols to highlight the sitter's majesty. Queen Elizabeth I was particularly astute about managing her public image. As an unmarried female monarch, it was important to overcome prejudice based on her gender. Unauthorised images were proscribed and official portraits were filled with codes and symbols that emphasised her authority. In the work known as the 'Ditchley portrait' (fig. 4), she is symbolically presented as a superhuman figure towering over England, with a divine command that extends even to controlling the weather.

Such conventions for representing power became increasingly obsolete as royal power was supplanted by new social structures, such as democracy and capitalism. Jillian Edelstein's photograph of Nelson Mandela (see p.57), one of the twentieth century's most revered political leaders, contains no allusion to his power; on the contrary, his lowered gaze creates an atmosphere of contemplative introspection. The central role of artists in shaping public perceptions has been eclipsed by public relations officers controlling media representation. Artists continue to play

Fig. 5 **Dame Ellen Terry (1847–1928) ('Choosing')**
George Frederic Watts, 1864
Oil on board, 472 × 352mm
NPG 5048

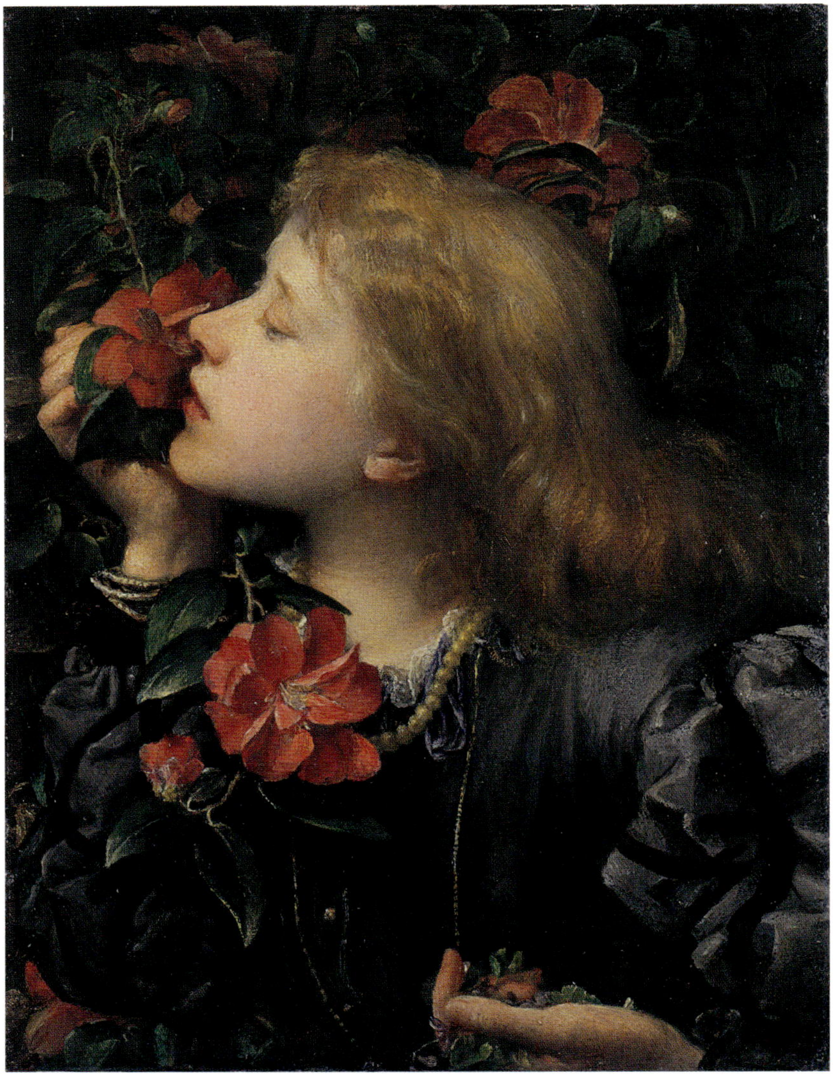

an important role either by creating more considered and enduring likenesses, or by questioning and contesting the relationships between image, power and society.

LOVE AND LOSS

The instinct to respond to portraits as though encountering a real person rather than an image gives them a talismanic quality. The sense of immediacy is particularly potent when the viewer feels love for the portrait's subject. If only fleetingly, portraits can serve as a substitute for the individual depicted, turning an absence into a presence and traversing distance, time and even death. The powerful emotional responses engendered by portraits means that for centuries they have served as tokens of love and as a means of recording key life events, such as marriage.

The depiction of romantic love can be especially intense when the loving gaze is that of the artists themselves. George Romney was introduced to the teenage Emma Hamilton in 1782 and painted her portrait with obsessive regularity over the next twenty years (see p.75). The nineteenth-century artist George Frederic Watts painted his young wife, the actor Ellen Terry, in the year of their marriage (fig. 5). The sensuality of the image, with its rich evocation of the pleasures of sight, touch and smell, is indicative of the artist's feelings for his wife. In the event, the painting

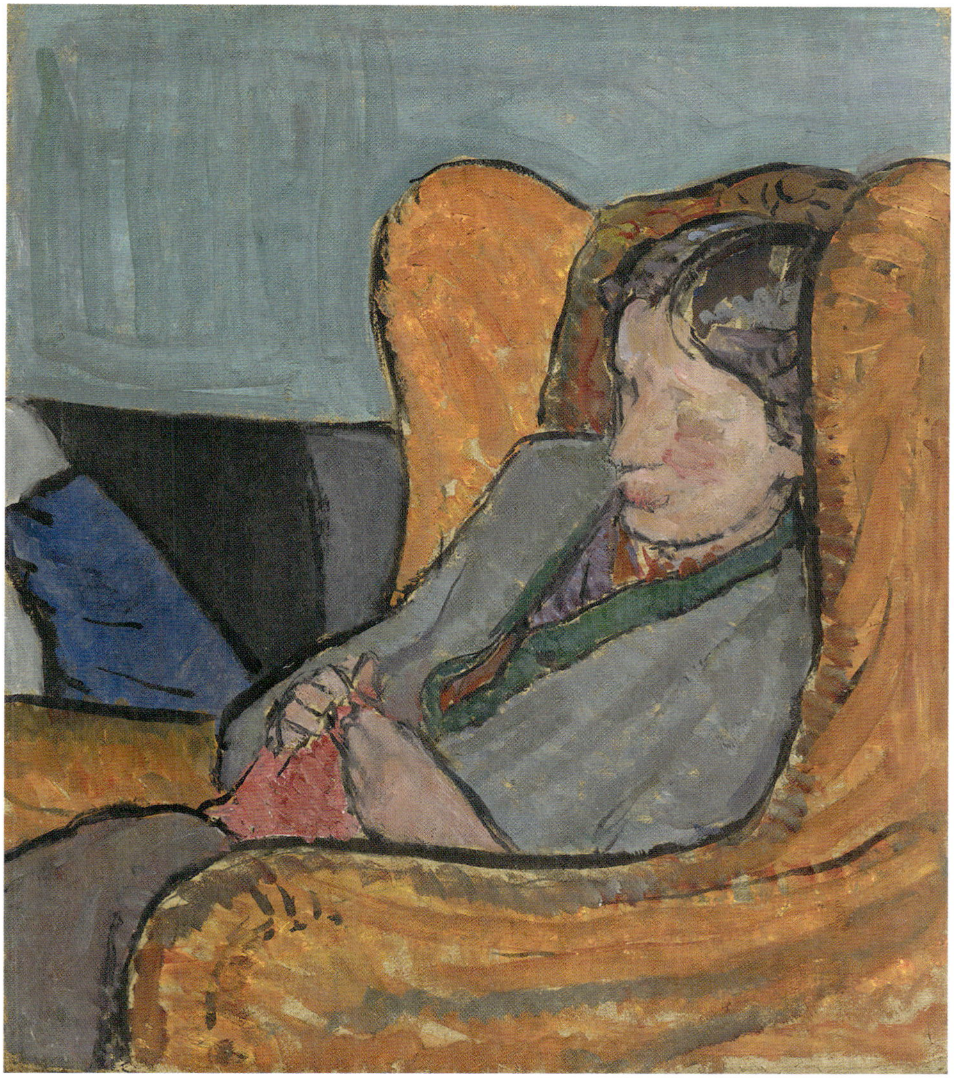

Fig. 6 **Virginia Woolf (1882–1941)**
Vanessa Bell, 1912
Oil on board,
400 × 340mm
NPG 5933

would be bittersweet for Watts, as the marriage lasted less than a year; it serves as a reminder that in some portraits the themes of love and loss are inseparable.

IDENTITY

The expression of identity is a central concern of portraiture. Identity can be defined as the characteristics that make people uniquely themselves. It combines the type of identity that can be determined by a DNA sample with the way that individuals think and feel about themselves and are seen by society. A person's sense of identity is likely to draw upon gender, ethnicity, age, sexuality, nationality, belief, social status and profession, amongst other factors. It is complex, multifaceted, mutable and profoundly personal, so transmitting an insight into the sitter's identity is one of the key challenges for portrait artists.

As the location of our most recognisable features and our main means of expressing emotion, it is no surprise that the face is the primary focus of the exploration of identity in portraits. However, in the modernist painter Vanessa Bell's portrait of her sister Virginia Woolf (fig. 6), Woolf's features are barely discernible, perhaps questioning the validity of the face's elevated status as the key to identity.

Artists also indicate aspects of a sitter's identity through pose, costume, props, setting and medium. William

Hoare's portrait of Ayuba Suleiman Diallo (see p.85) draws attention to the sitter's West African identity and Islamic faith through the use of costume and a Quran around his neck. Contemporary artists have developed innovative methods to explore current concepts of identity. Stephan Willats's collaborative portrait of the performance artist Leigh Bowery (fig. 7) includes photography, text and everyday objects taken from the sitter's flat to represent the transformation from his daytime to nighttime personas.

INNOVATION

From sixteenth-century panel paintings to the use of digital technology by contemporary artists, the National Portrait Gallery's Collection illustrates the profound changes that have taken place within portraiture over the centuries. Wider social and technological factors have exerted an enormous influence on the art form, but it has been innovative artists developing new techniques and ways of seeing that have been key to challenging conventions and expanding its boundaries. Exceptional artists who have made an indelible impact on the art of portraiture include Sir Peter Paul Rubens (see p.101) and John Singer Sargent (see p.103).

The most significant technological impact on portraiture since the Renaissance was the invention of photography in the nineteenth century. The new means of accurately recording a likeness challenged traditional media at the same time as expanding the possibilities of art. Julia Margaret Cameron was a pioneer of portrait photography in the 1860s. She recognised that photographs were more than merely mechanical means of producing a likeness. Her creative compositions, lighting and framing of sitters, and her experimentation with lens focus and darkroom techniques helped to establish the status of photography as an art form. She enjoyed a fruitful creative collaboration with her niece Julia Stephen (fig. 8), who in turn would become mother to two of the most innovative artists of the next generation, the painter Vanessa Bell and the writer Virginia Woolf.

SELF-PORTRAIT

Self-portraits occupy a unique place within portraiture. Most portraits involve the interpretation and display of aspects of the sitter's character and identity that can never be fully known to the artist. When making a portrait of

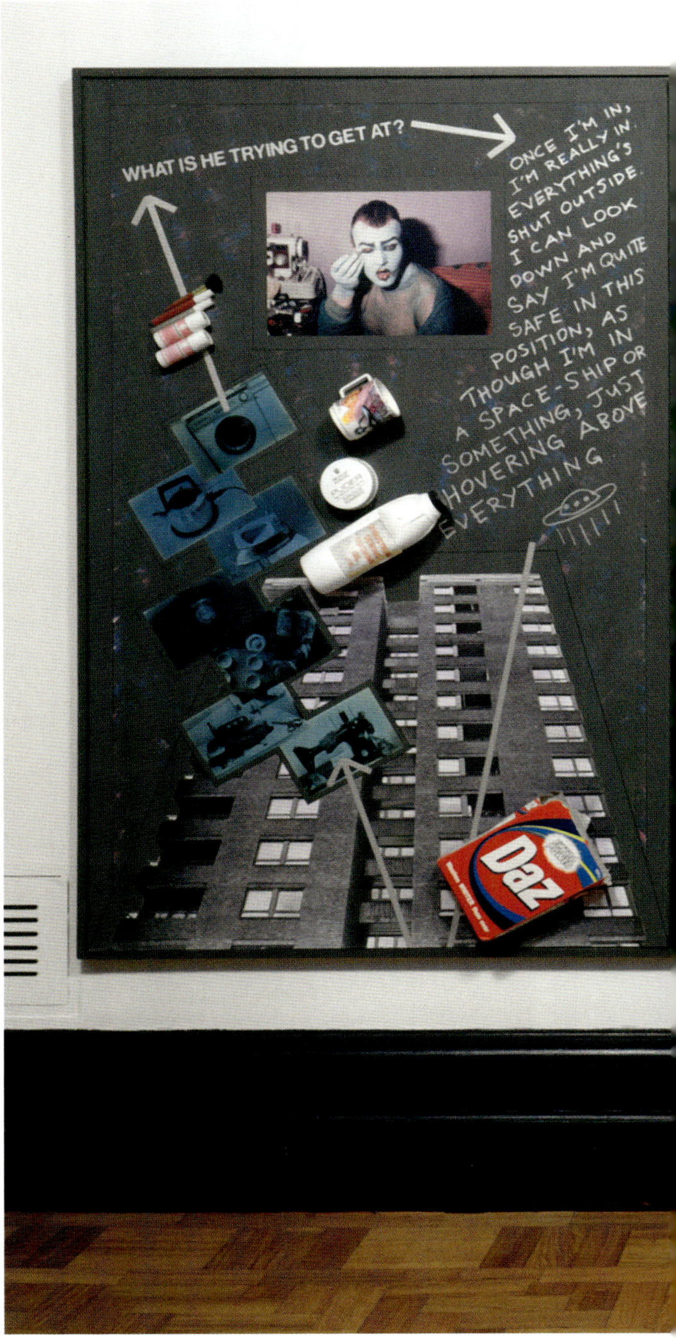

Fig. 7 **Leigh Bowery (1961–94)**
('What is he trying to get at? Where does he want to go?')
Stephen Willats, 1984
Mixed media, panel one 1520 × 980mm,
tower 2000 × 440mm, and panel two 1520 × 980mm
NPG 6660

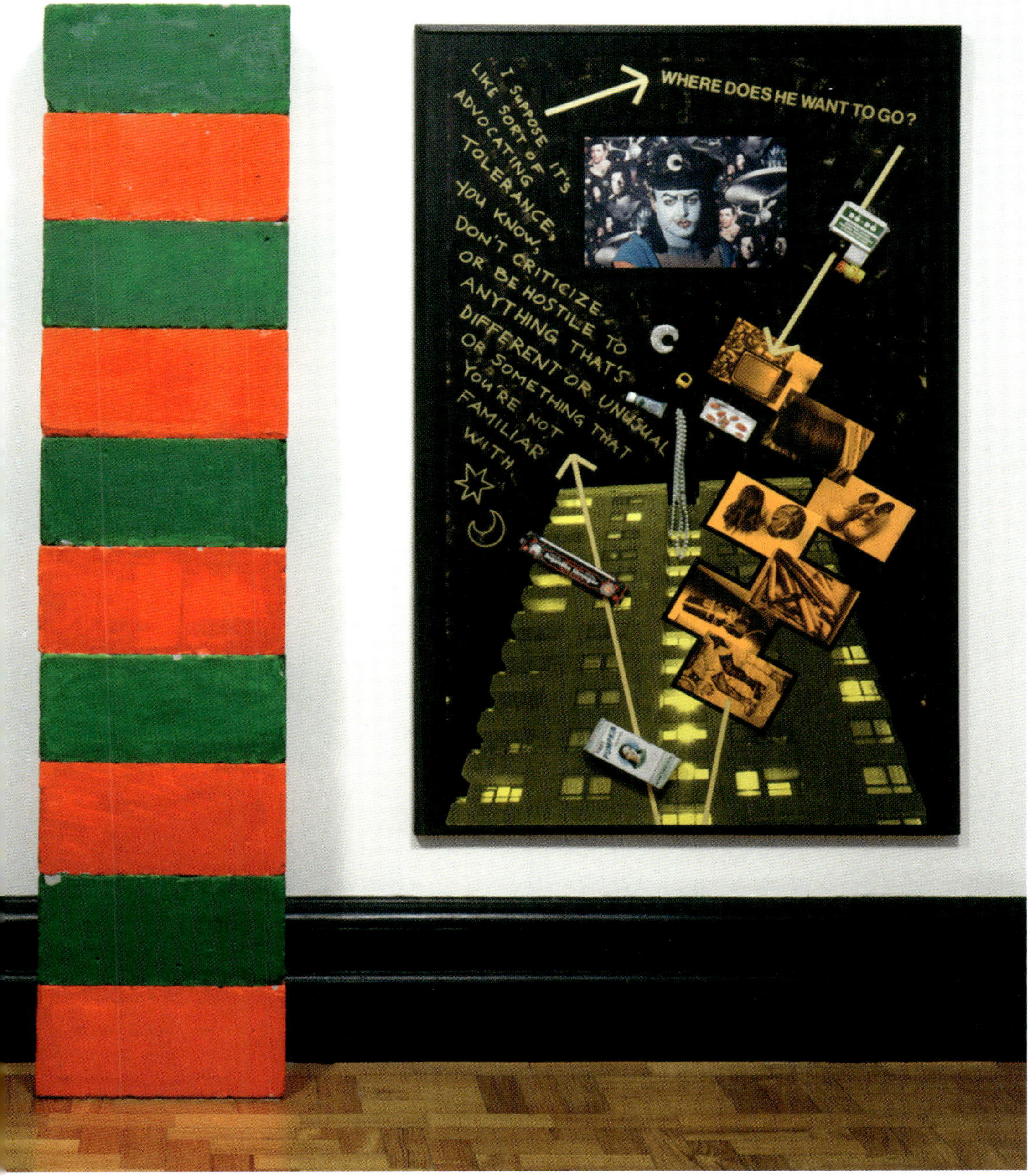
I SUPPOSE IT'S
LIKE SORT OF
ADVOCATING
TOLERANCE,
YOU KNOW,
DON'T CRITICIZE
OR BE HOSTILE TO
ANYTHING THAT'S
DIFFERENT OR UNUSUAL
OR SOMETHING THAT
YOU'RE NOT
FAMILIAR
WITH.
WHERE DOES HE WANT TO GO?

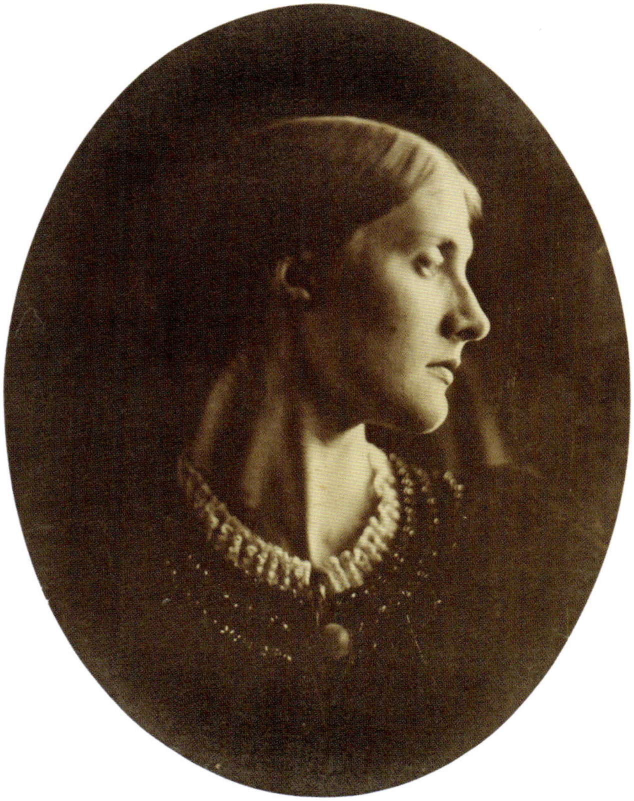

themselves, artists can draw upon the rich fusion of experiences, emotions and ideas that make them who they are. For this reason, self-portraits are rarely an entirely straightforward record of an artist's physical appearance.

There are many reasons for artists to depict themselves. At the most practical level, they are a free and willing model with whom to practise their art and experiment with techniques, gestures or expressions. An example of this type of self-portrait is the chalk study made by John Constable (see p.121) during the period that he was a student at the Royal Academy Schools. Self-portraits can also serve as promotional tools that enable prospective clients to appreciate the style and skill of an artist by comparing the artwork to the model (and artist) before them. Self-portraits often simultaneously accommodate these worldly concerns with more profound speculations about personal identity and existence. Marc Quinn's *Self* (fig. 9) comprises a cast of his head made entirely from his own frozen blood. Encountering the sculpture, encased in the refrigeration unit that keeps it from melting, viewers are invited to contemplate their own vulnerabilities and mortality.

CONCLUSION

Portraiture is an art form that consistently and intensely investigates the lived experience of being human. The development of new media and the expansion of the functions that portraits serve has not detracted from this core concern. Within an enormous variety of form and style, a common feature of portraiture is a sense of encounter with another person that is mediated by the artist to excite our curiosity about the life and identity depicted.

Portraits have traditionally conveyed likeness and a sense of the sitter's social status, profession or character. They have been used to mark significant life events, promote individual ambitions, or display affection, loyalty or solidarity. Increasingly, artists have used portraits as a vehicle for self-expression and the exploration of complex issues of identity and the body. The energy and fascination of the genre transcends boundaries of time and geography. The thematic presentation of works in *Icons and Identities* aims to challenge expectations and open up a space in which stimulating and provocative visual conversations can take place. Whether they are the product of the sixteenth or twenty-first century, portraits reveal and celebrate our shared humanity.

Fig. 8 **Julia Stephen (1846–95)**
Julia Margaret Cameron, 1867
Albumen print, 344 × 263mm
NPG x18018

OPPOSITE Fig. 9 **Marc Quinn (b.1964) ('Self')**
Marc Quinn, 2006
Blood (artist's), liquid silicone, stainless steel, glass, perspex and refrigeration equipment,
2050 × 650 × 650mm
NPG 6863

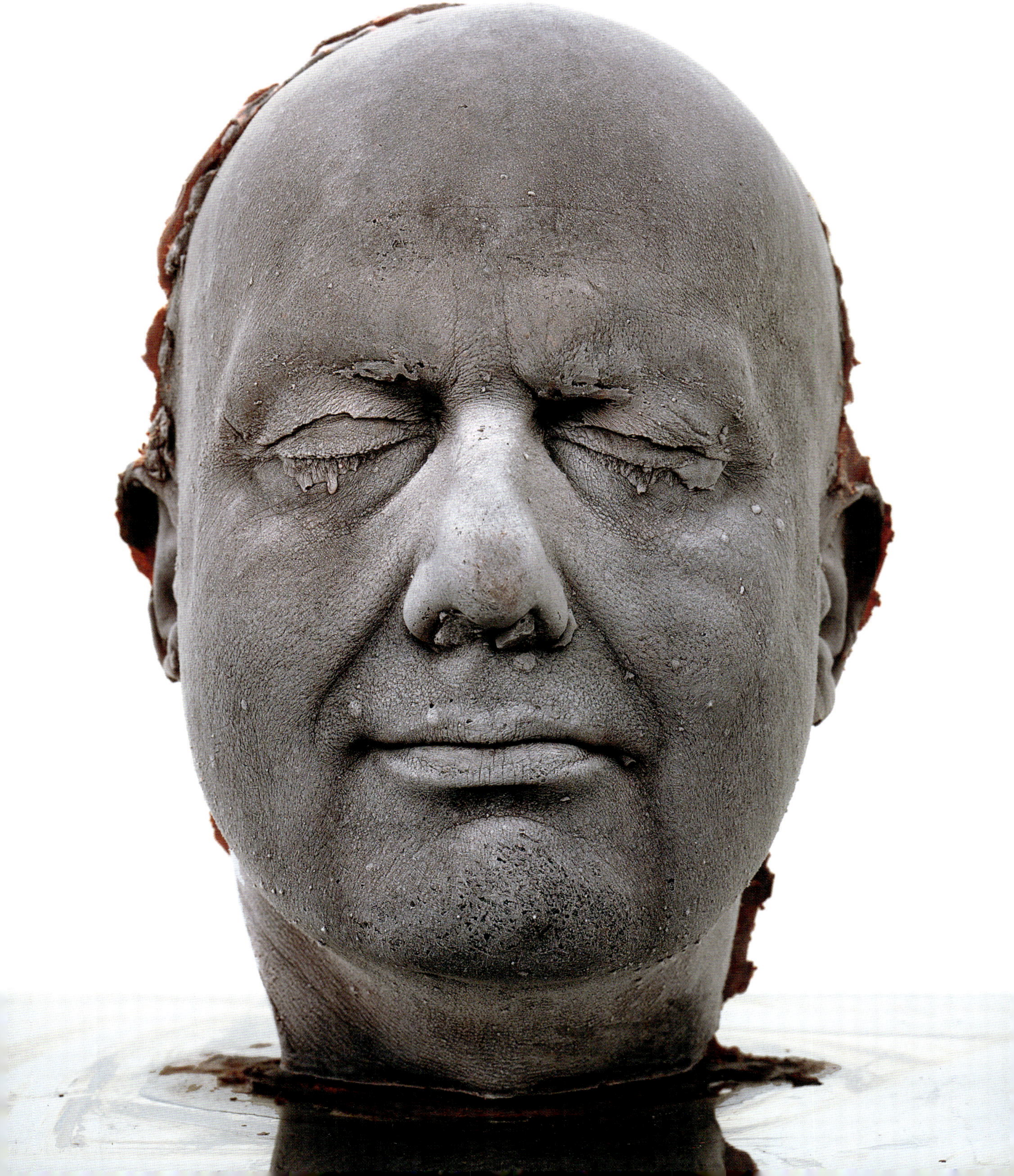

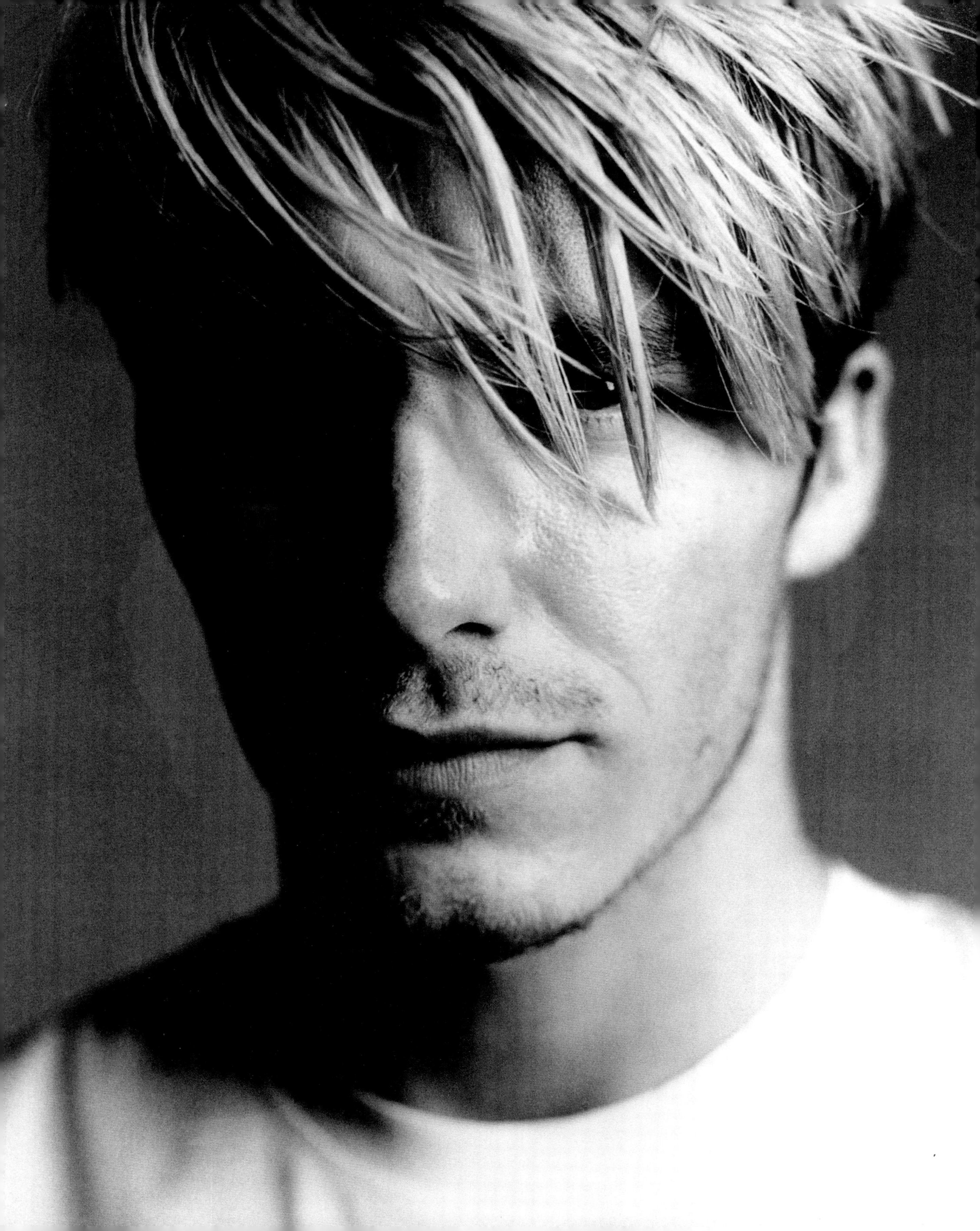

Fame

Almost by definition, being famous is reliant on wide recognition. People need to be seen if they are to enhance and extend their fame, while the public, eager for a connection with their favourite star, scrutinise and idolise their portraits. Charles Dickens (see p.27) was adept at using his image in self-promotion, as were the actors Sarah Siddons and Elizabeth Taylor (see p.31 and p.34). There are also many people who were famous in their day but for whom the bias in the recording of history has not been favourable; despite their fame at the time, their images and biographies became obscure and are now often missing from popular histories.

In today's globally connected world, a seemingly limitless supply of images of public figures can be accessed by the swipe of a screen. The Internet has also democratised fame by providing a platform in which practically anyone can become famous, if only for a while. Some, like Ed Sheeran (see p.30), have utilised the power of the Internet to achieve lasting fame. Whilst our fascination with celebrities has been facilitated by digital technology, this section will show that it is by no means a new phenomenon.

The seventeenth-century diarist Samuel Pepys obsessively sought out printed images of his favourite female actor Nell Gwyn (see p.26). Women had only recently been permitted to perform on the public stage, and 'pretty witty Nell', as Pepys called her, was London's theatrical star. She was also a canny manager of her public profile, and collaborated with the artist Simon Verelst on a series of sexualised portraits that knowingly exploited her notoriety as a royal mistress. Throughout history, physical beauty has been an advantage for the attainment of fame. In the late twentieth century, a generation of fashion models attracted such public interest that they became household names. Supermodels such as Naomi Campbell (see pp.38–9) cultivated their worldwide recognition to take command of their careers and expand their influence.

Fame can be fleeting, particularly in popular culture, but the renown of some people has increased over time to an extent that they could never have foreseen. The scientist Charles Darwin (see p.28) was reluctant to step into the public eye, but his features are today recognised around the world. The death of the playwright William Shakespeare in 1616 went unmarked beyond his home town of Stratford-upon-Avon. Indeed, it took over a century for his reputation and international fame to be secured. His modest picture in the National Portrait Gallery (see p.24) may be of limited artistic merit, in comparison to the extravagant portraits of courtiers and the royal family made by court artists during the same period, but it is one of the Gallery's greatest treasures because it is likely to be his only lifetime portrait.

DETAIL **David Beckham, 1998**

1

1 **William Shakespeare** **(1564–1616)**
John Taylor, *c.*1600–10
Oil on canvas, 552 × 438mm
NPG 1

Poet and playwright William Shakespeare was described by his contemporary Ben Jonson as the 'soul of the age'. He was born in Stratford-upon-Avon, the son of a glover, and attended the local grammar school, the King's New School. He married Anne Hathaway in 1582, and in the later 1580s joined a company of actors. He spent most of his working life in London, first as an actor and then as a playwright, providing plays for the immensely popular public theatres and the royal court. The posthumous publication of *Mr. William Shakespeares Comedies, Histories, & Tragedies* ('the First Folio') in 1623 was a milestone in the recognition of plays as lasting, influential works of literature, as they were commonly considered to be ephemeral texts that belonged to the theatre by which they were commissioned.

This is the only painted portrait of Shakespeare that has a good claim to have been painted from the life. The notebooks of the eighteenth-century antiquarian George Vertue record that the portrait was at one point owned by Shakespeare's godson, William Davenant, and that it was painted by 'one Taylor, a Player and painter', who was a contemporary of Shakespeare; this is believed to be a reference to John Taylor, who was a member of the Painter-Stainers' Company. The significance of this painting of Britain's most famous literary hero is such that in 1856 it became the founding portrait of the National Portrait Gallery.

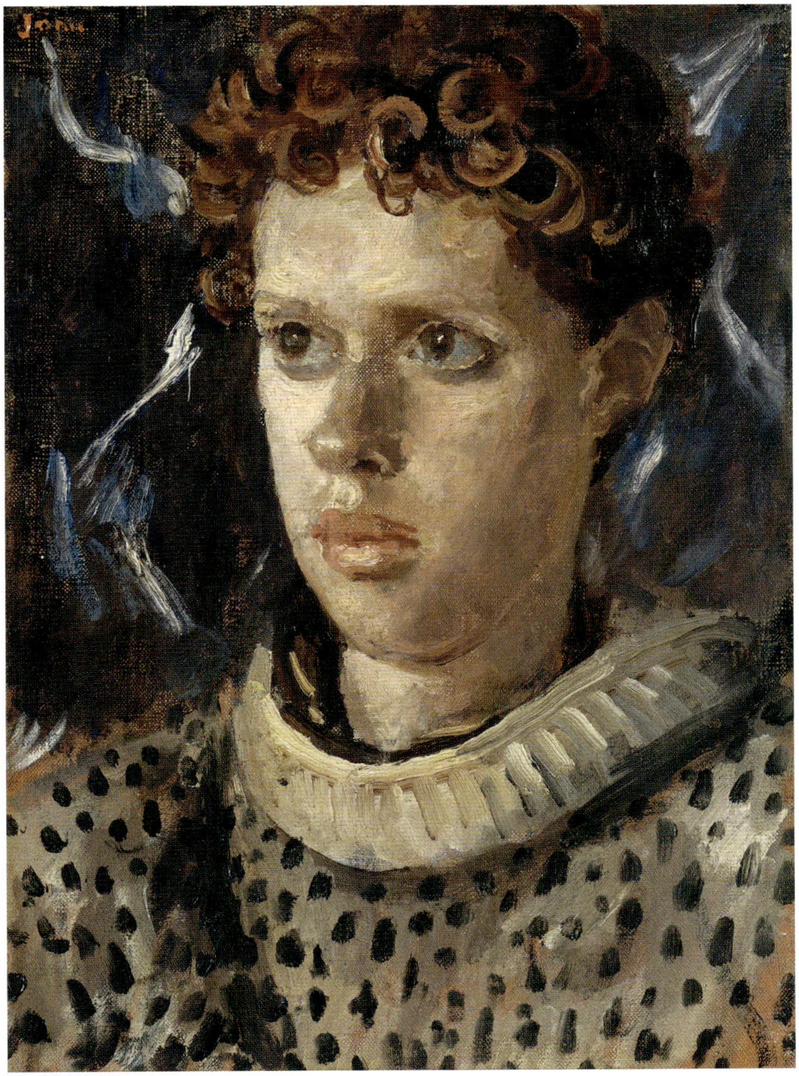

2 **Dylan Thomas** **(1914–53)**
Augustus John, *c.*1937–8
Oil on canvas, 457 × 337mm
NPG 7049

The poet Dylan Thomas was born in Swansea, South Wales, where he worked briefly as a journalist. By the age of 19, Thomas had filled four exercise books with 200 poems, many of which were published as *Eighteen Poems* (1934) and *Twenty-Five Poems* (1936), and are the foundation of his literary reputation. Much of his writing, including the short story collection *Portrait of the Artist as a Young Dog* (1940), evokes his early life in Wales. From 1940 Thomas wrote scripts for the BBC and worked as a broadcaster. He was a brilliant performer of his poetry, and his public readings and recordings helped to cement his international fame. His four tours of the USA were significant in popularising the performance of poetry, and were an influence on the Beat poets and musicians such as Bob Dylan, who changed his name in honour of the poet. Thomas was affected by alcoholism but completed the radio play *Under Milk Wood* in May 1953, shortly before his death in New York.

As his literary reputation grew in the early 1930s, Thomas gravitated to London and was a distinctive figure in bohemian circles in Soho and Fitzrovia. Here he met the painter and fellow Welshman Augustus John, who introduced Thomas to his future wife, Caitlin Macnamara. Shortly after their marriage, when the newlyweds were staying in Hampshire, close to John's studio, Thomas sat for John twice. Of his exuberant sitter, John wrote in his autobiography that when 'provided with a bottle of beer he sat very patiently'.

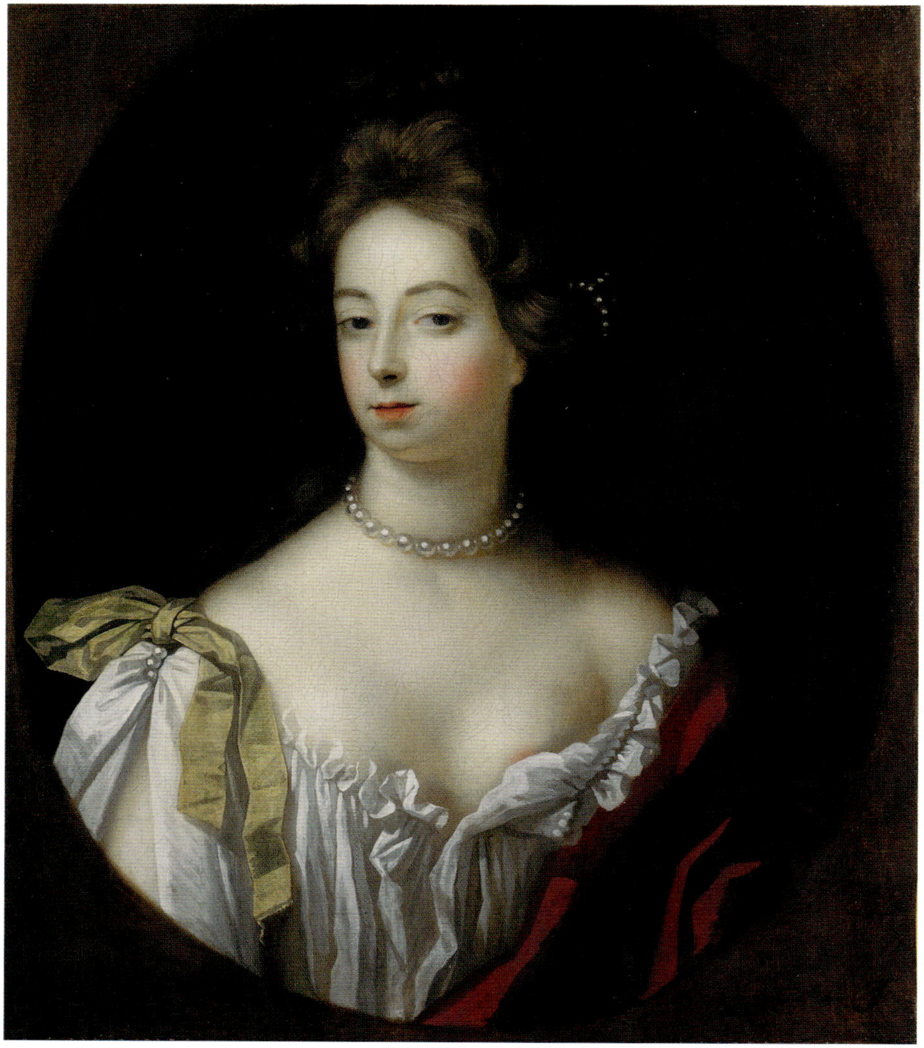

3 **Nell Gwyn** **(c.1651–87)**
Simon Verelst, *c.*1680
Oil on canvas, 737 × 632mm
NPG 2496

The actor Eleanor 'Nell' Gwyn was one of the first women to perform on the English public stage. She was also the most famous and popular of King Charles II's many mistresses. She had two sons by him: Charles, later Duke of St Albans, and James. Most likely born in London, Gwyn grew up in its slums in the shadow of the English Civil War (1642–51). She never knew her father, and her mother, who drank to excess, died by drowning. After living hand-to-mouth, apparently selling oranges to theatregoers and shucking oysters, Gwyn established herself as a comic actor in London's Drury Lane. It was a role that she also enacted in King Charles II's court, where her wits as much as her looks ensured her favour.

Simon Verelst was a Dutch artist who painted most of the prominent figures at court at least once, and his theatrical style was perhaps particularly suited to Gwyn, whose portrait he painted on a number of occasions. In this sexualised image, she is shown wearing just her shift, or underwear. The fabric is gathered loosely by a drawstring around the neckline and opens down the centre front to partially reveal her shoulders and chest. Actors were not expected to conform to the usual behavioural norms; Nell allowed the diarist Samuel Pepys (and presumably others) to watch her dressing for her roles.

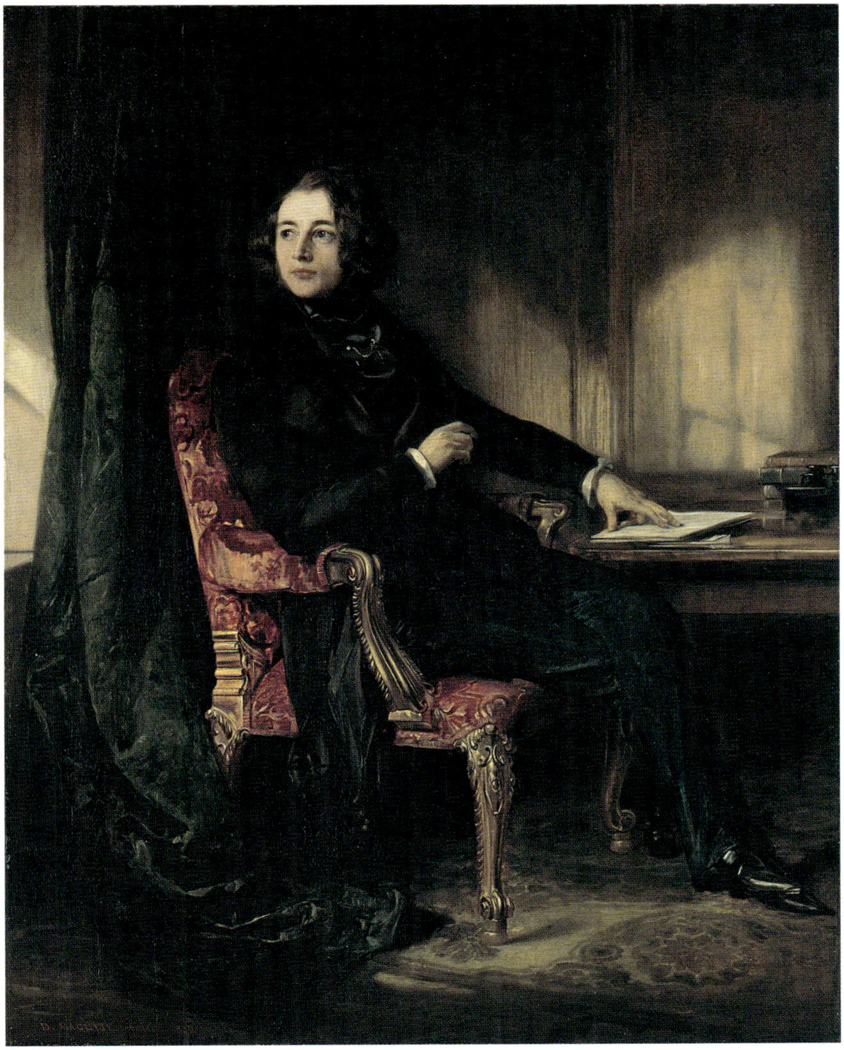

4 **Charles Dickens** (1812–70)
Daniel Maclise, 1839

Oil on canvas, 914 × 714mm
NPG 1172

Charles Dickens was one of the greatest novelists of his age, with an international reputation. A prolific writer, he established his name with *The Pickwick Papers* (1836–7) and went on to write a total of fifteen novels. These include some of the best-known works in the English language, such as *Oliver Twist* (1837–9), *A Christmas Carol* (1843), *Bleak House* (1852–3) and *Great Expectations* (1860–1). Most were initially published as serials in literary journals, such as *Household Words*, which Dickens co-founded and edited. In addition to his novels, he worked extensively as a journalist.

This portrait was painted in 1839, while the reading public were gripped by the monthly serialisation of Dickens's third novel, *Nicholas Nickleby*. He had met the artist Daniel Maclise the previous summer and they had become close friends. Maclise painted him on several occasions, and also made portraits of Dickens's wife and children. In a letter dated 28 June 1839, Dickens wrote that 'Maclise has made another face of me, which all people say is astonishing'. He assumes the role of a dandy and man of letters, clothed in a pristine wide-collared black coat and waistcoat, trousers with foot-straps to preserve an unwrinkled line over his boots, and an elegant black satin diamond-studded cravat. Subsequently, an engraving of the portrait by William Finden was used as the frontispiece to the first book edition of *Nicholas Nickleby* and the work was exhibited at the Royal Academy, helping to consolidate the young author's fame.

5 **Charles Darwin** (1809–82)

John Collier, 1883

Oil on canvas, 1257 × 965mm
NPG 1024

This portrait of the naturalist Charles Darwin is a copy by the artist of a painting he made for the Linnean Society in 1881. It was given to the National Portrait Gallery by Darwin's eldest son, William Erasmus Darwin, who in 1896 wrote to the Director, Lionel Cust, that 'as a likeness, it is an improvement on the original'. Darwin's career as a scientist began properly in 1831, when his university tutor secured him a place on the *Beagle* voyage around the world. The expedition lasted five years, during which he visited South America, the Galapagos Islands, Australia and South Africa. Darwin's experiences and the samples that he collected provided the foundations of his controversial work on evolution, *On the Origin of Species by Means of Natural Selection* (1859).

John Collier was the son-in-law of Thomas Huxley, Darwin's defender in the furore surrounding the publication of his work. Collier's portrait, which depicts Darwin as an old man in the year before his death, was much admired. Darwin's son Francis wrote in his *Life and Letters of Charles Darwin* (1887), 'Many of those who knew his face most intimately, think that Mr Collier's picture is the best of the portraits and in this judgement the sitter himself was inclined to agree.'

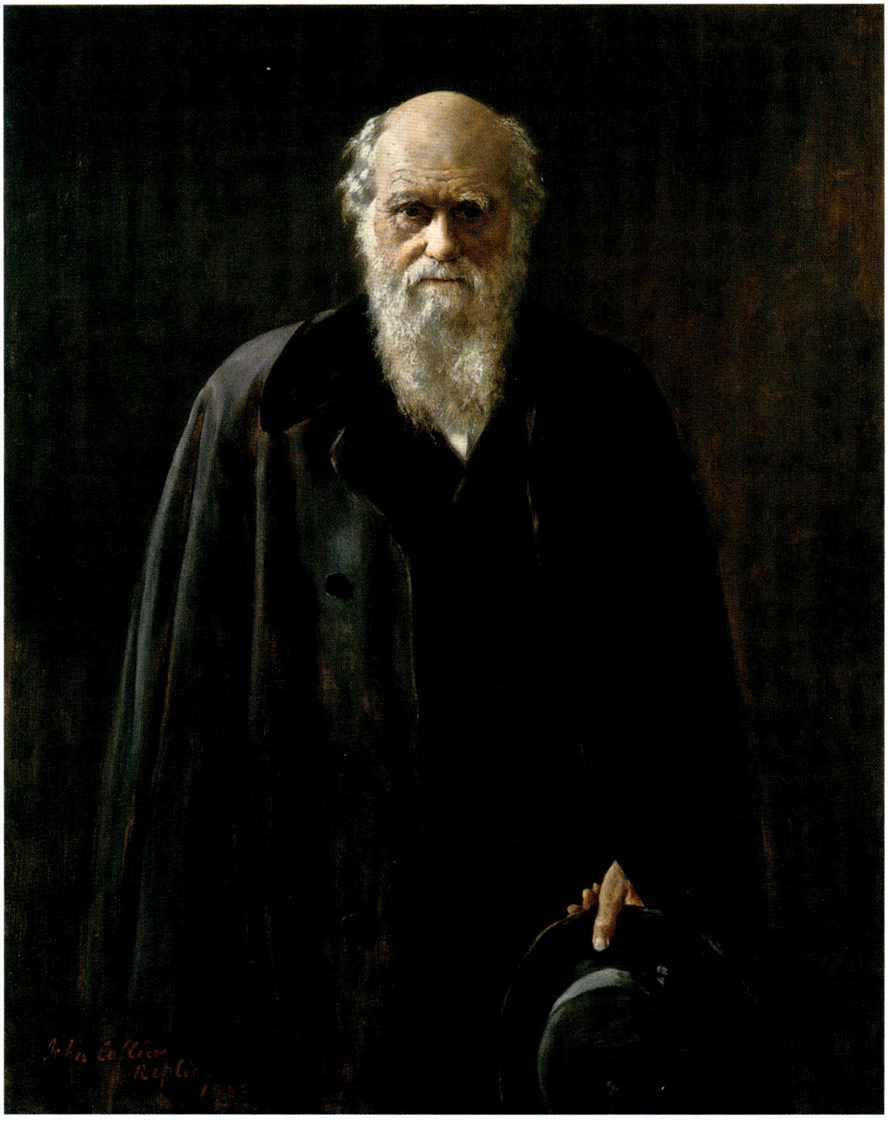

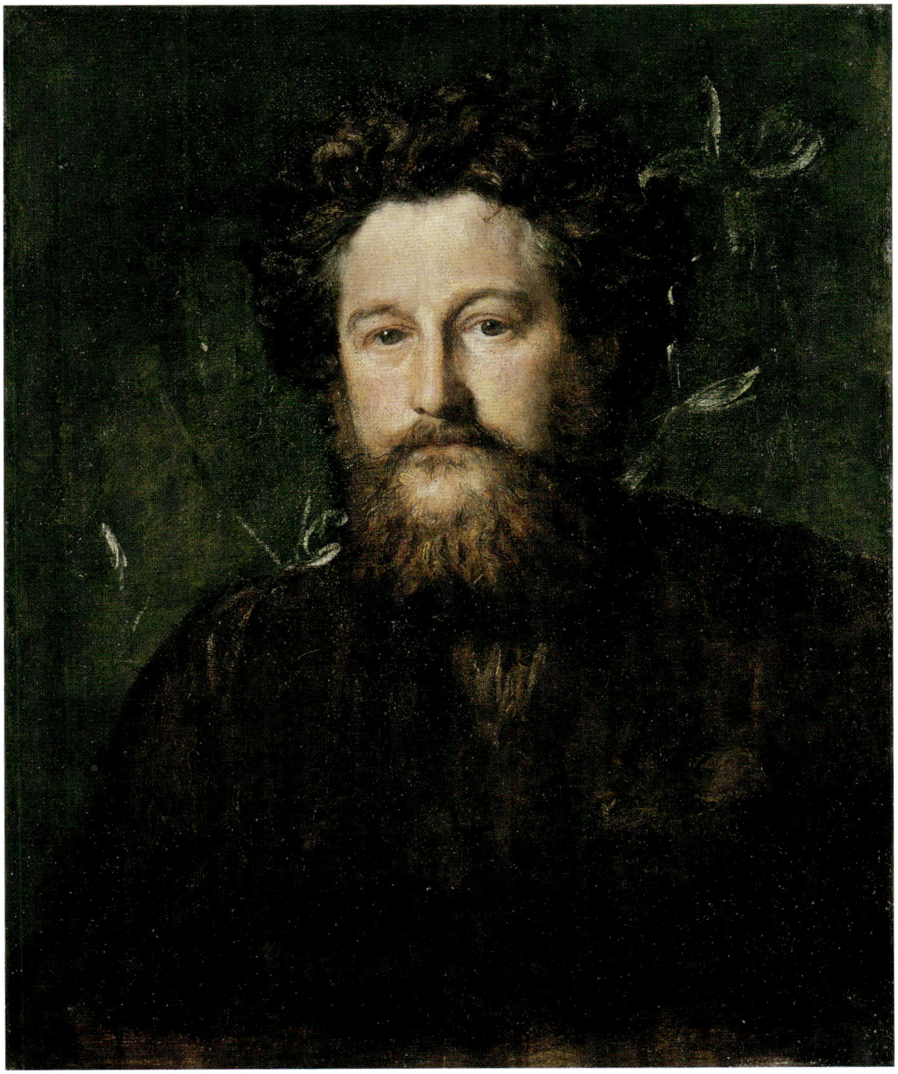

6 **William Morris** (1834–96)
George Frederic Watts, 1870
Oil on canvas, 648 × 521mm
NPG 1078

This is a rare painted portrait of William Morris, one of the most influential artistic figures of the Victorian period. His name has become synonymous with the Arts and Crafts movement, which embraced standards of medieval craftsmanship in order to oppose factory mass-production. At the time of Watts's portrait, Morris, then in his late thirties, was reaching the height of his considerable powers as a designer of wallpapers and textiles, and also stained-glass windows, mainly in collaboration with his life-long friend Edward Burne-Jones. He was immersed in the manual disciplines of craftwork, having taught himself embroidery and wood engraving, and revived lost techniques in illumination and calligraphy. He would soon turn his attention to hand-weaving, setting up a loom in his bedroom in Hammersmith.

His industriousness and apparent dislike of portraiture made him an elusive subject. According to Mary Seton Watts, wife of the artist George Frederic Watts, there may have been just one sitting for the picture, on 15 April 1870. In 1880 the work was submitted to the Summer Exhibition at the Grosvenor Gallery, for which it was possibly reworked. Ultimately, it made a worthy addition to Watts's 'Hall of Fame', a series of more than fifty portraits depicting eminent Victorians. The Gallery's acquisition of this portrait eschewed the usual ten-year rule regarding the acceptance of deceased sitters into the Collection, testament to Morris's celebrity at the time of his death.

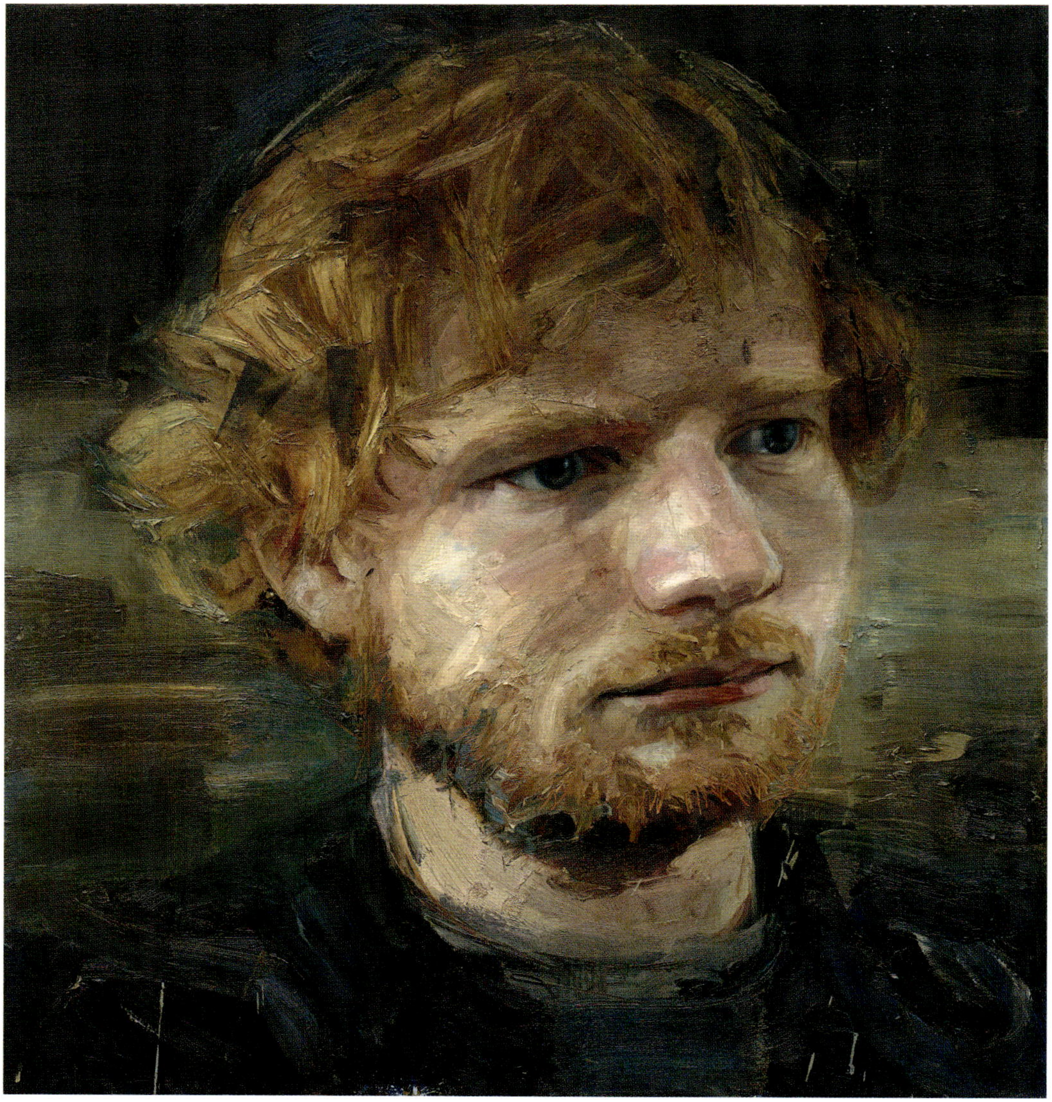

7 **Ed Sheeran (b.1991)**
Colin Davidson, 2016
Oil on linen, 1270 × 1170mm
NPG 7035

The internationally acclaimed musician Ed Sheeran began playing the guitar and writing songs at a young age. His style is a blend of acoustic, pop, folk and hip-hop, which reflects his diverse influences from Bob Dylan to Eminem. He began recording in 2005, self-releasing EPs and playing small gigs (312 in 2009 alone). He built a strong fan base on social media, before his first single 'The A Team' (2011) entered the UK chart at number three. His 2011 debut album + (*Plus*) and 2014 album *x* (*Multiply*) gained international acclaim – *x* becoming a UK and US number one. In April 2017 he began a world tour of ÷ (*Divide*), which made history as the fastest-selling album by a male artist. His fourth studio album *No.6 Collaborations Project* (2019) spawned three UK number one singles. He has won Ivor Novello, BRIT and Grammy awards.

Sheeran was introduced to the Northern Irish portrait painter Colin Davidson through his father, an art historian and curator. This portrait, one of two larger-than-life portrait heads Davidson painted of the musician, represents Sheeran in a moment of quiet introspection. Davidson commented: 'I deliberately didn't want Ed to perform and that was odd for him.' The portrait is based on a sitting at Sheeran's home in Suffolk, during which Davidson made around twenty drawings from life and took reference photographs.

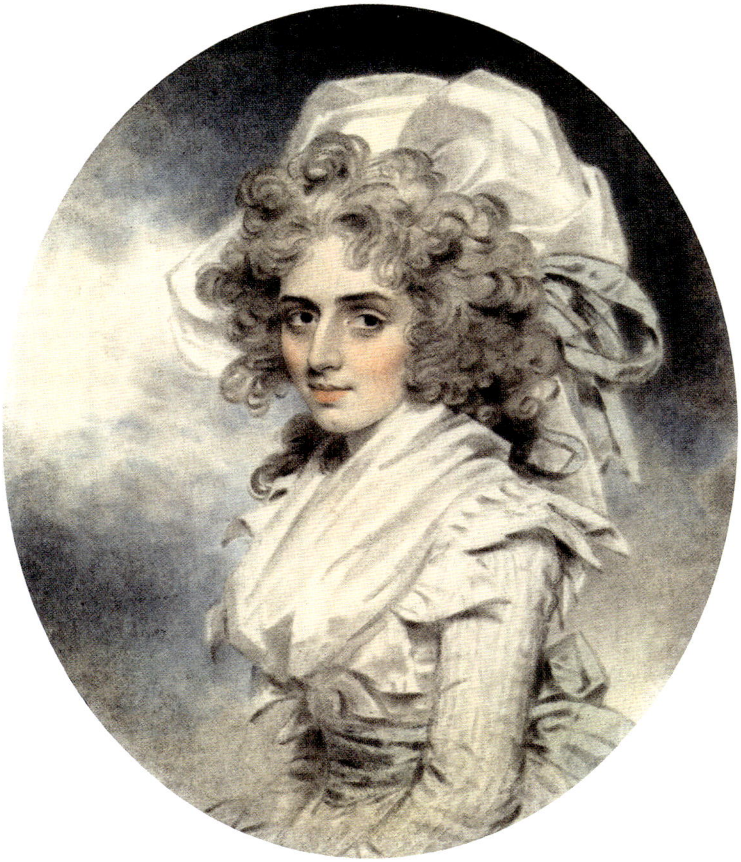

8 **Sarah Siddons** **(1755–1831)**
John Downman, 1787
Chalk, 203 × 171mm
NPG 2651

The English actor Sarah Siddons was a forerunner of modern thespians – such as Dames Judi Dench and Maggie Smith – pioneering a more psychological approach to the craft. The eldest of actor-manager Roger Kemble's twelve children, she toured with his company throughout her childhood, marrying company member William Siddons in 1773. Her first major success came in 1782 with her portrayal of Isabella in the *Fatal Marriage*, written by David Garrick, the leading actor-manager of the period. It led to a sequence of other tragic roles, and her renown as the peerless tragic actor of her day; the critic William Hazlitt proclaimed her 'tragedy personified'. Her portrayal of Lady Macbeth in a production of 1812 was her swansong. Painted by leading English portrait artists Sir Joshua Reynolds, Sir Thomas Lawrence and Thomas Gainsborough, she became a respected celebrity, her portraiture securing her fame. Her funeral in 1831 drew more than 5,000 mourners.

John Downman studied under Benjamin West and exhibited at the Royal Academy between 1770 and 1802. This fine chalk drawing of Siddons comes from a series of portraits of contemporary 'beauties' commissioned by the 3rd Duke of Richmond for the scenery of his private theatre productions in Richmond House. Siddons is pictured in ordinary, fashionable dress. Downman noted of the portrait, 'Off the Stage I thought her face more inclined to the Comic.' However, revealing her informal, 'comic' side, in contrast to her status as the great tragic actor, led to the work being criticised as a portrait of 'a pastoral coquette' when shown at the Royal Academy in 1788.

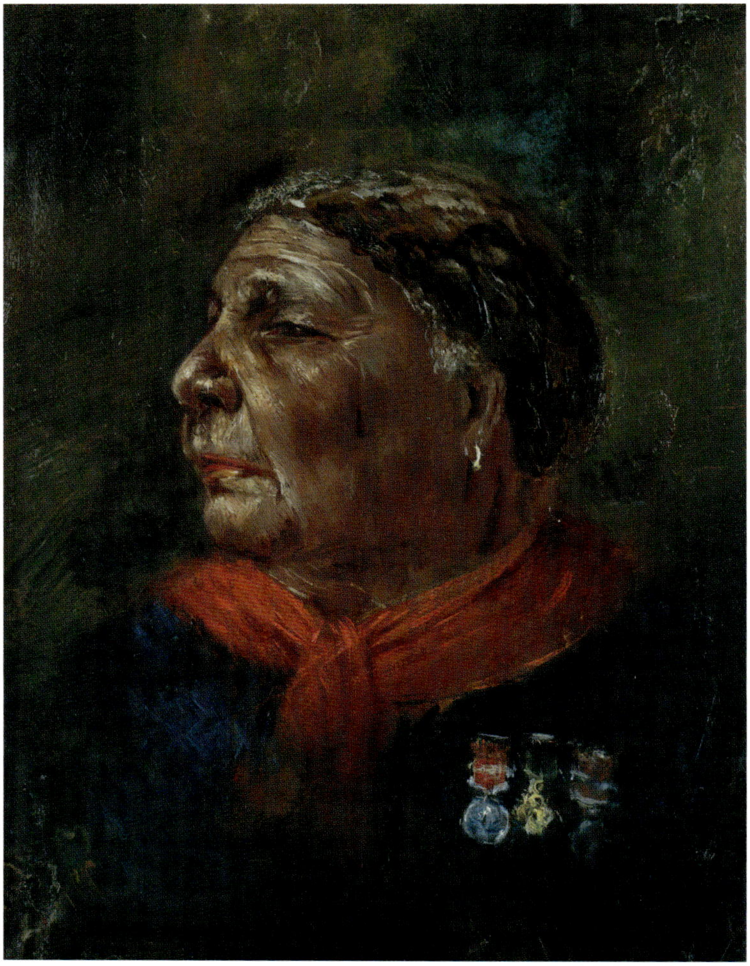

9 **Mary Seacole** **(1805–81)**
Albert Charles Challen, 1869
Oil on panel, 240 × 180mm
NPG 6856

Born in Kingston, Jamaica, Mary Seacole was the daughter of a Scottish army officer and a Jamaican businesswoman and practitioner of traditional Jamaican medicine. During her early career, she travelled between the Caribbean, Britain and Central America before coming to public prominence through her nursing activities during the Crimean War (1853–6). Rebuffed, probably due to her mixed-race background, when she tried to join Florence Nightingale's nursing sisters, she travelled independently to Balaklava, which served as an officers' club, a canteen for troops and a base for her nursing activities. She remained in the Crimea until July 1856, returning to England after financial difficulties. She published her memoir *Wonderful Adventures of Mrs Seacole in Many Lands* in 1857. While she was certainly the most famous black British woman of the nineteenth century, her historical significance following her death was largely forgotten in Britain until the 1970s, when revisionist historians started to recognise her important position in British history. She was posthumously awarded the Jamaican Order of Merit in 1991, and voted the greatest black Briton in a public poll of 2004.

This portrait dates from the last period of Seacole's life, when she was in her sixties. She wears a traditional Caribbean scarf and three roughly delineated medals commemorating her involvement in the Crimean War. Although she received no official British honour, she no doubt wore her medals to demonstrate pride in her achievements and her strong sense of comradeship with Crimean war veterans.

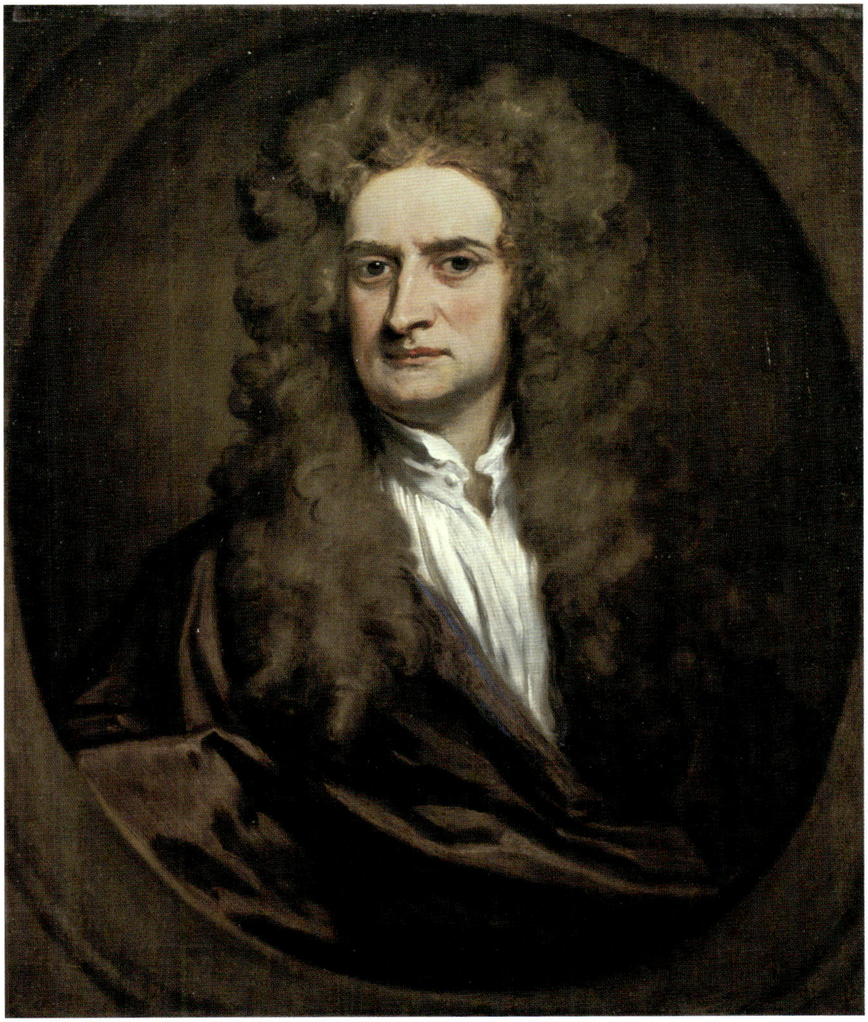

10 **Sir Isaac Newton** (1642–1727)

Sir Godfrey Kneller, 1702

Oil on canvas, 756 × 622mm
NPG 2881

One of the greatest of all scientists and thinkers, Sir Isaac Newton was the most important influence on theoretical physics and astronomy before Albert Einstein. However, his wide-ranging achievements include theories concerning light, colour and calculus. His most significant contribution to scientific thought is the theory of universal gravitation, an idea that supposedly first came to him when he saw an apple falling from a tree. His most important theories were published in two seminal works: *Principia Mathematica* (1687) and *Opticks* (1704). He was knighted by Queen Anne in 1705 and presided over the Royal Society, the oldest scientific academy in continuous existence, from 1703 until his death.

There was great demand for Newton's portrait among friends and associates, and by institutions with which he was connected. This demonstrates Newton's enormous fame and the desire of others to acquire some reflected glory by owning portraits of him. Newton understood the benefits of his fame and was a willing sitter. The portrait above was painted when Newton and Sir Godfrey Kneller, painter to numerous British monarchs, were at the indisputable pinnacle of their respective professions. It is the second of four portraits Kneller painted of Newton. The picture is conventional in almost every sense – the head-and-shoulders composition, the wig and the arbitrary swathe of drapery. However, Kneller's vigorous and swift handling of the paint gives the picture an exceptional vividness, while the piercing intensity of the sitter's gaze provides a sense of his genius. Newton kept the portrait in his possession until he died.

11 **Dame Elizabeth Taylor** (1932–2011)
Yousuf Karsh, 1946

Gelatin silver print, 338 × 268mm
NPG P490(74)

Born in London to American parents living in Britain, Dame Elizabeth Taylor made her film debut aged 10 in 1942. Her career moved with increasing acclaim from roles as a child in films such as *National Velvet* (1944) and *Little Women* (1949) to parts in Tennessee Williams adaptations, including *Suddenly Last Summer* (1959). Taylor fell in love with Richard Burton on the set of the 1963 film *Cleopatra* and married him in 1964. They appeared together in several films, including *Who's Afraid of Virginia Woolf?* in 1966, for which she won a second Academy Award, and *The Taming of the Shrew* in 1967. Latterly she devoted her energies to raising funds for AIDS research.

This photograph was taken at the height of Taylor's early fame by the renowned Armenian-Canadian photographer Yousuf Karsh. Karsh was fascinated by the 'greatness' of eminent contemporary figures, and through careful manipulation of pose and artificial lighting imbued all his sitters with a sense of timeless dignity.

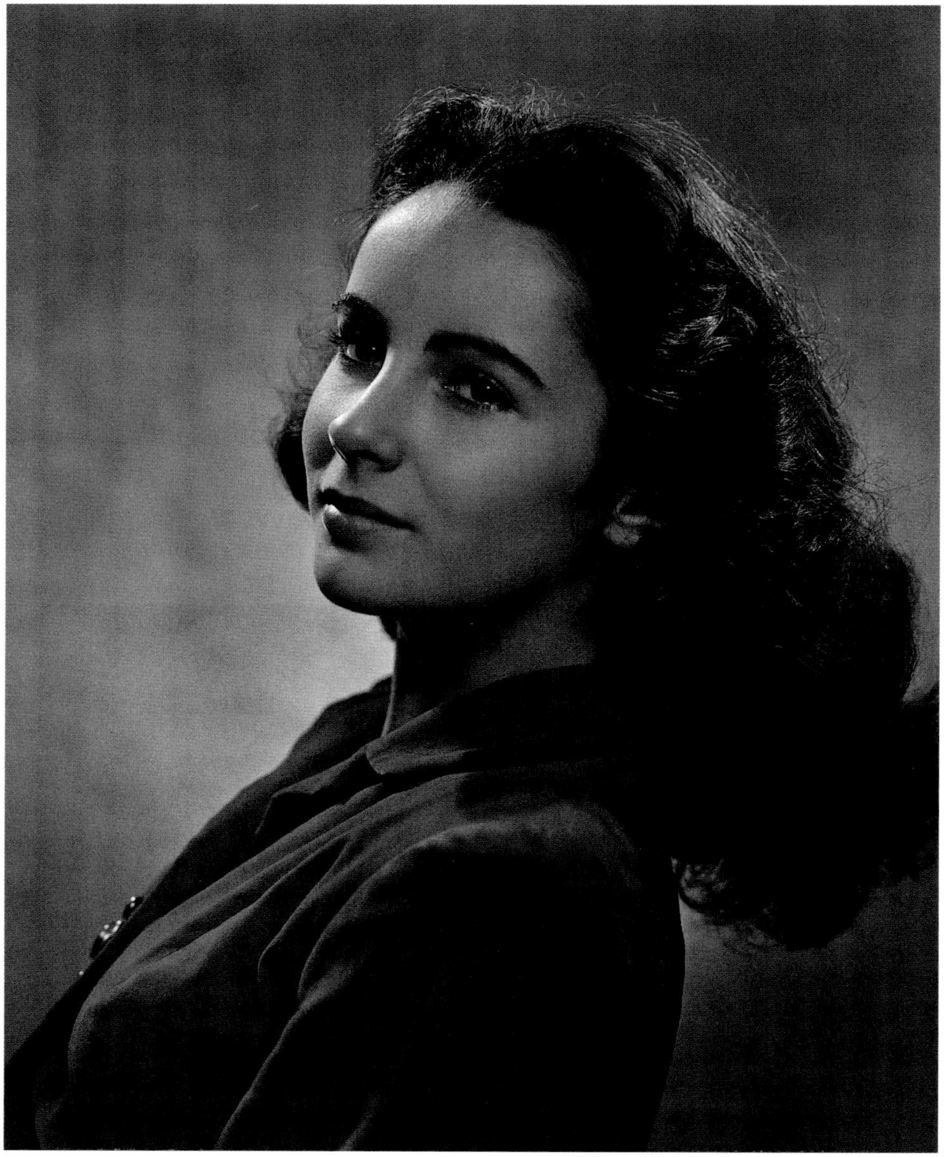

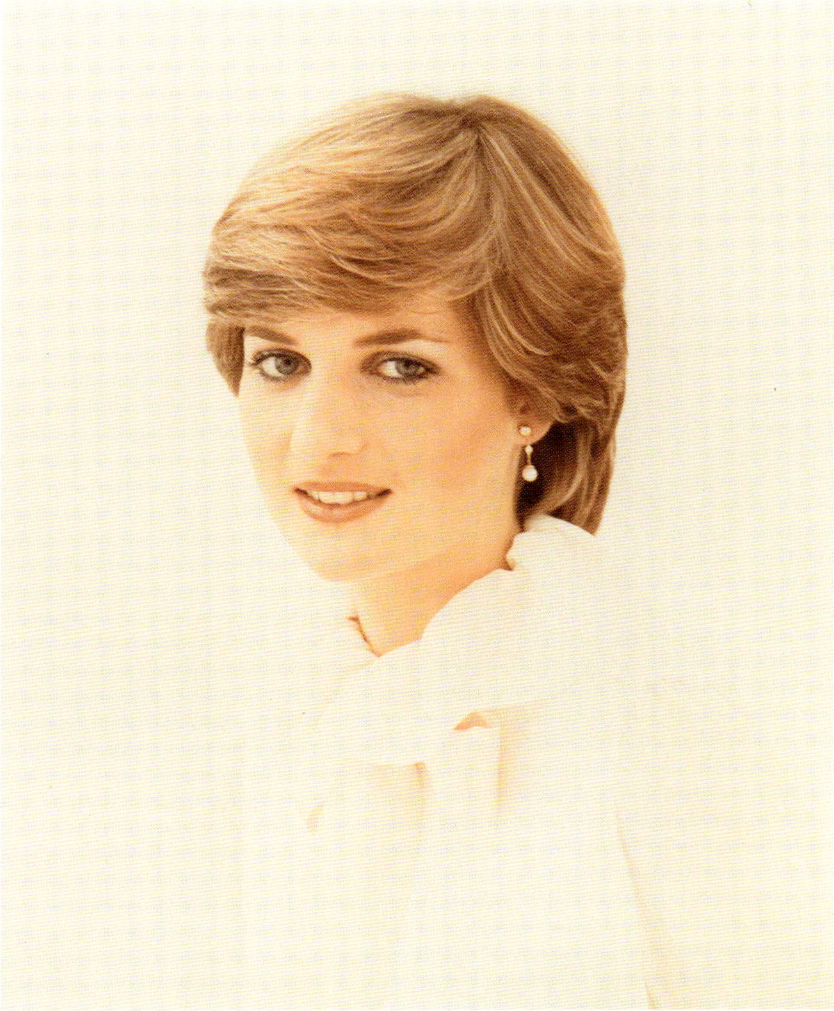

12 **Diana, Princess of Wales** **(1961–97)**
Lord Snowdon, 1981
Cibachrome print, 508 × 406mm
NPG P218

Diana, Princess of Wales, was born into an aristocratic British family and at the age of 20 married Charles, Prince of Wales, eldest son of Queen Elizabeth II. She was known as the 'People's Princess' and embodied many roles throughout her life: as a representative of the royal family, as wife and mother, as ambassador for numerous charities, and as an icon of fashion and beauty. Diana was renowned for her empathy, which made the public feel closer to her than to other royal figures. She drew huge crowds at her public engagements, and her fame reached immense heights around the world, affording her a single-name identifier.

This photograph was published in British *Vogue* in February 1981, coinciding with the announcement of her engagement. It was commissioned by *Vogue* as part of a 'Portrait Portfolio' of young aristocratic women by the photographer Lord Snowdon, who had recently divorced Princess Margaret, but continued to photograph the royal family. Lady Diana Spencer, as she then was, is presented as a demure 'English rose', wearing a chiffon blouse with a satin ribbon necktie by David and Elizabeth Emanuel, the designers who went on to create her wedding dress. Although she had dated Prince Charles for only six months prior to the engagement, she was quickly launched into the spotlight. From the outset, their relationship was subjected to public scrutiny, and the teenage Lady Diana had to adapt to constant media presence, becoming over the years one of the most photographed people in the world. The couple had two sons, the princes William and Harry, but their marriage was dissolved in 1996. A year later Diana, Princess of Wales, died in a car accident in Paris.

13 **George Harrison** (1943–2001), **Sir Paul McCartney** (b.1942), **Sir Ringo Starr** (b.1940) **and John Lennon** (1940–80) **('The Beatles')**

Norman Parkinson, 1963

Gelatin silver print, 392 × 591mm (image size)
NPG x128893

Widely considered the most important band of all time, The Beatles defined the Swinging Sixties and contributed to the rise of British bands on the international stage. Arguably the most famous Britons of the era, The Beatles sold 150 million albums during the recording lifespan of the band, from *Please Please Me* in 1963 to *Let it Be* in 1970. 'Beatlemania' erupted in the year that Norman Parkinson's photograph was taken in a hotel in Russell Square on an early visit to London, and for the next seven years the group needed police protection wherever they appeared. The Beatles remain the best-selling band of all time and continue to influence music today.

Although the youngest member of The Beatles, George Harrison wrote two of the band's most enduring songs, 'Something' and 'Here Comes the Sun'. He introduced the band to Eastern spiritualism and Indian music, and went on to enjoy a solo career, including financing successful British films such as Monty Python's *Life of Brian* (1979).

Paul McCartney became lead in the band *Wings*, formed with his first wife, Linda, and later launched a successful solo career. An outspoken vegetarian and activist, McCartney is a patron of a number of international charities. A seminal influence on popular culture, he was knighted in 1997.

Ringo Starr joined The Beatles as drummer in 1962. He occasionally sang lead vocals, including 'With a Little Help from My Friends' on *Sgt. Pepper's Lonely Hearts Club Band* (1967). Following the break-up of the group he frequently collaborated with his former bandmates and was knighted in 2018 for services to music.

Born in Liverpool, John Lennon married Cynthia Powell in 1962, and later married Yoko Ono, whom he met in 1966 at the Indica Gallery in London. In 1970, when the Beatles split, he embarked on a solo career. On 8 December 1980, he became a victim of an assassination by a crazed fan and died aged 40.

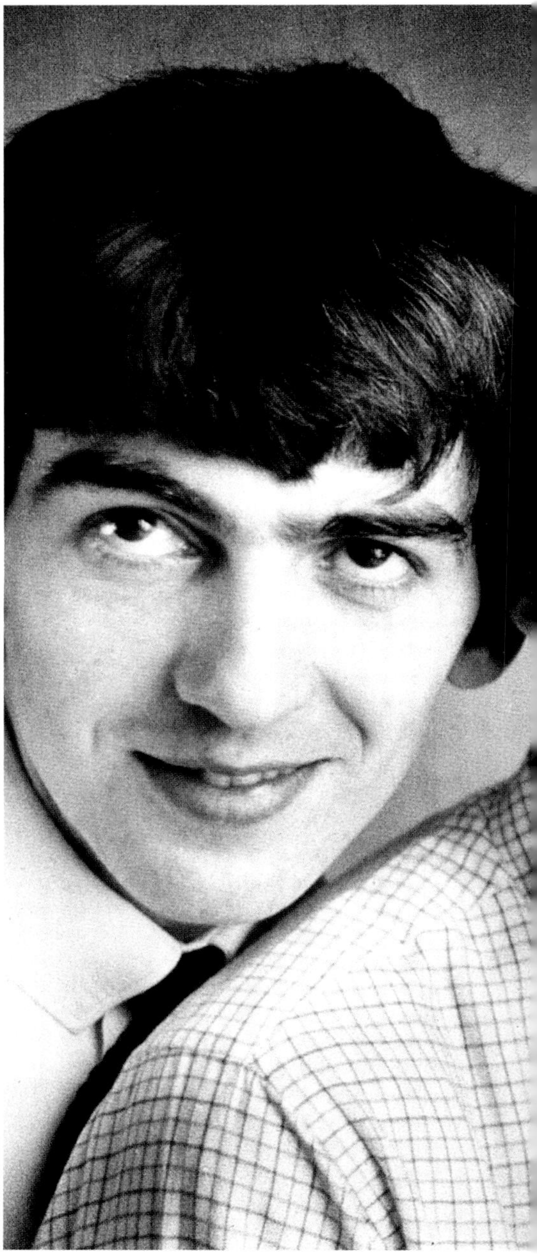

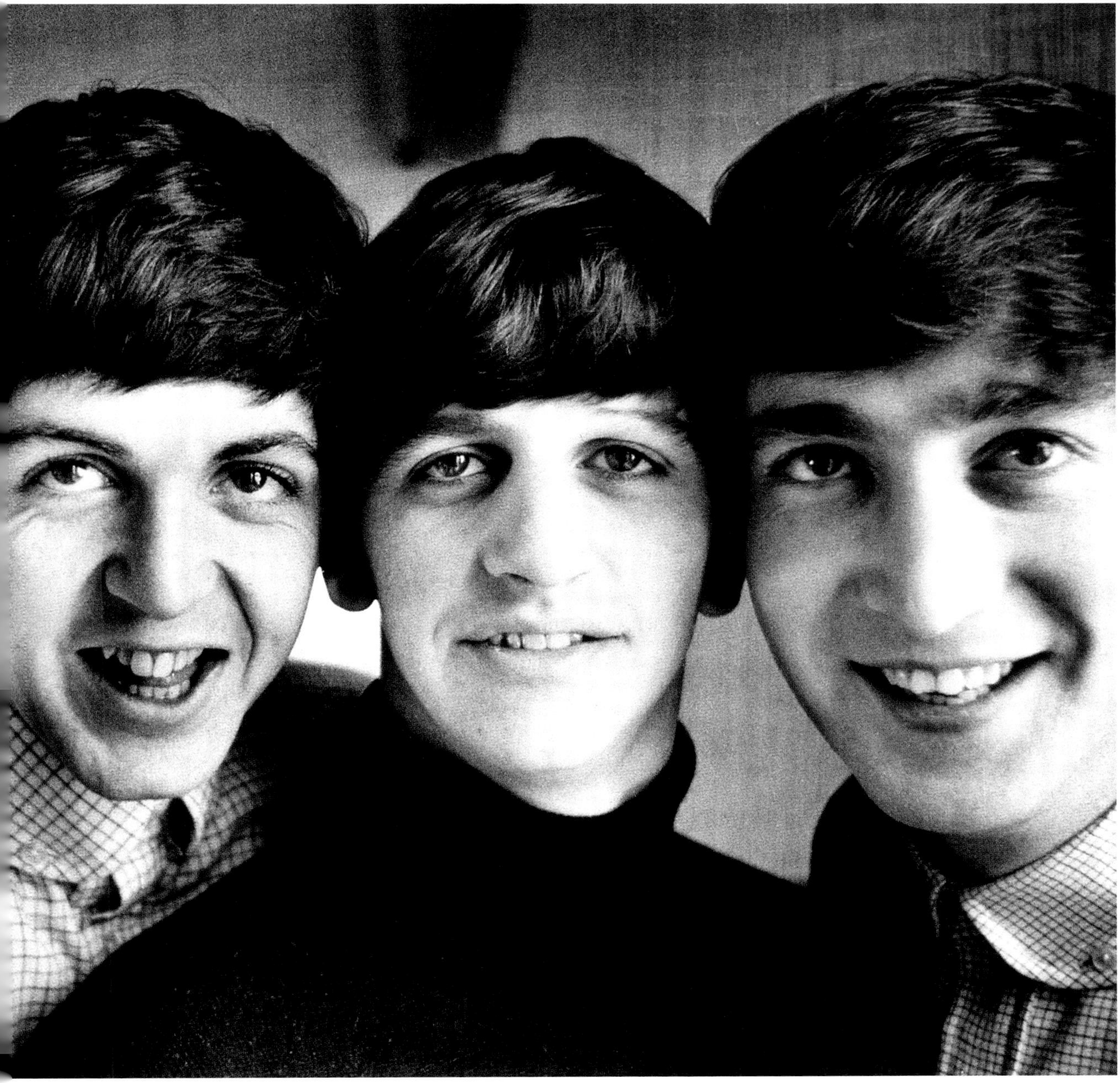

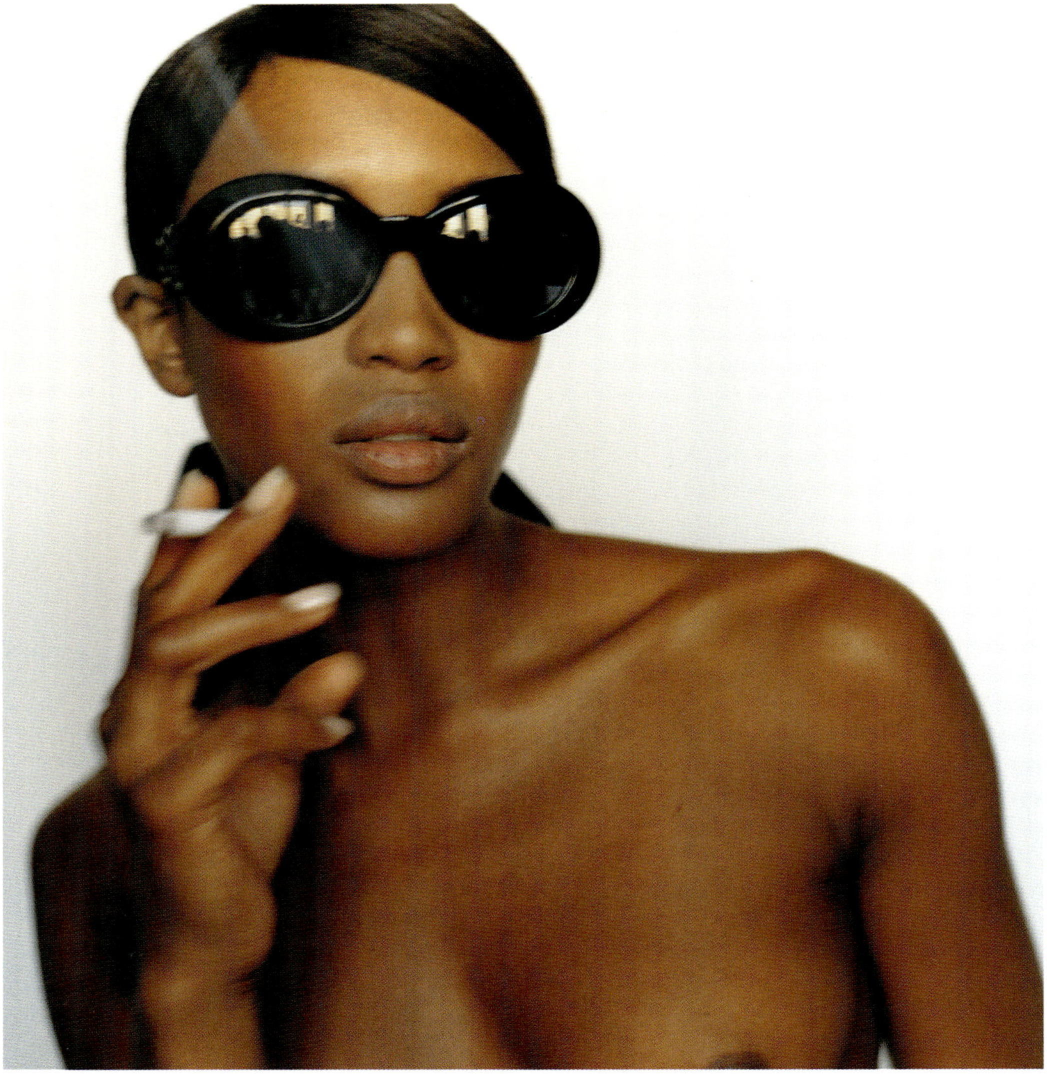

14 Naomi Campbell (b.1970)
Mario Testino, 1996
Chromogenic print, 510 × 407mm
NPG P1012

London-born Naomi Campbell attended stage school aged 5 and worked in television and on music videos before signing with a model agency in 1985. She became one of the most recognised and sought-after models of the 1980s and 1990s, dubbed one of the six supermodels of her generation. She has appeared on more than 500 magazine covers, was the first British black model to appear on the cover of British *Vogue* (December 1987, see opposite), and was the first black cover model for French *Vogue* (August 1988), *TIME* magazine (September 1991) and Russian *Vogue* (September 2000). Her early experiences of performing and auditioning led to a sense of being overlooked: 'I understood what it meant to be black … You had to be twice as good.' She has fronted high-profile campaigns for prestigious couture houses, and stands against racism and for diversity in her industry. Her advice, reported by *Elle*, to those insecure in an industry that seems not to value them: 'Do not give up or give in.' A contributor to British *GQ*, *Interview* and other magazines, including British *Vogue* since 2017, she also fundraises for the Nelson Mandela Children's Fund and is a Fashion for Relief spokesperson.

This seemingly informal photograph by Mario Testino was taken in Paris for the fashion label Versace. Wearing nothing but a pair of sunglasses, Campbell exudes self-confidence. The photographer can be seen as a diminutive figure reflected in the sunglasses.

15 **Naomi Campbell** (b.1970)
Patrick Demarchelier, 1987
Chromogenic print, 1158 × 865mm
NPG x199692

This image by fashion photographer Patrick Demarchelier was Naomi Campbell's debut British *Vogue* cover in December 1987 and shows her wearing a shimmering dress by Chanel. With this image, Campbell also became the first British black model on the cover of British *Vogue*; there would be many more cover shoots in her journey from south London teenager to world-renowned supermodel.

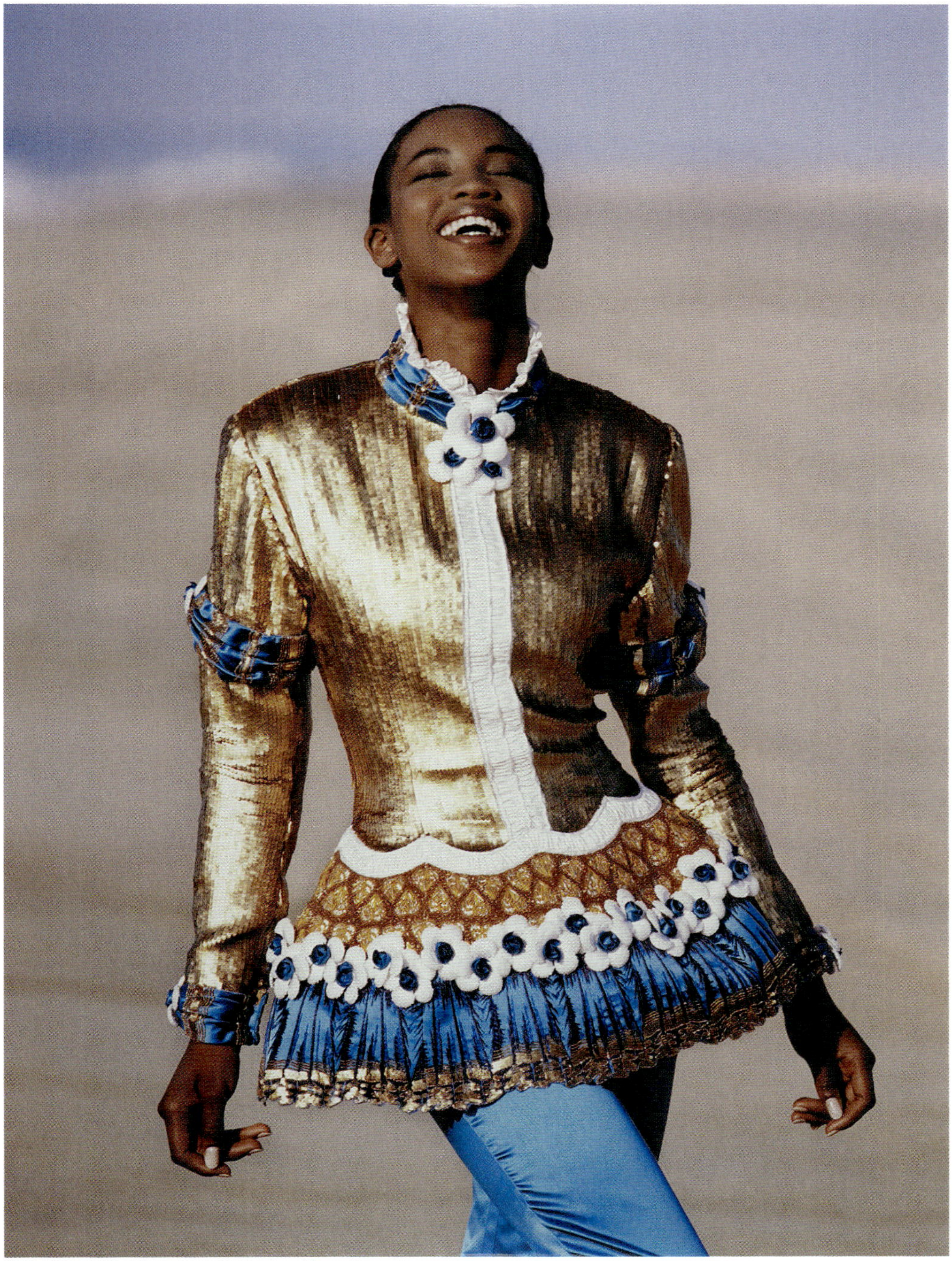

16 **Frank Bruno** (b.1961)
Sir Don McCullin, 1983

Gelatin silver print, 347 × 280mm
NPG x26502

Frank Bruno started boxing at Wandsworth Boys Club in London when he was 9 years old. His professional boxing career began in 1982, and he went on to win twenty-one consecutive fights through knockouts, becoming well known for his punching prowess. During his career he made unsuccessful bids for the world title against Tim Witherspoon (1986), Mike Tyson (1989) and Lennox Lewis (1993), before taking the WBC title on a unanimous points decision over Oliver McCall at Wembley on 2 September 1995. He was awarded an MBE in 1990. In 2003 he was diagnosed with bipolar disorder, and has since helped to raise awareness of the stigma attached to mental health.

Sir Don McCullin is recognised as one of the greatest British photographers of the twentieth century, renowned for his photojournalism documenting the horrors of war around the world, but also for his poignant landscapes, still lifes and commissioned portraits. McCullin photographed Frank Bruno as part of a series of sporting figures. When this photograph was taken, Bruno was undefeated and on his way to cementing his reputation as one of Britain's best-loved sports personalities.

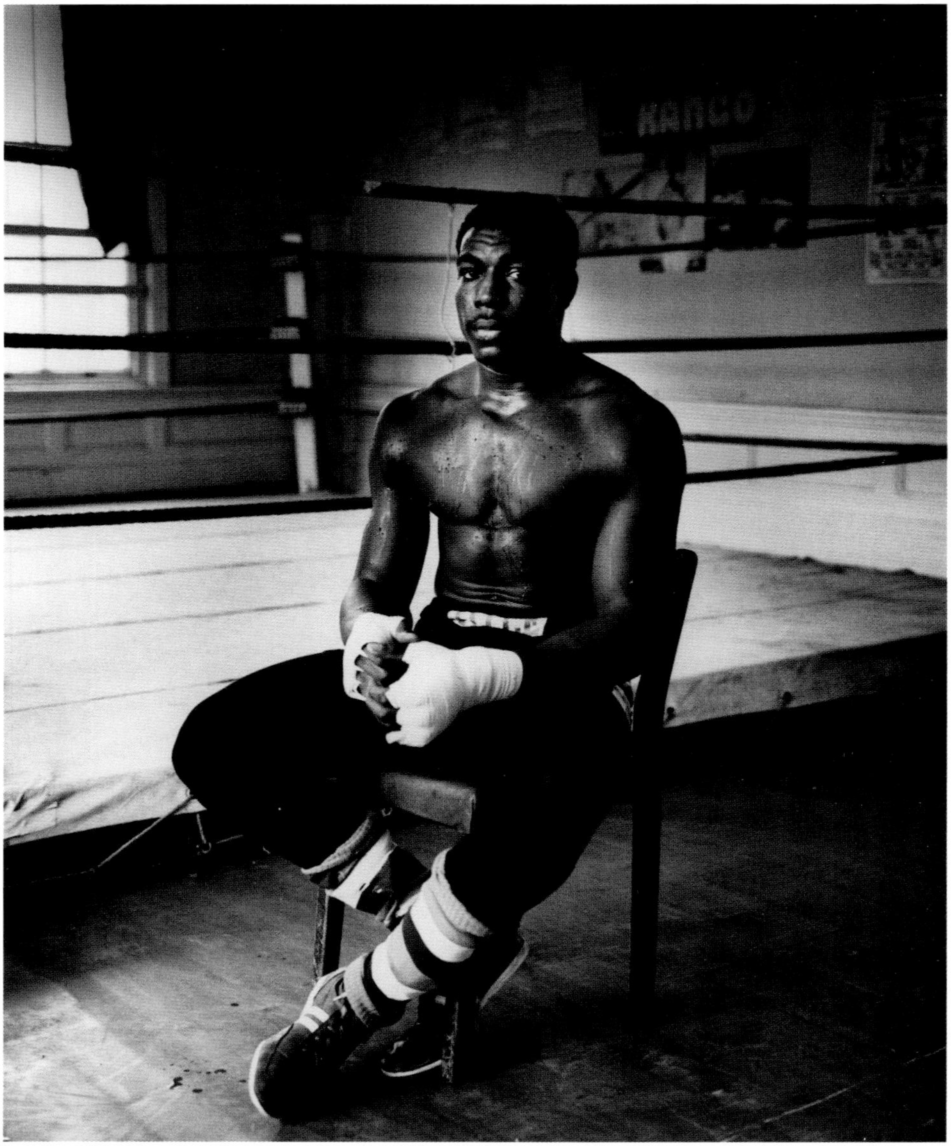

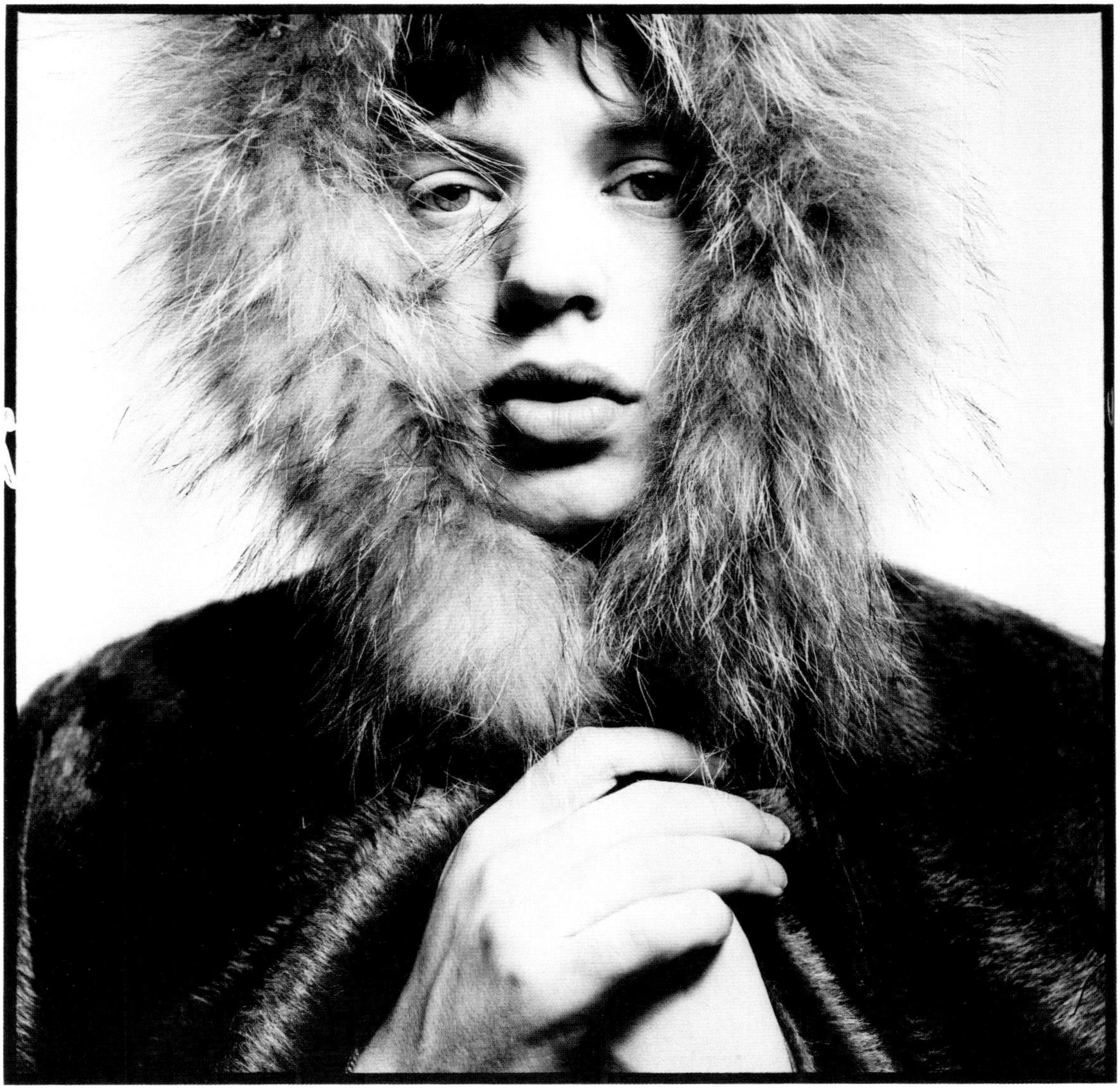

17 **Sir Mick Jagger** **(b.1943)**
David Bailey, 1964
Gelatin silver print, 410 × 408mm
NPG P952

Born in Dartford and educated at Dartford Grammar School and the London School of Economics, Sir Mick Jagger formed the rock band The Rolling Stones in 1962 with Keith Richards and Brian Jones. Bill Wyman and Charlie Watts joined soon after. One of the most successful and enduring bands of all time, The Rolling Stones' hits include *Satisfaction* (1965), *Street Fighting Man* (1971) and *Angie* (1973). Jagger also starred in films such as *Performance* and *Ned Kelly* (both 1970). A cultural icon for over fifty years, he was knighted in 2003 for services to popular music.

The photographer David Bailey is the most famous chronicler of London in the 1960s, with two defining portrait publications: *David Bailey's Box of Pin-Ups* (1965) and *Goodbye Baby and Amen* (1969). This photograph of Jagger appeared on the back cover of the *Box of Pin-Ups* publication and is one of thirty-six portraits, mainly of male leading figures from London's new cultural and fashionable elite. The portfolio includes many of the actors, artists, musicians and models who have since become synonymous with the Swinging Sixties. Collectively, they reveal a new celebrity culture that evolved during a decade of great change. In the accompanying text, the writer Francis Wyndham observed: 'In the age of Mick Jagger, it's the boys who are the pin-ups.'

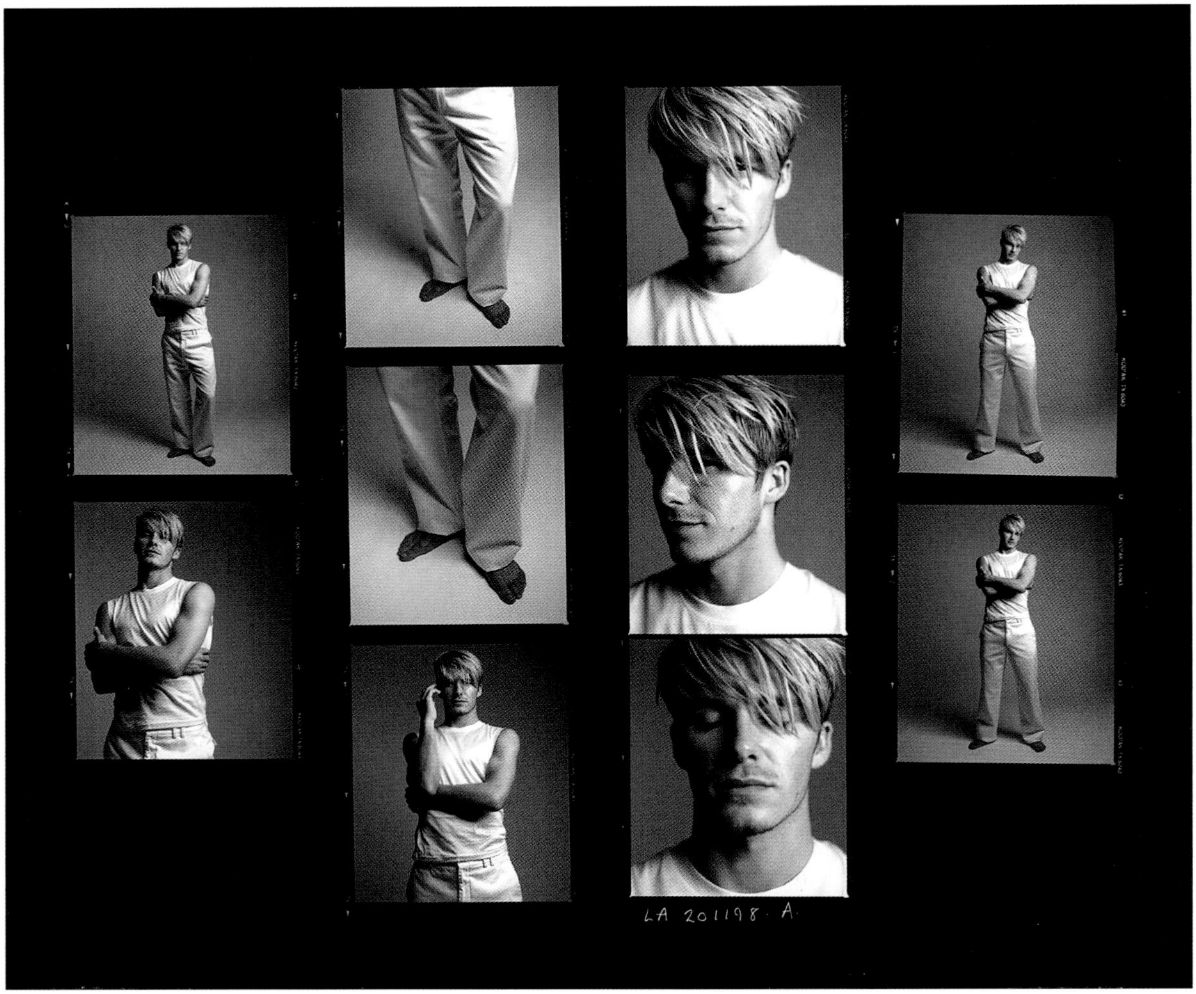

18 **David Beckham (b.1975)**
Lorenzo Agius, 1998
Contact sheet, 270 × 320mm
NPG x88384

19 **David Beckham (b.1975)**
Lorenzo Agius, 1998
Gelatin silver print, 500 × 370mm
NPG x88370

Beckham contributed to nineteen major footballing trophy wins in a career where he played for Manchester United (1992–2003), Real Madrid (2003–7), LA Galaxy (2007–12) and Paris Saint-Germain (2013). He captained the English national team fifty-eight times over a six-year period.

This close-up head-and-shoulders photograph, and the accompanying contact sheets showing Beckham in multiple poses, were taken by Lorenzo Agius in 1998, the same year Beckham proposed to Victoria Adams, then a Spice Girl. Known as 'Posh and Becks', their relationship has been the subject of considerable media attention ever since. Beckham has modelled extensively, appearing in campaigns for his own clothing lines, fragrances and even whisky. His instantly recognisable appearance has become a desirable brand. He received an OBE in 2003, and in 2010 was presented with the BBC Sports Personality of the Year Lifetime Achievement Award. In 2018, Beckham announced his newly established Major League Soccer team, Inter Miami CF.

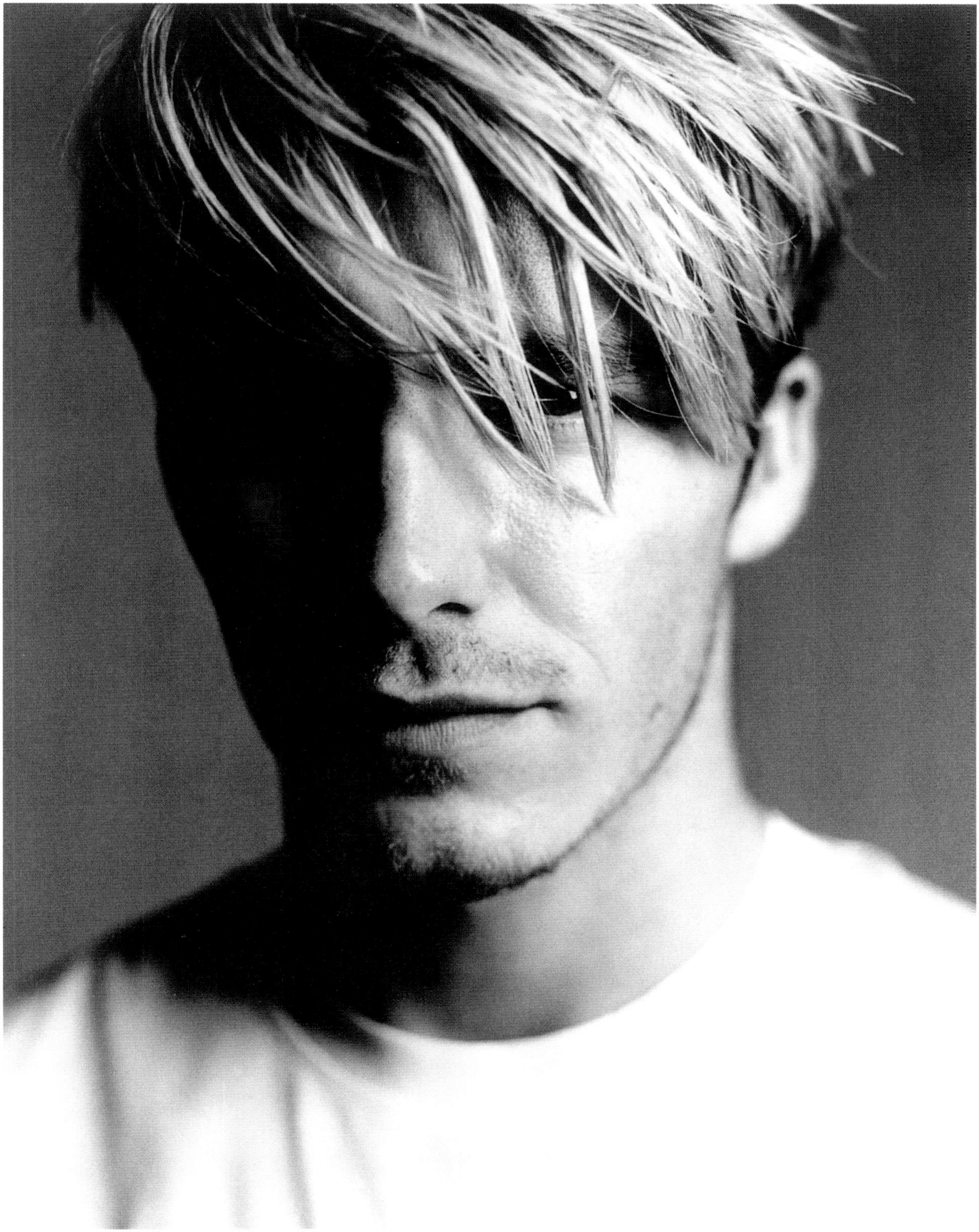

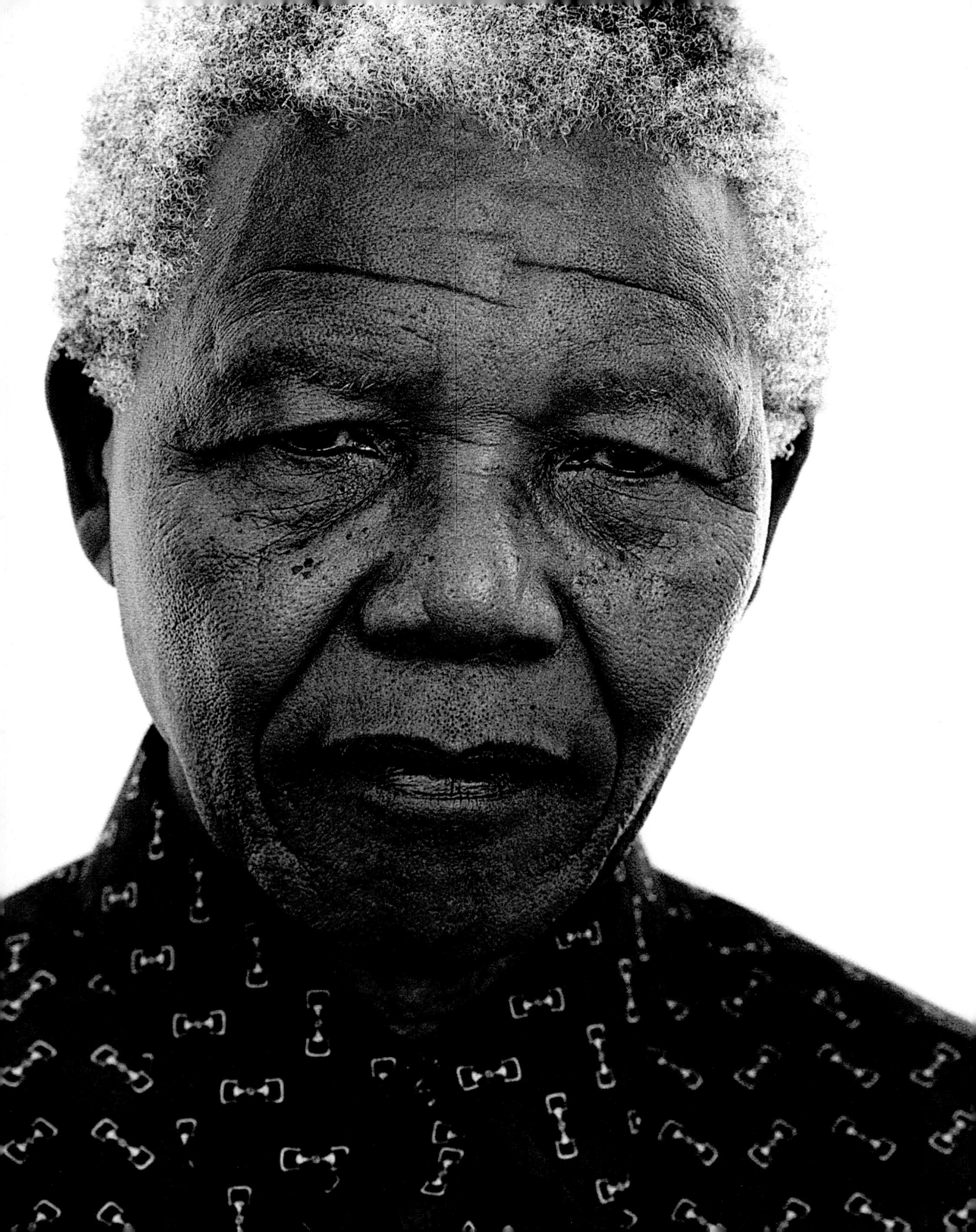

Power

There are many types of power – political, economic, military, social and cultural – and these often intersect or reinforce one another. The representation of power in portraiture is similarly varied, ranging from outright propaganda to more complex and subtle works in which the theme may not be immediately apparent. An illustrative comparison can be made between the portraits of King Charles I by Gerrit van Honthorst (see p.48) and Oliver Cromwell by Robert Walker (see p.49).

King Charles is presented informally, unburdened by the usual trappings of monarchy, but his elevated status is nevertheless indicated by his dignified expression and the refinement and luxury of his clothes. Perhaps the key indication of his power is the fact that the portrait is evidence of his ability to secure the services of one of the most fashionable artists in continental Europe. An alternative approach is employed in the portrait of Oliver Cromwell, the king's nemesis during the English Civil War (1642–51), who is presented as the stern embodiment of military authority. However, despite overthrowing the monarchy and executing the king, Cromwell's portrait is far from revolutionary, as all the elements have been copied from earlier royalist portraits by Sir Anthony van Dyck.

Representations of power may be largely illusory, as with Louis Gabriel Blanchet's grandiose portrait proclaiming the royal authority of Prince Charles Edward Stuart (see p.50), even though it was painted fifty years after his grandfather, King James II, had been deposed from the British throne and the prince and his family were living in exile in Rome. Portraits may be produced as part of an official programme of image making, as with Nicholas Hilliard's portrait of Queen Elizabeth I (see p.47). Other types of power explored in this section include the imperial military power that is casually referenced in James Jacques Tissot's portrait of Frederick Burnaby (see pp.52–3) and the intellectual and moral authority celebrated in Sir Thomas Lawrence's portrait of the slavery abolitionist William Wilberforce (see p.51).

Contemporary artists continue to explore and question the conventions of how to convey power in portraits. The scale and optical domination of Alex Katz's portrait of Anna Wintour (see pp.58–9) complements her standing in the world of fashion. Sean Henry's sculpture of the Internet pioneer Tim Berners-Lee (see p.56) – presented casually, as if caught off guard on his way to work, his laptop bag swung over his shoulder – invokes the power the World Wide Web has brought to the 'everyman', rather than the prestige of its inventor. Photographs of the twentieth-century prime minister Margaret Thatcher (see p.55) and the human rights activist Malala Yousafzai (see p.62) depict people with very different life experiences and claims to authority, yet their portraits share a steadfast gaze that is characteristic of portraits of power.

DETAIL **Nelson Mandela, 1997**

2

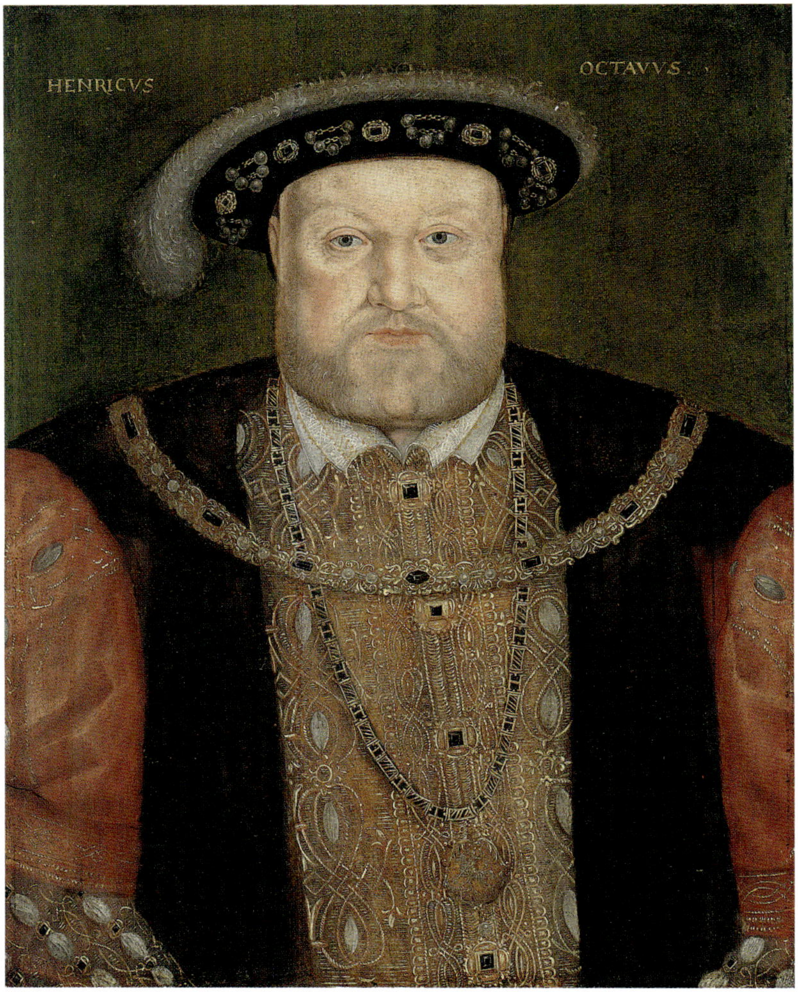

20 King Henry VIII (1491–1547)

Unknown artist, c.1597–1618

Oil on panel, 582 × 450mm (uneven)
NPG 4980(14)

King Henry VIII acceded the throne in 1509, shortly before his eighteenth birthday. Perhaps most popularly known for his six marriages, Henry's reign was characterised by ambition abroad and ruthlessness at home. Henry married his brother Arthur's widow, Katherine of Aragon, just before his coronation, and they ruled the country together for over twenty years. The pressure to provide the realm with a male heir to the throne ultimately caused Henry to doubt the legitimacy of their union and he sought to have the marriage annulled in order to marry Anne Boleyn. He initiated the break from the Catholic Church in Rome and transferred the Church's assets to the Crown and nobility, following the dissolution of religious houses in England.

With the possible exception of his daughter Queen Elizabeth I, no English monarch has matched Henry VIII's ability to control his public image and impose it on posterity. The work shown here is part of an important portrait set of early English kings and queens that formerly hung in Hornby Castle. It comprises sixteen portraits of English rulers from William the Conqueror to Queen Mary I. Similar sets of portraits were popular in later Elizabethan and Jacobean houses, and were used to decorate long galleries. Portrait sets celebrated the hereditary claim of the reigning monarch – in this case probably Elizabeth I – affirming their position as the rightful heir. Their growing popularity in the late sixteenth century was in part due to an increased interest in the history of the nation. The portraits in the set were likely based on an early printed set of portraits; the images of the earliest kings are mostly fictitious, while those from Edward III onward relate to a painting, print, or effigy believed to be from life. Henry VIII's portrait derives from a type created by Hans Holbein the Younger.

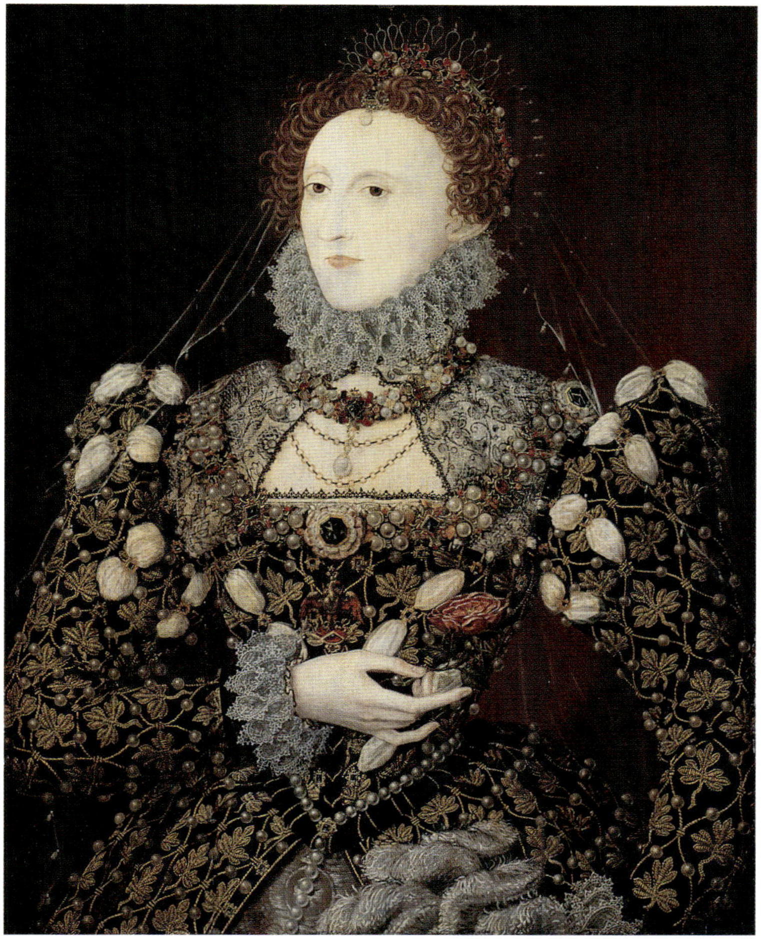

21 Queen Elizabeth I (1533–1603)

Associated with Nicholas Hilliard, c.1575

Oil on panel, 787 × 610mm

NPG 190

The only surviving child of Henry VIII of England and his second wife, Anne Boleyn, Elizabeth was 25 years old when she inherited the throne from her half-sister Mary. In 1557 the Venetian ambassador described her as 'comely rather than handsome ... tall and well formed, with a good skin ... she has fine eyes and above all a beautiful hand of which she makes a display'. On becoming queen, Elizabeth I surrounded herself with able advisers and together they brought about the re-establishment of the Church of England. She was expected to marry, but was constrained in her choice by the fact that an English nobleman would have been beneath her status and risked the development of factions at court, while a European prince raised the spectre of foreign influence in English affairs. Robert Dudley, Earl of Leicester, and Hercule-François, Duc d'Alençon, were Elizabeth's most persistent suitors, but, ultimately, Elizabeth chose to retain her authority and rule in her own right.

The use of clothing and jewellery as symbols of power, authority and wealth predates the emergence of the painted portrait. It is in portraiture, however, that we have clear visual evidence of the ways elaborate clothing could represent royal power. This portrait of Elizabeth shows her wearing a jewel in the form of one of her favourite emblems, the phoenix, which symbolised both virginity and renewal. She also adopted black and white as her colours, their association with constancy and purity being highly appropriate for the 'Virgin Queen'.

She clasps a red rose, a symbol of the house of Tudor, which together with the phoenix and the vast number of pearls – also a symbol of purity – serve as a reassurance that Elizabeth would regenerate and sustain the dynasty. The portrait was most likely completed in the studio or under the supervision of the artist Nicholas Hilliard, who was called upon by Elizabeth's ministers and courtiers to make images filled with codes and symbols that emphasised the queen's royal power.

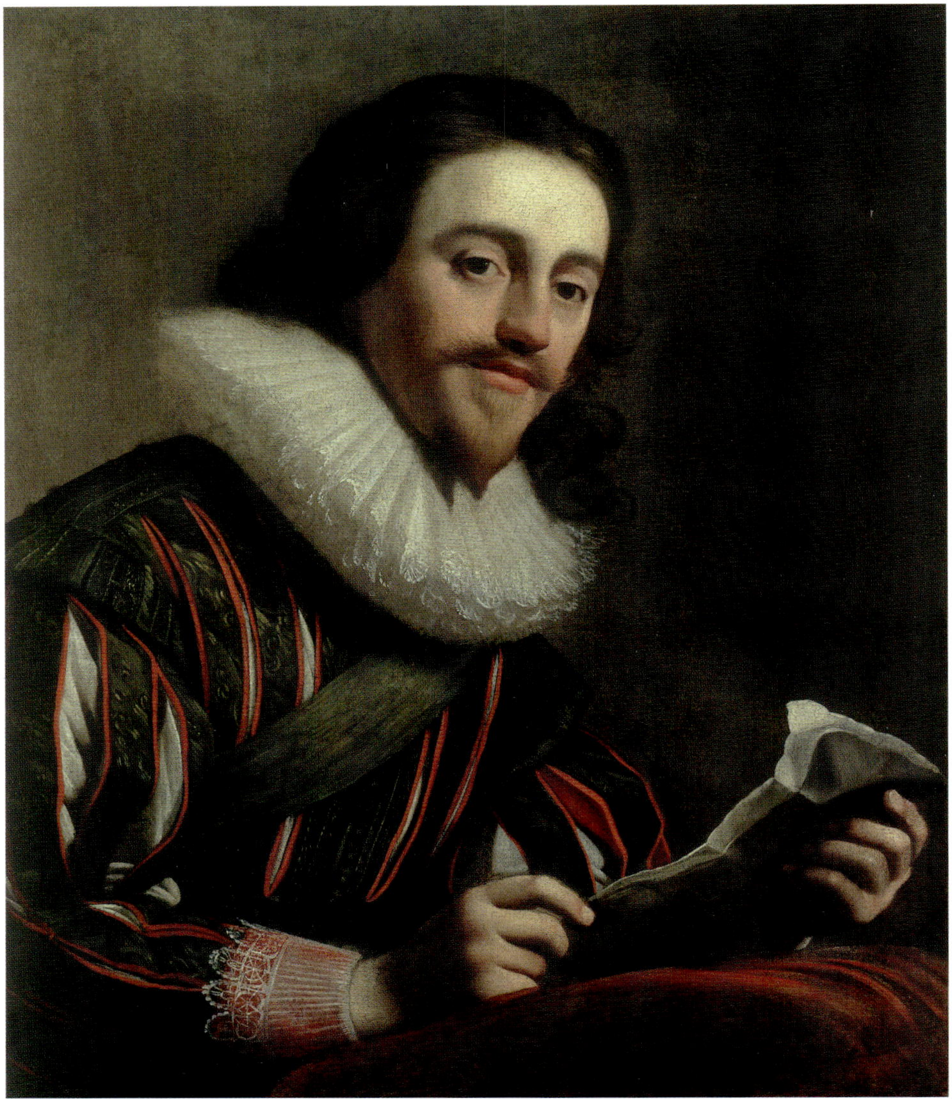

22 **King Charles I** (1600–49)

Gerrit van Honthorst, 1628

Oil on canvas, 762 × 641mm
NPG 4444

The younger son of King James I and Anne of Denmark, Charles became heir to the throne on the death of his brother Henry in 1612. He suffered from a speech impediment and physical disabilities as a child, and from comparisons with his much-admired elder brother as a young man, but his personal life flourished, with a successful marriage to Henrietta Maria of France, and six children who survived beyond early childhood. However, his dismissal of Parliament, his imposition of unpopular taxes and his attempts to impose religious uniformity contributed to increasing civil and political unrest, and eventually to civil war, culminating in his execution outside the Banqueting House on Whitehall on 30 January 1649.

This informal and intimate portrait made from life captures something of the king's serious-minded, scholarly character. It was painted during the period that Gerrit van Honthorst was working on a large allegorical group portrait now at Hampton Court. Charles, a passionate collector and patron of art, had invited the Dutch artist to come to England in 1628. He commissioned a huge painting that shows himself and his queen as Apollo and Diana, along with his favourite, the Duke of Buckingham, as Mercury, presenting the Seven Liberal Arts.

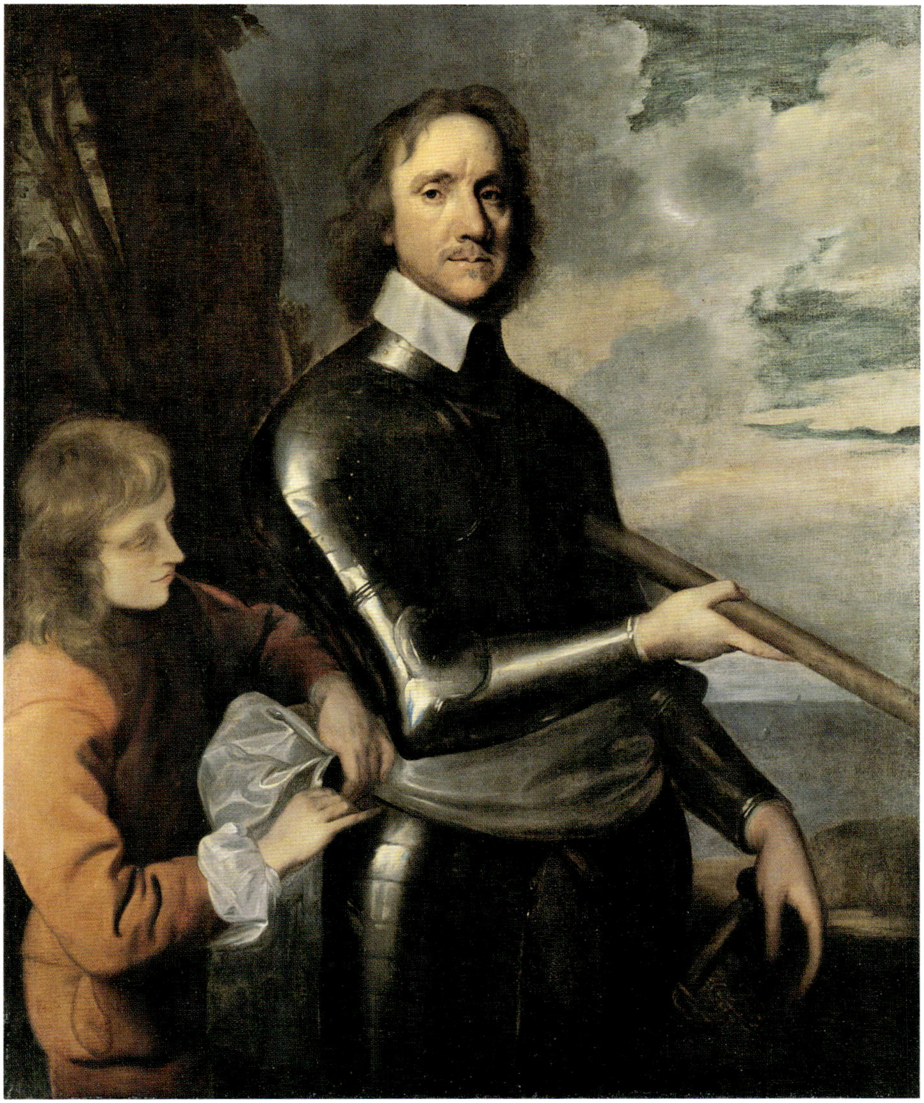

23 **Oliver Cromwell** **(1599–1658)**
Robert Walker, *c.*1649
Oil on canvas, 1257 × 1016mm
NPG 536

Oliver Cromwell rose from the position of a country gentleman to become a leading statesman, soldier and finally head of state as Lord Protector (1653–8). His political and military career was shaped by strongly held religious beliefs. As a Puritan, he was distrustful of King Charles I and felt that the Church of England was insufficiently Protestant. As the country descended into civil war, Cromwell emerged as a natural leader, and his military skill was a decisive factor in the Parliamentarian victory. Following the execution of the king in 1649, he led the New Model Army in brutal campaigns in Ireland and Scotland. He refused the crown in 1657, and his death left a power vacuum that would only be filled by the restoration of the monarchy in 1660.

This portrait was painted soon after the execution of the king at a time when the new regime was searching for appropriate forms of self-representation. The solution provided by Robert Walker was to base Cromwell's portrait on elements taken from Sir Anthony van Dyck's portraits of Charles I's court. Cromwell's armour, baton and the sash being tied around his waist by an attendant were all symbols of military command, borrowed from the regime that he had just overthrown.

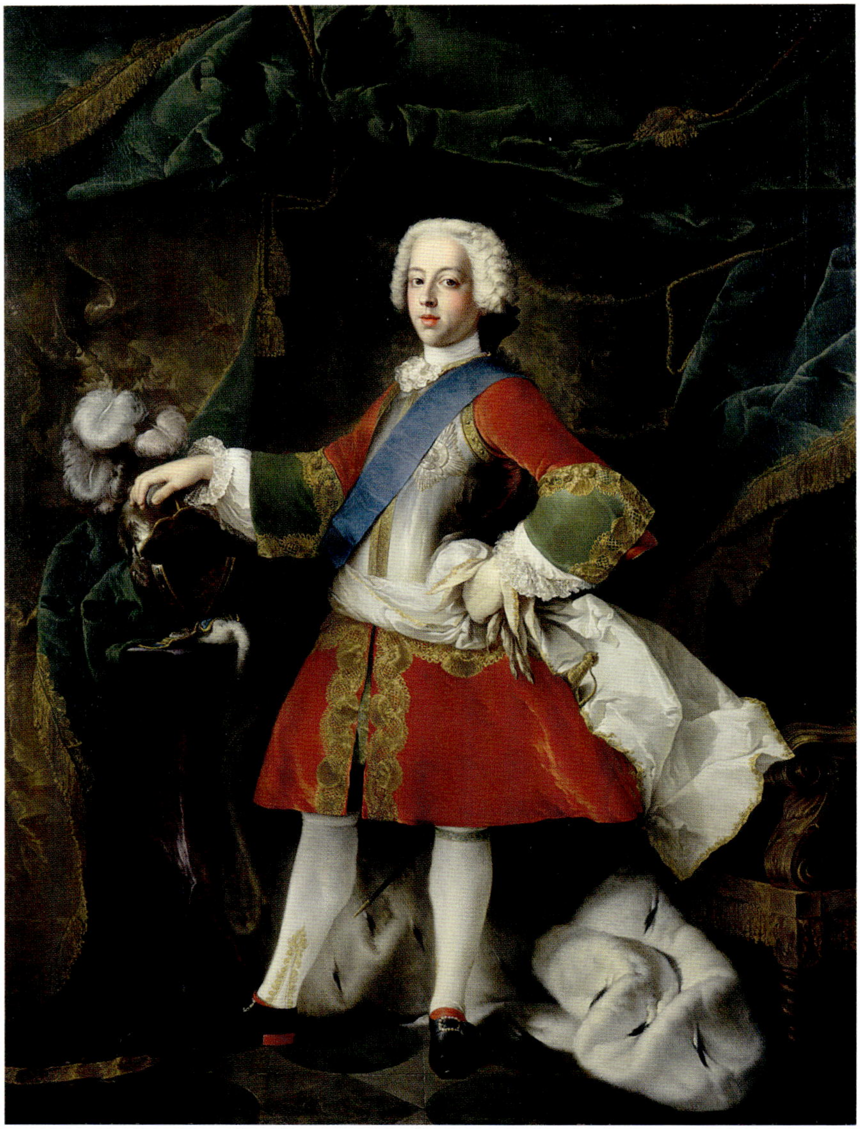

24 **Prince Charles Edward Stuart** (1720–88)
Louis Gabriel Blanchet, 1738
Oil on canvas, 1905 × 1410mm
NPG 5517

Born in Rome, Prince Charles Edward Stuart – also known as 'Bonnie Prince Charlie' and the 'Young Pretender' – was the grandson of James II, who had been deposed from the British throne in 1688, largely because of his Catholicism. The Stuart royal family lived in exile, moving around the courts of Europe and attempting to assert their claims to the British throne. Portraiture in a variety of media played an important role by serving as a rallying point for their so-called 'Jacobite' supporters in Britain and elsewhere.

In this flamboyant portrait, painted in Rome by the French artist Louis Gabriel Blanchet, Prince Charles is shown aged 17 wearing royal regalia and armour as a projection of Jacobite ambition, identity and military intentions. In 1745, seeking to reclaim the British throne, Charles landed in Scotland and led a rising of Highland clansmen as far south as Derbyshire but, forced to turn back, many of his men were massacred by the better-equipped government troops at the Battle of Culloden. Charles fled, disguised as a maidservant and assisted by his supporter Flora Macdonald. He evaded capture and eventually escaped to France but his hopes of regaining the throne were crushed. He died in exile in 1788.

25 **William Wilberforce** (1759–1833)

Sir Thomas Lawrence, 1828

Oil on canvas, 965 × 1092mm
NPG 3

The Conservative Member of Parliament William Wilberforce was renowned for his high principles and great personal charm. A leading member of the Clapham Sect, an influential group of evangelicals, Wilberforce devoted his career to social reform. His life's work was as parliamentary leader of the abolitionist movement. Having campaigned tirelessly for twenty years to end the slave trade, declaring to Parliament in 1791 that 'never, never will we desist till we ... extinguish every trace of this bloody traffic', Wilberforce's Bill was eventually passed with a standing ovation in 1807. He then campaigned for the total abolition of slavery, dying one month before the Slavery Abolition Act was passed in 1833.

This portrait was begun in 1828, after Wilberforce, suffering from extreme skeletal degeneration, retired from Parliament on account of ill health. His constant discomfort helps explain the awkward pose and unfinished state of this painting by Sir Thomas Lawrence. With only one sitting, Lawrence managed to capture both 'the intellectual power and winning sweetness of the veteran statesman', as his friend John Harford described it, in the image.

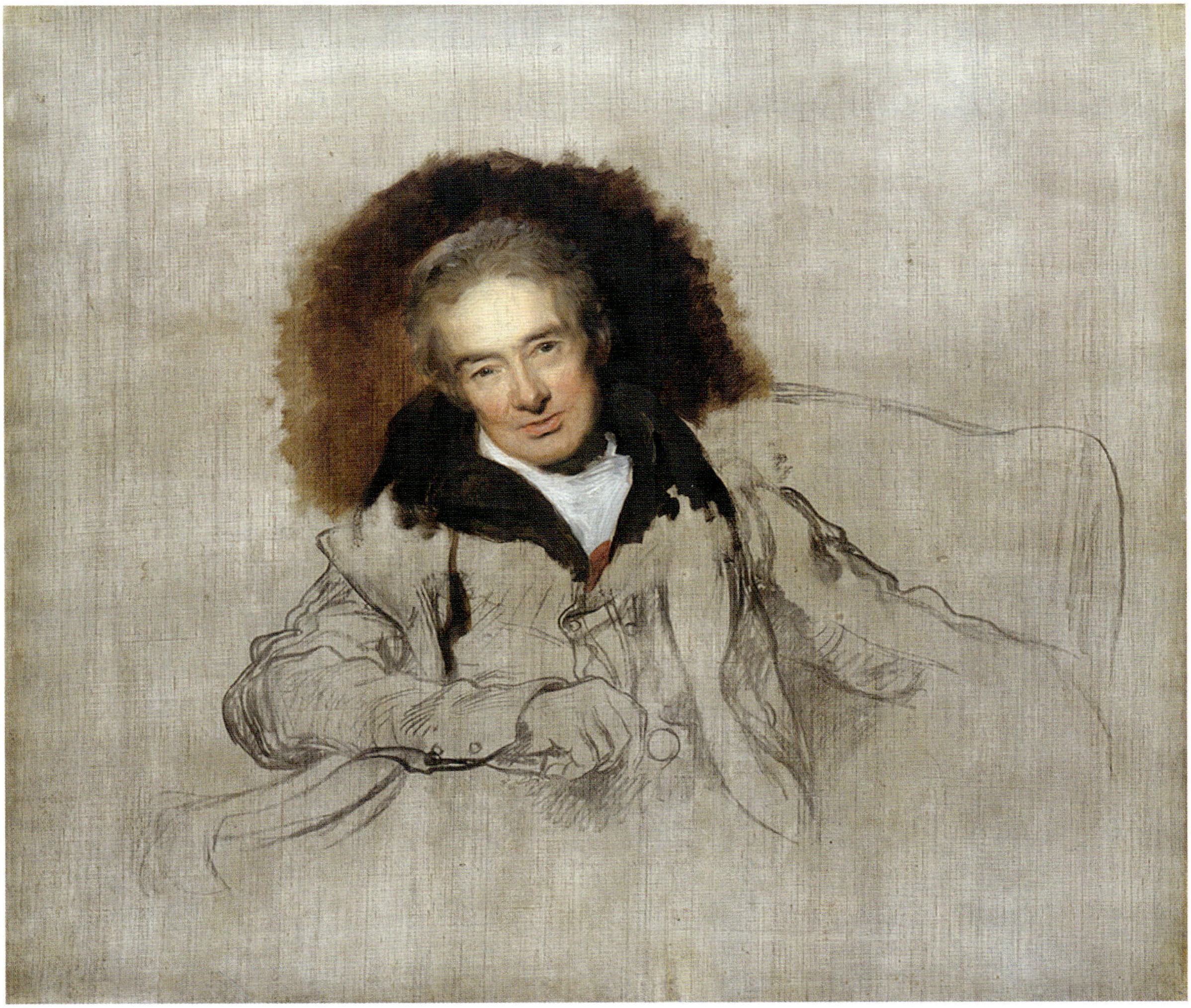

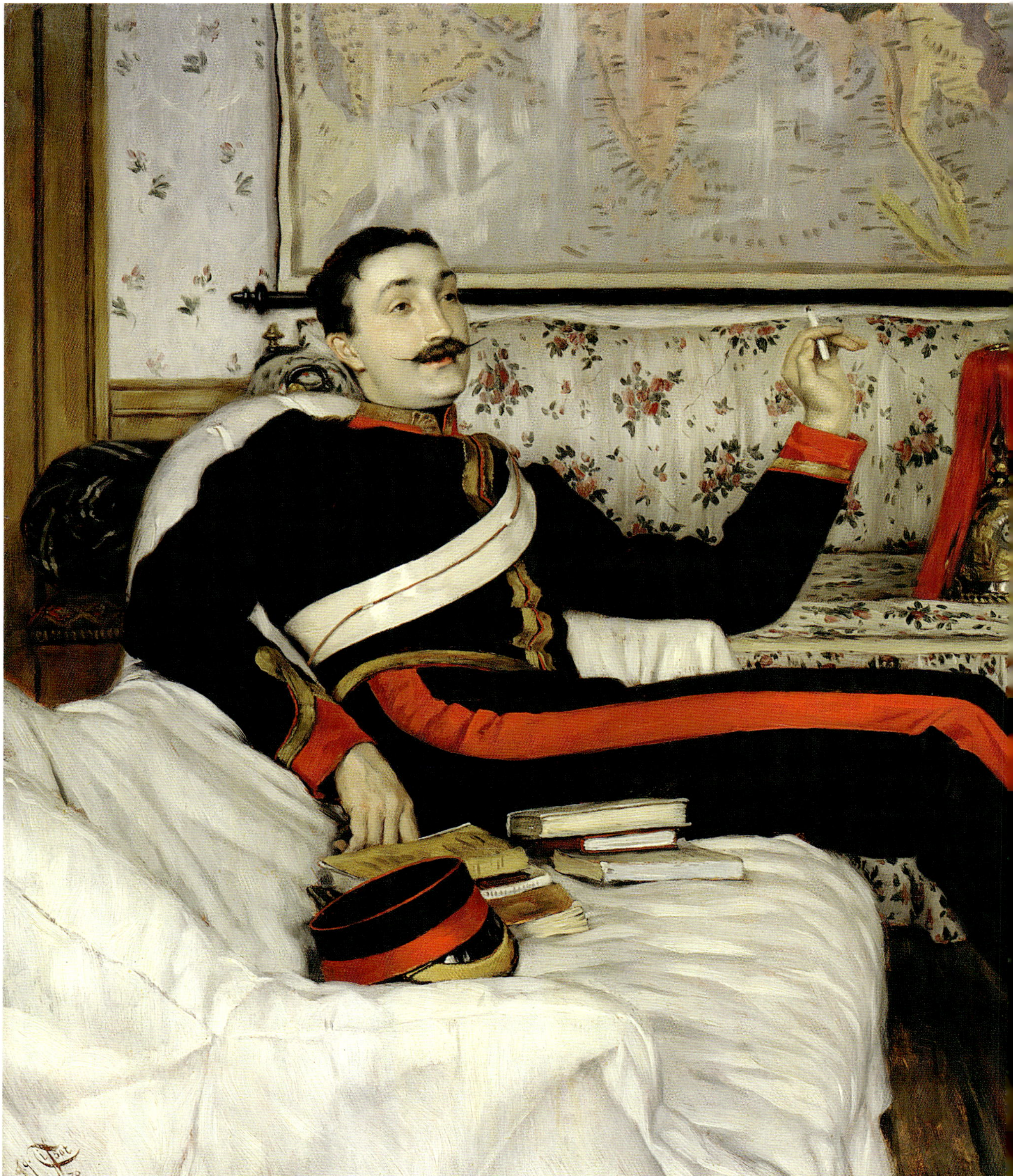

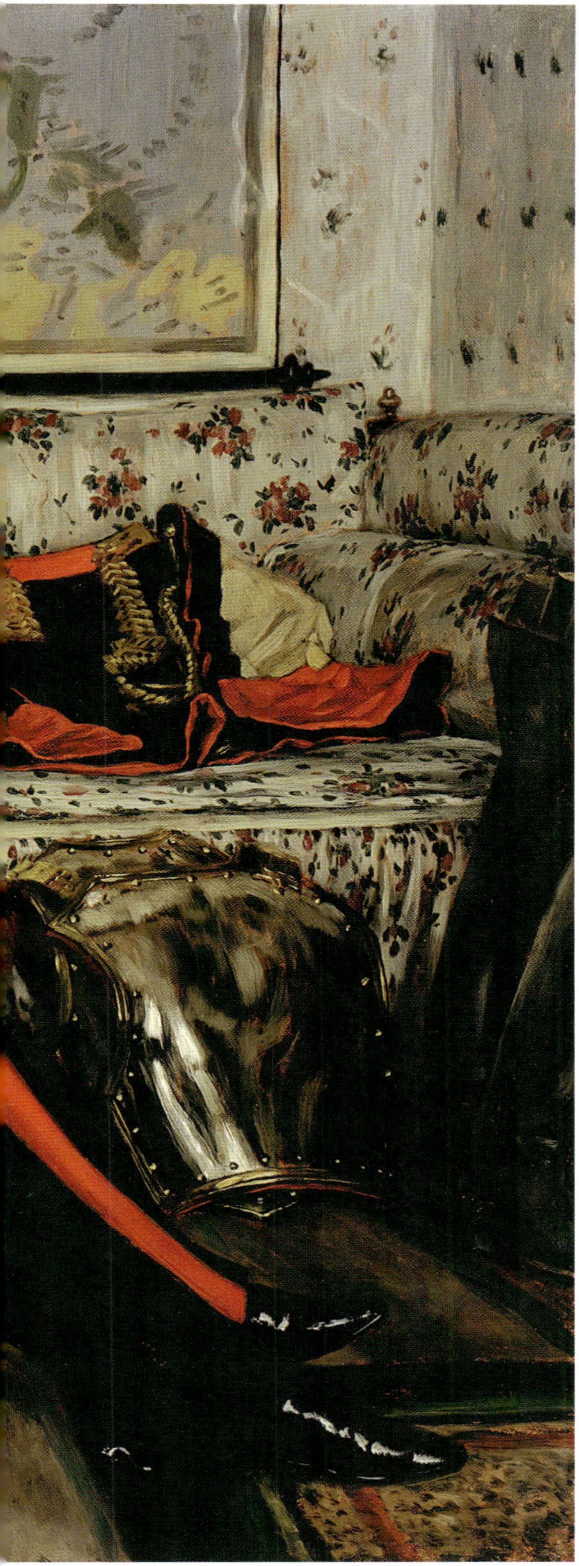

26 **Frederick Burnaby** (1842–85)

James Jacques Tissot, 1870

Oil on panel, 500 × 610mm

NPG 2642

Frederick Burnaby is here portrayed as a dashing young officer, with waxed moustache and nonchalantly posed with cigarette. He lounges on a sofa in his uniform as a captain in the 3rd Household Cavalry. This picture presents a generalised depiction of the easy confidence of an army officer of the period. The informal presentation contrasts with the conventional full-length standing or mounted military portrait. However, the prominent inclusion of a map centred on India provides a stark indication of the military's role in exerting British imperial interests during this period, including the brutal suppression of resistance movements.

An officer of the Royal Horse Guards with a gift for languages and a penchant for travel and adventure, Burnaby became renowned for both his exploits and his writings about them. *A Ride to Khiva* (1876), the narrative of a journey on horseback across 3,000 miles of the Russian steppes in winter, and *On Horseback through Asia Minor* (1877), which described a tour during which he fought on behalf of the Turks against the Russians, were both bestsellers. A tall figure, nearly two metres in height, he was reputed to be the strongest man in the British army, and was said to have once carried two ponies, one under each arm.

The picture was commissioned by Thomas Gibson Bowles, a friend and associate of Burnaby, with whom he founded *Vanity Fair* in 1868. It is likely that the idea for the portrait was conceived in 1869, the year that Bowles met James Jacques Tissot in Paris and when the French artist's first caricatures of European monarchs were published in the magazine under the pseudonym 'Coïdé'.

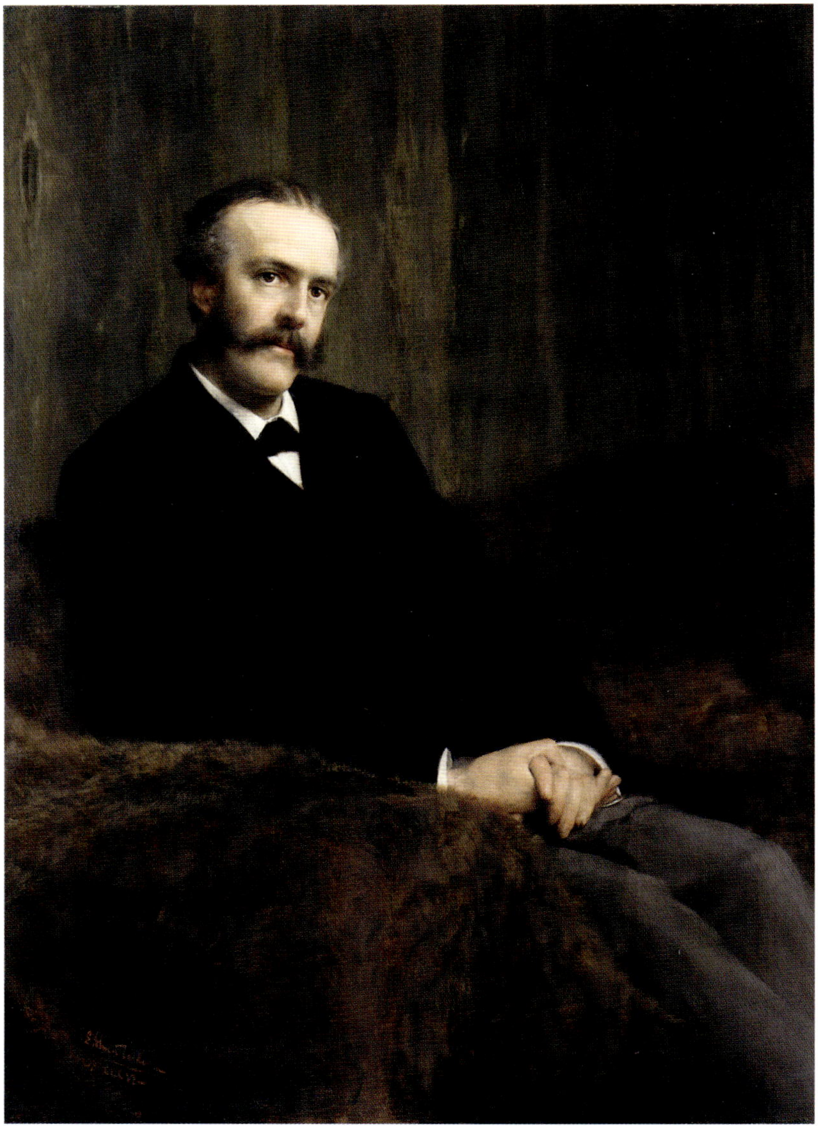

27 Arthur Balfour, 1st Earl of Balfour (1848–1930)

Sir Lawrence Alma-Tadema, 1891

Oil on canvas, 1270 × 921mm
NPG 2949

Born at Whittingehame House, East Lothian, and educated at Eton College followed by Trinity College, Cambridge, Arthur Balfour first made his mark as a philosopher, publishing *A Defence of Philosophic Doubt* in 1879. He entered politics in 1874 through the patronage of his uncle, Lord Salisbury, as a Conservative member for Hertford. Succeeding Salisbury as prime minister in 1902, he was unable to keep together a party divided by issues of free trade and protectionism, and resigned in 1905. He served as First Lord of the Admiralty during the First World War and, as Foreign Secretary in 1917, he issued the Balfour Declaration, which was a step in the foundation of modern Israel.

Sir Lawrence Alma-Tadema was born in the Netherlands and trained in Antwerp, before exhibiting at the Paris Salon and the Royal Academy. Following his move to London in 1870, he enjoyed enormous popularity and success with his highly detailed classical scenes. His portrait of Balfour has an atmosphere of quiet reflection, presenting his subject as a man of thought rather than political action. It is a rare picture in Alma-Tadema's body of work as he avoided formal portrait commissions.

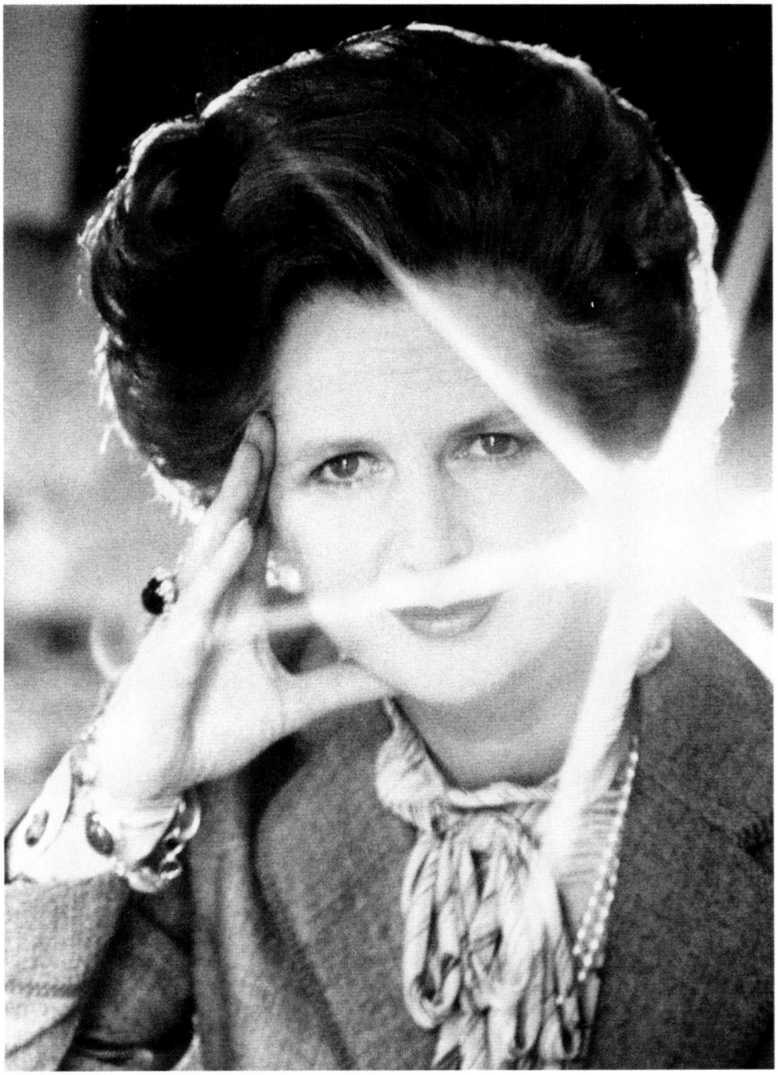

28 **Margaret Thatcher** (1925–2013)
Norman Parkinson, 1981
Gelatin silver print, 486 × 340mm
NPG P176

Margaret Thatcher was Conservative prime minister from 1979 to 1990. She was the first woman to hold the office in Britain, and was re-elected twice, in 1983 and 1987. Educated at Kesteven and Grantham Girls' School and Somerville College, Oxford, her first career was as a research chemist. She was called to the Bar in 1954 and specialised in tax law. Her career at the House of Commons began when she was elected MP for Finchley in 1959. During her first term in office, she led the country into war against Argentina in the Falkland Islands. In her second term, the government pursued a controversial programme of privatisation and deregulation that would introduce market mechanisms into areas such as health and education, with wide-ranging impacts upon public services in Britain.

In this photograph, the prime minister is shown wearing a tailored suit chosen by Norman Parkinson for the portrait. The outfit is redolent of the order and efficiency associated with her public image. In the 1980s 'power suits' and 'power dressing' became a popular choice for women. A beam of light from behind cuts across Thatcher's face, softening and glamorising the image. Parkinson said, 'I like to make people look as good as they'd like to look, and with luck, a shade better.' Another photograph from this sitting was selected as the prime minister's official portrait, and hung at 10 Downing Street when Thatcher was in office, indicating her approval.

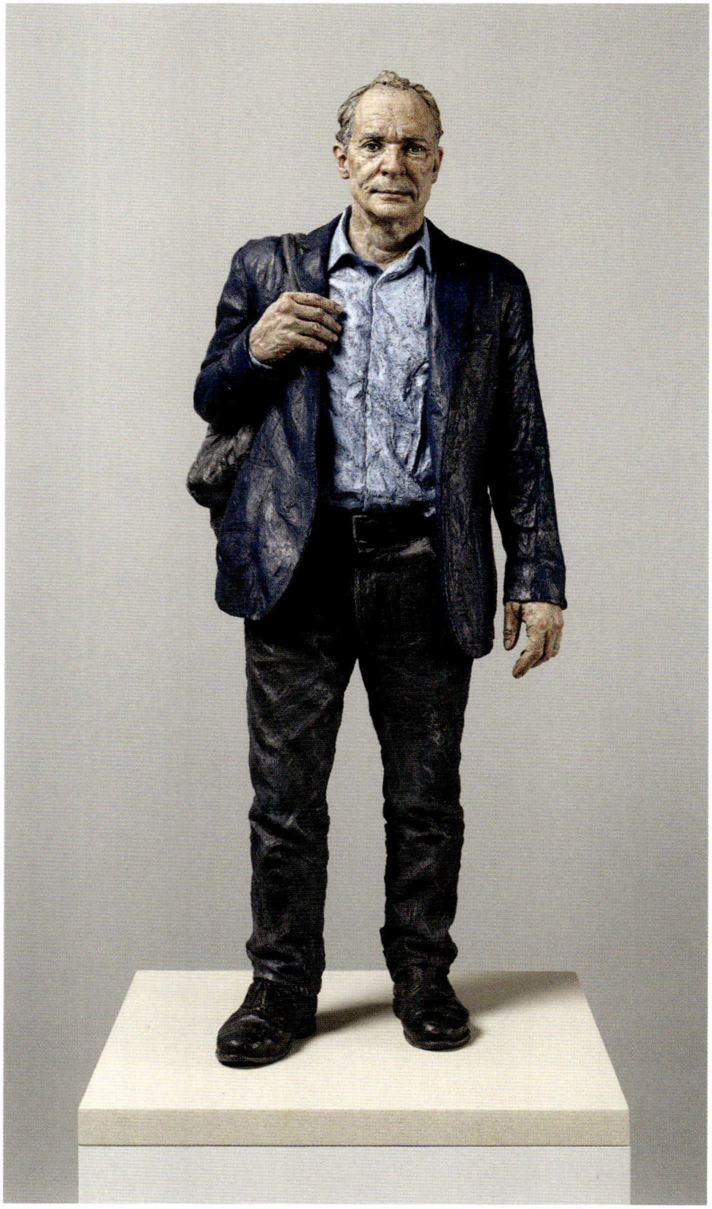

29 **Sir Tim Berners-Lee** (b.1955)

Sean Henry, 2015

Painted bronze, 1170 × 440mm
NPG 6996

Tim Berners-Lee graduated from Queen's College, Oxford, in 1976. There he built his first computer with a soldering iron, a processor and an old television. He began his career in telecommunications before inventing the World Wide Web in 1989, which is widely regarded as the most transformative technological innovation of modern times. In 1994, he joined the Laboratory for Computer Science at the Massachusetts Institute of Technology.

Cast in bronze and painted, the sculpture depicts Berners-Lee standing and is two-thirds life-size, displayed on a plinth. Sean Henry spent two days with Berners-Lee in Boston, observing him at work and visiting him at home. The pose for the portrait is taken from a number of photographs Henry took of his sitter walking outside, carrying the indispensable leather rucksack in which he keeps his laptop. Henry was interested in the paradox inherent in the impact of Berners-Lee's world-changing invention and his self-effacing demeanour. His sculpted figures are usually anonymous, and in this portrait he has retained the idea of his subject as an 'everyman' through the casual pose and his simply dressed appearance. The depiction of his sitter is resolutely contemporary, but the use of bronze has a timeless and permanent quality appropriate for a sitter with such a significant legacy.

30 **Nelson Mandela** (1918–2013)

Jillian Edelstein, 1997

Gelatin silver print, 480 × 340mm (image size)
NPG x128760

Nelson Mandela was the first president of South Africa to be elected in fully representative democratic elections, serving from 1994 to 1999. A member of the African National Congress from 1944, Mandela secretly left South Africa in January 1962 using the adopted name David Motsamayi. After travelling around Africa, he visited England in June that year to gain support for the ANC's struggle against the apartheid policies of the ruling National Party. On his return to South Africa, Mandela was arrested on 5 August 1962. He served a continuous term of imprisonment for his involvement in the struggle against apartheid until 1990. During this time he became an international symbol for freedom, human rights and racial equality. Among numerous international awards and honours, Mandela received the Nobel Peace Prize in 1993.

The photographer Jillian Edelstein was born and grew up in South Africa. She graduated as a social worker before starting work as a press photographer in Johannesburg in 1981 and moving to London in 1985. This powerfully introspective portrait was taken in a ten-minute sitting at the presidential house as part of Edelstein's four-year project documenting participants in South Africa's Truth and Reconciliation Commission hearings.

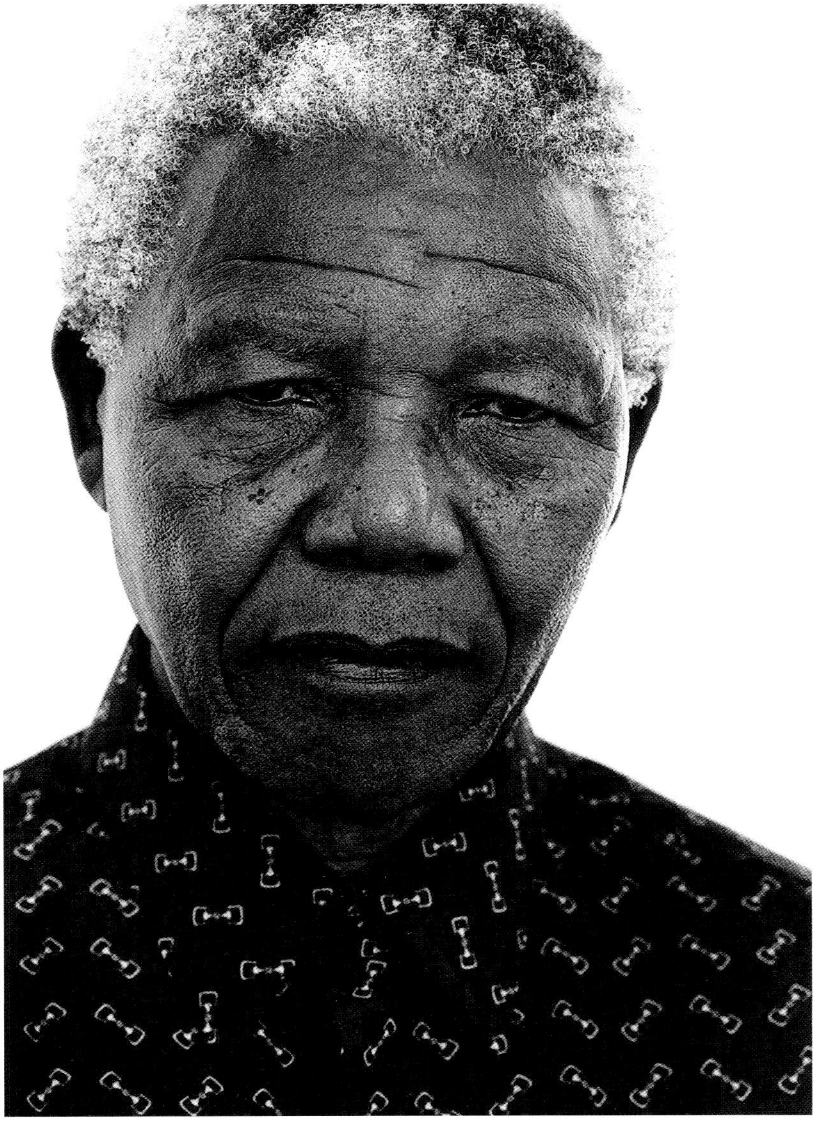

31 Dame Anna Wintour (b.1949)

Alex Katz, 2009

Oil on linen, 1524 × 2134mm
NPG 6908

As editor-in-chief of American *Vogue* since 1988, British-born Anna Wintour has made a significant contribution to the international fashion industry. Previously editor of British *Vogue* from 1984 to 1987, Wintour is credited with boosting the circulation and reinvigorating both titles. In 2013, she became artistic director for Condé Nast, *Vogue*'s publisher. Her powerful personality was the inspiration for Lauren Weisberger's novel *The Devil Wears Prada* (2003), which was made into a successful film starring Meryl Streep in 2006. In 2017, she was made a dame for services to fashion and journalism.

Born in Brooklyn in 1927, Alex Katz is one of America's most respected and influential artists. Based on studies from life, this painting was the first time Wintour sat for a portrait. Katz has said: 'Some people you want to paint, others you don't … Painting Anna was like shooting a fish in a barrel. There was no way I could miss it. She's made to order. Highly styled.'

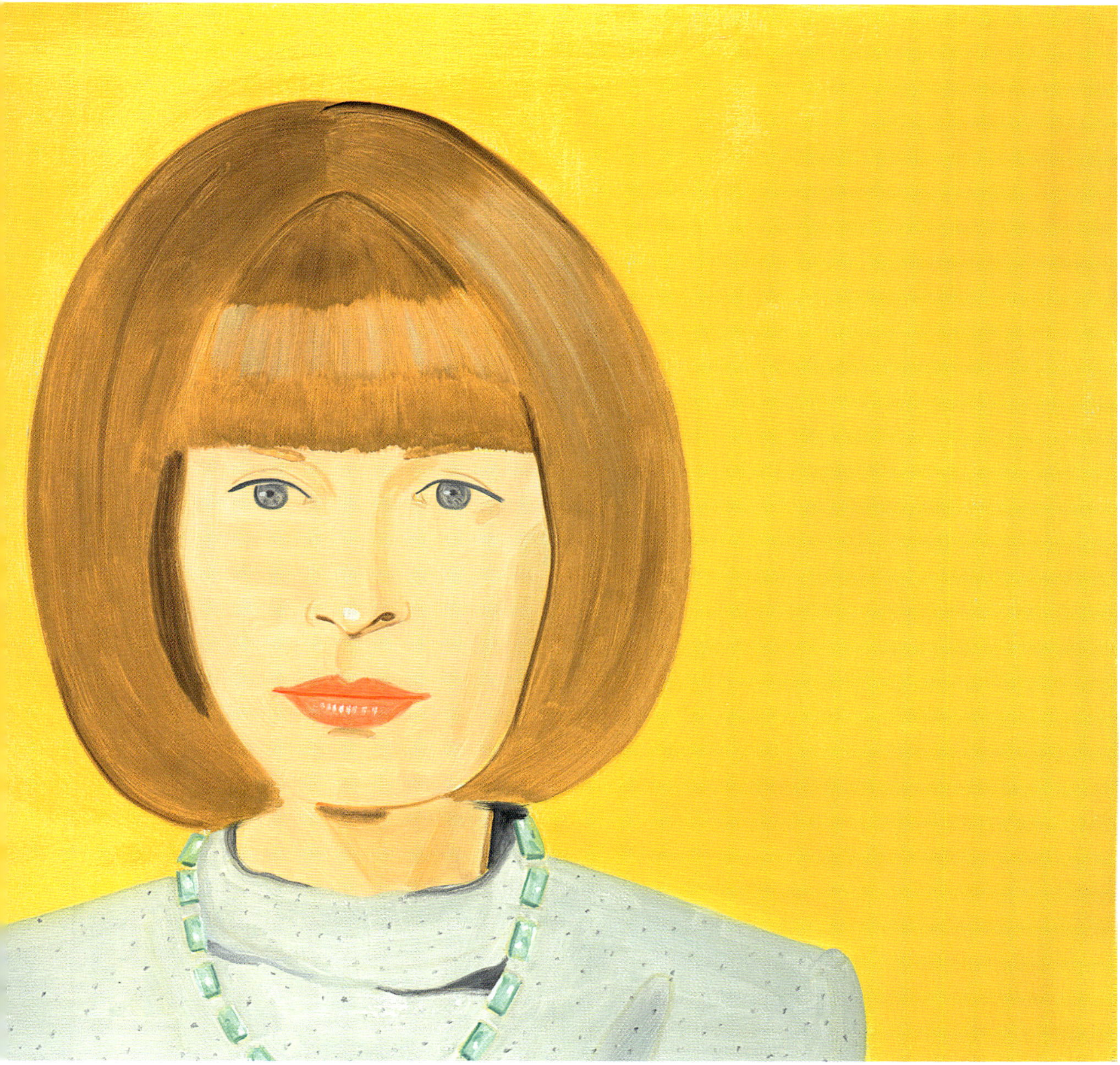

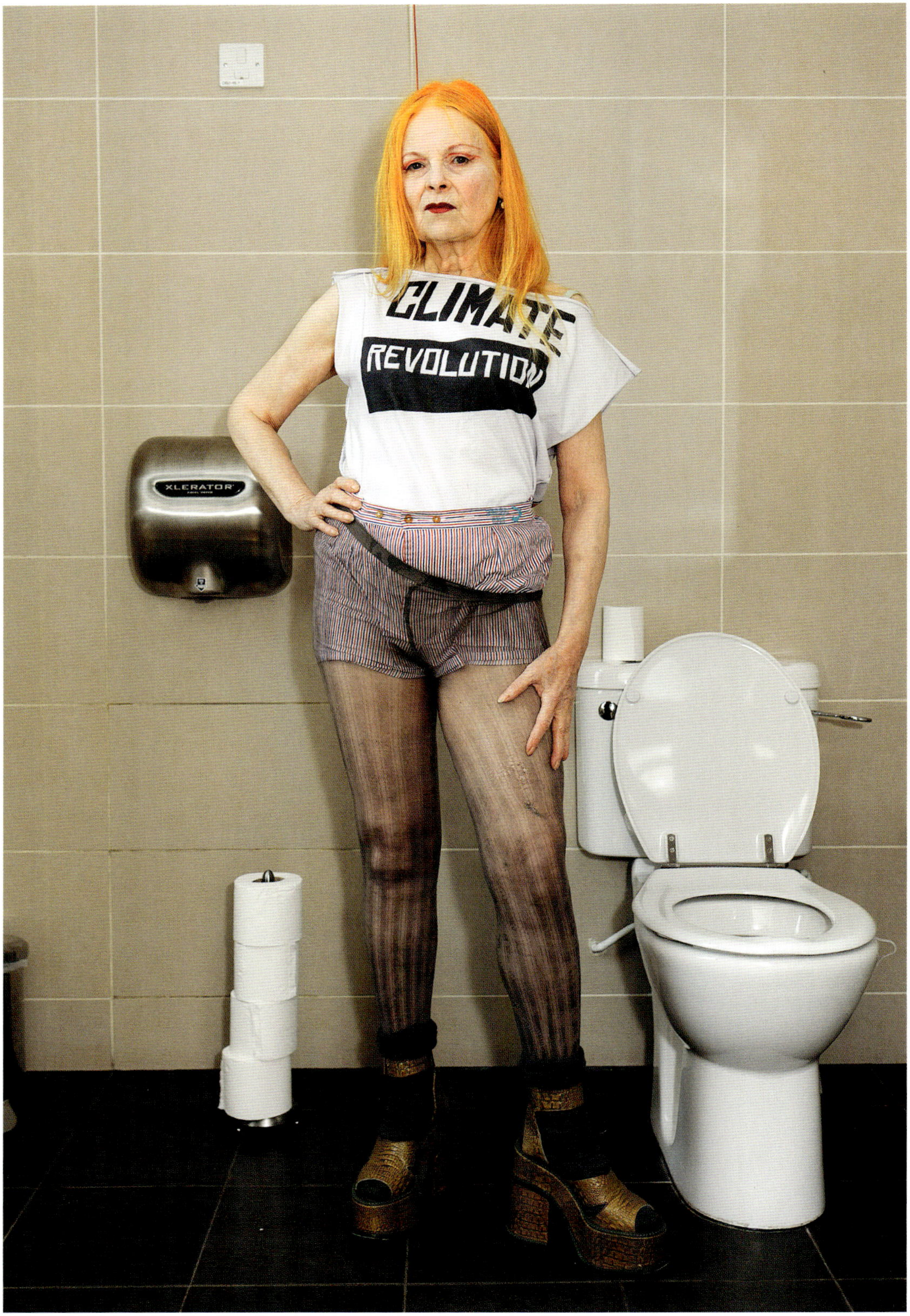
CLIMATE
REVOLUTION
XLERATOR

32 **Dame Vivienne Westwood** (b.1941)
Martin Parr, 2012
Pigment print, 1528 × 1052mm overall
NPG P2089

Dame Vivienne Westwood is one of Britain's leading fashion designers. In the 1970s she co-founded the boutique *Let It Rock* on London's King's Road with her partner Malcolm McLaren. Later renamed *SEX*, the shop helped define British punk. Twice named Designer of the Year (1990, 1991), Westwood was honoured with a retrospective exhibition at the Victoria and Albert Museum, London, in 2004.

Martin Parr is one of the most celebrated and influential British photographers. Over four decades, he has transformed British social documentary photography and revealed the eccentricities of modern life with affection and insight. When the commission involves celebrity portraiture, he approaches each sitting with the same distinct visual language that he brings to the rest of his work, posing sitters in incongruous settings, often with a hint of mischief and humour, as exemplified in his portrait of Westwood posed in a toilet. Despite the crude, inelegant setting, Westwood exudes confidence, and her T-shirt proudly proclaims her activism on environmental issues.

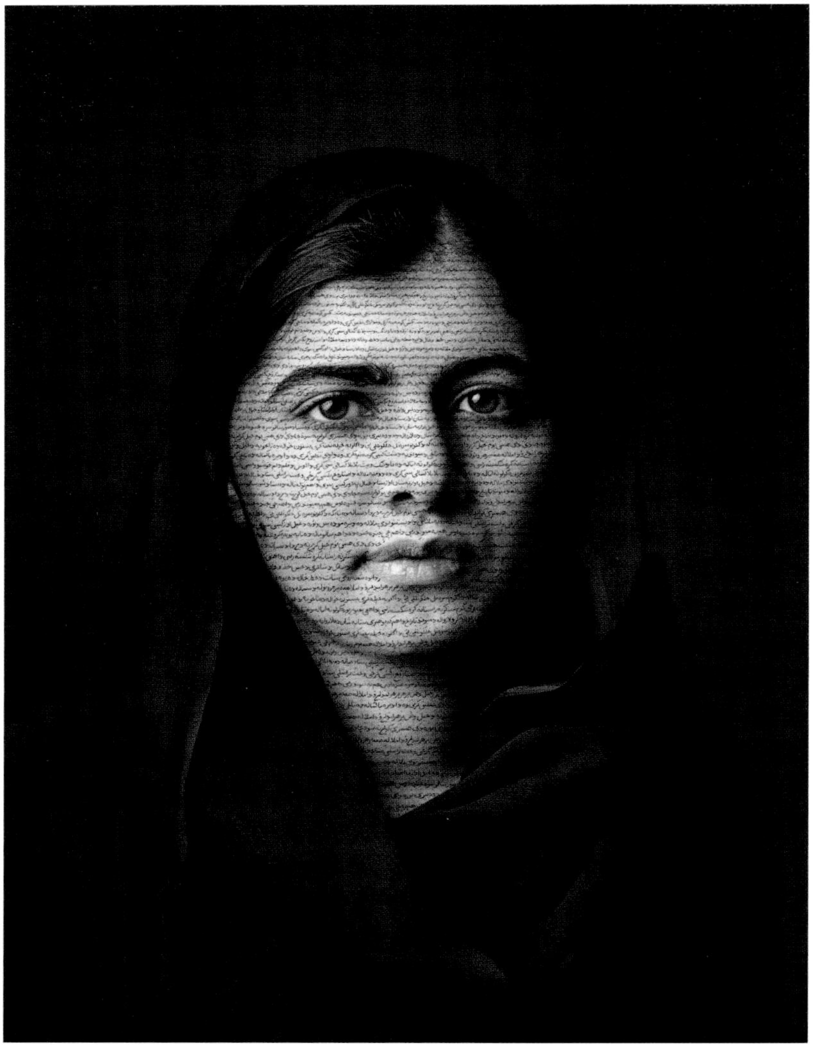

33 **Malala Yousafzai** (b.1997)
Shirin Neshat, 2018

Archival ink on gelatin silver print, 1524 × 1016mm
NPG 7052

Born in Mingora, Pakistan, Malala Yousafzai is a human rights activist for female education. She came to prominence in 2009 after writing about her life during the Taliban occupation of the Swat Valley and the ban on girls' education. In October 2012, she was shot on the left side of her head in an attack by a Taliban gunman on her school bus. She recovered in Birmingham, UK, where she chose to remain with her family. In 2013, Malala was awarded the International Children's Peace Prize, and in 2014 she became the youngest recipient of the Nobel Peace Prize with Indian activist Kailash Satyarthi. She founded the Malala Fund in 2013, which is dedicated to giving all girls access to twelve years of free, safe, quality education. She graduated with a degree in philosophy, politics and economics from the University of Oxford in 2020.

This is one of a pair of portraits by Iranian-born artist and film-maker Shirin Neshat. Neshat took a series of photographs before selecting two, onto which she has used calligraphy to inscribe a poem in Pashto by Rahmat Shah Sayel, written in 2011. The poem addresses the legendary Pashtun heroine Malala of Maiwand and praises her namesake Malala Yousafzai, while making connections between the two formidable young women. The artist recalled: 'I knew of Malala as an extraordinary young woman ... when I look back on our encounter, I am left with impressions of humility, wisdom and a rare sense of inner beauty.'

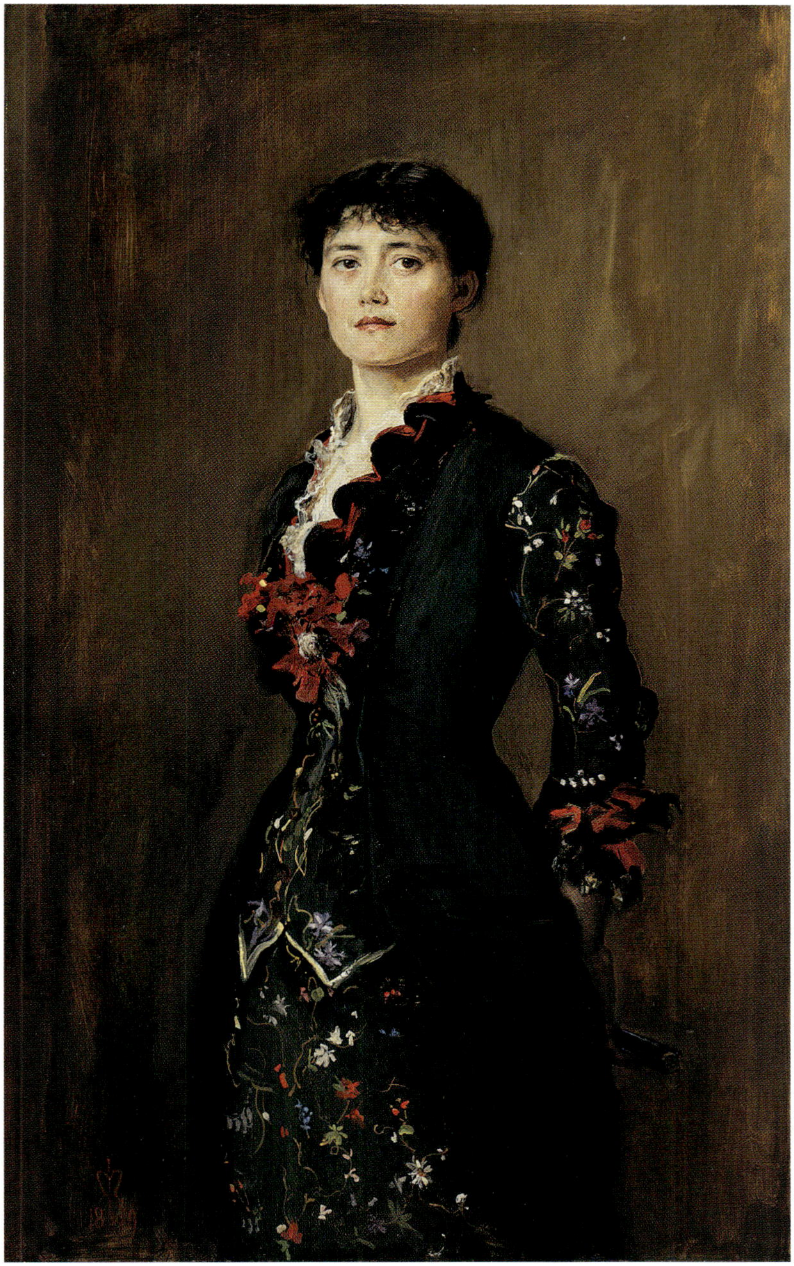

34 **Louise Jopling** (1843–1933)

Sir John Everett Millais, 1879

Oil on canvas, 1240 × 765mm
NPG 6612

Louise Jane Jopling, portrait painter, teacher and suffragist, was prominent in an era when women in the arts were often dismissed as dabbling in 'amateurism'. Joplin established a painting school for women in 1887 and she also published a book of art instruction. Her essay 'On the Education of the Artistic Faculty' (1903) supported women's education on equal terms with men. A member of the National Union of Women's Suffrage, she pushed for women to be allowed to work from nude models, and in 1901 became one of the first women admitted to the Royal Society of British Artists, where she exhibited alongside men. Nonetheless, she felt frustrated at the limitations of being a woman in a man's world, saying: 'I hate being a woman … Women never do anything.' She expanded further on these feelings in her memoir, *Twenty Years of My Life: 1867–87* (1925).

This picture – in which Jopling holds a 'defiant, rather hard' expression, as she described it – was painted for her husband Joseph Jopling in John Everett Millais's London studio at Palace Gate, Kensington. In the late 1870s Millais's portrait practice was thriving; his recent subjects included Thomas Carlyle, Lillie Langtry and William Ewart Gladstone. Jopling said she sat 'with all the knowledge of a portrait painter', which enabled the portrait to be painted quickly, requiring just five short sittings. Jopling noted in her memoir: 'We had great discussions as to what I should wear. I had at that time a dress that was universally admired. It was black, with coloured flowers embroidered on it. It was made in Paris.' The portrait exemplifies the fluency of Millais's later style and displays a strong sense of design. It was exhibited at the Grosvenor Gallery in 1880, where James McNeill Whistler declared it 'superb'.

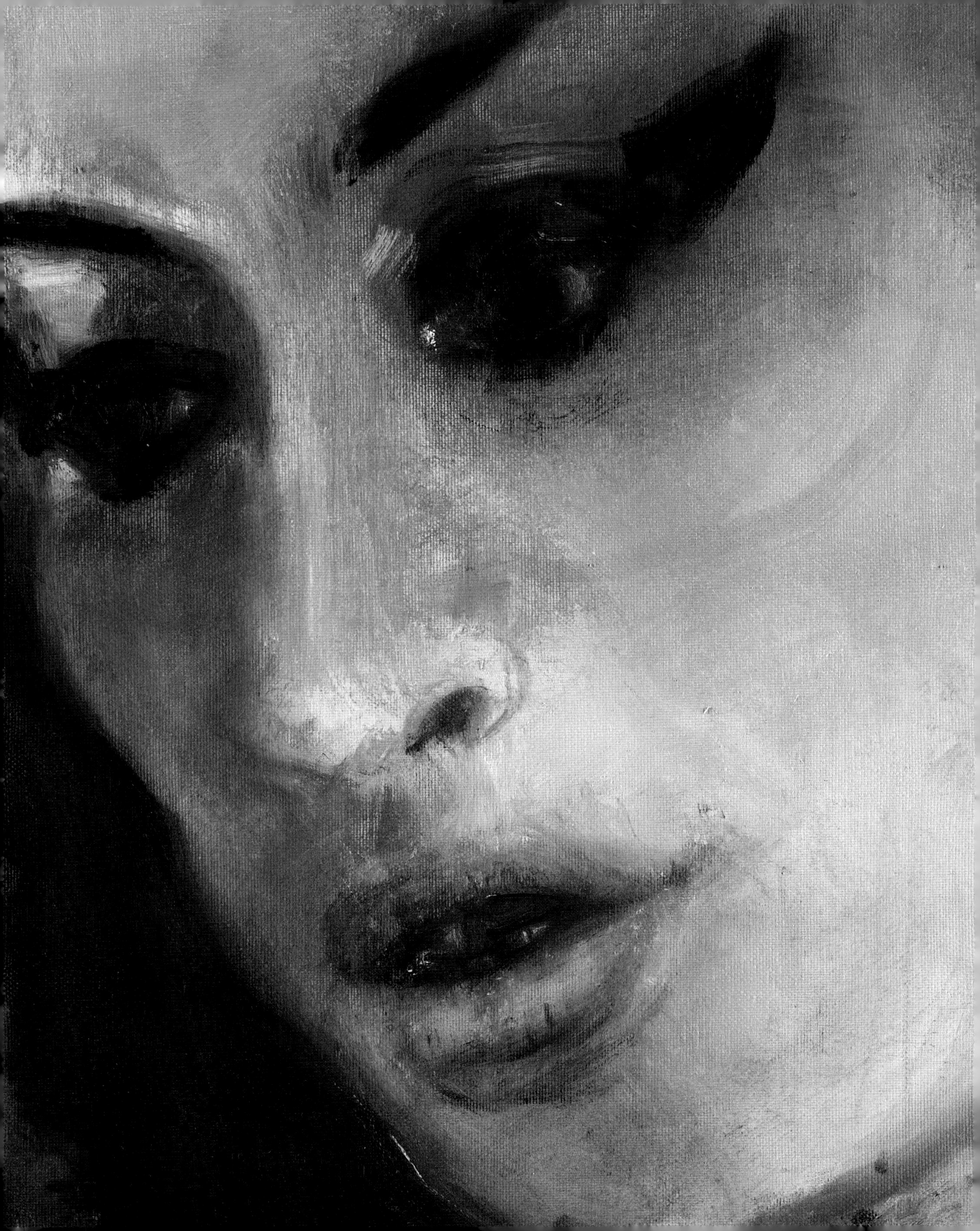

Love and Loss

More than simply depicting someone, portraits can powerfully evoke the sitter's living presence. For this reason, there has always been a strong association between portraiture and the themes of love and loss. Portraits have served as visual substitutes for an absent lover and provided a sense of immortality by keeping the memory of the dead alive in the hearts and minds of those they have left behind.

The theme of love is not always immediately apparent. The key to Sir Anthony van Dyck's portrait of Lord George Stuart in the guise of an Arcadian shepherd (see p.67) is only revealed by the Latin inscription *ME FIRMIOR AMOR* (Love is stronger than I am). Painted at the time of his secret marriage to Lady Katherine Howard, against the wishes of her parents, the portrait can be interpreted as a visual validation of the union. As in this case, the National Portrait Gallery Collection does not always include a portrait of both partners in a couple. Although painted for different occasions, portraits of Horatio Nelson and Emma Hamilton (see pp.74–5) help to illustrate one of the great love affairs of British history. Peter Lely's double portrait of Anne Hyde, Duchess of York, and King James II (see p.73) shows a husband and wife in the same frame but was painted only after their secret marriage was made public.

Portraits were customarily used as proxies in marriage negotiations between European royal families. The full-length portrait of the adolescent Princess Elizabeth Stuart (see p.72) advertises her wealth, status and beauty at around the age at which such dynastic marriages were arranged. A generation later, the Capel family portrait (see pp.70–1) celebrates the love, fertility and stability of the marriage between Arthur and Elizabeth Capel. Family portraits serve a similar role today, even if the scale is smaller, the composition more relaxed, and the medium more likely to be a digital photograph.

Some of the most striking portraits occur where the sitter and artist share a romantic relationship as well as an artistic one. The supermodel Kate Moss was a little-known 19-year-old when she was photographed by her boyfriend Mario Sorrenti (see p.78) in a series of images that capture all the rawness and intensity of first love and youthful desire. Recording their fleeting romance in 1946, Cecil Beaton's photographs of Hollywood actor Greta Garbo (see pp.68–9) recall informal and intimate snapshots taken by doting lovers.

DETAIL **Amy Winehouse, 2011**

3

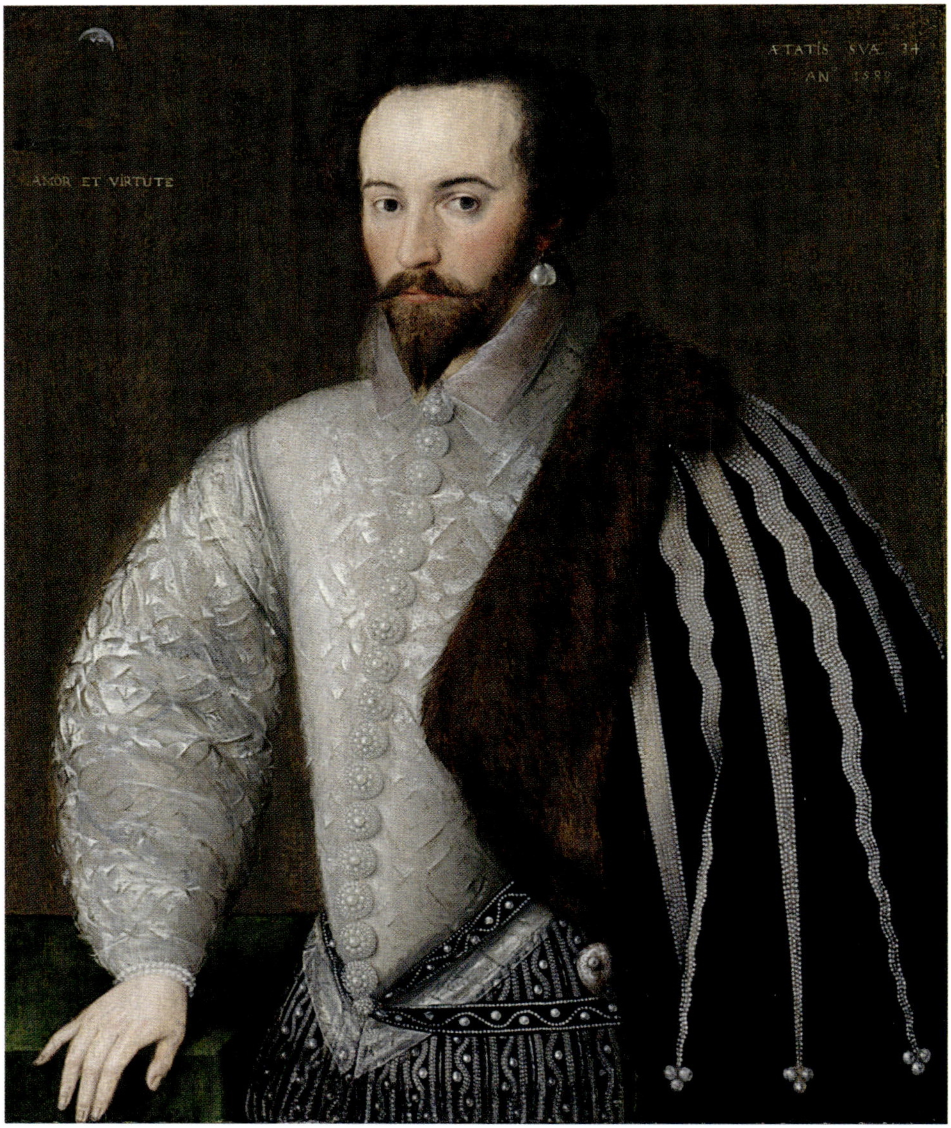

35 Sir Walter Ralegh (1554–1618)
Unknown English artist, 1588

Oil on panel, 914 × 746mm
NPG 7

A true 'Renaissance man', Walter Ralegh was a poet, explorer and soldier, as well as being a favourite of Elizabeth I. Much of his literary work is lost, but about thirty short poems and various prose works survive, including *The History of the World* (1614) and a cycle of poems to 'Cynthia' that were addressed to Elizabeth I. He organised and financed a number of expeditions to North America, and later in life made several unsuccessful attempts to find gold in South America. Ralegh spent much of the reign of James I in the Tower of London, and was executed for treason in 1618.

This portrait is a visual statement of Ralegh's devotion to Elizabeth I. His dramatic costume, in the queen's colours of black and white, is lavishly embroidered with pearls – precious stones much favoured by the queen. Conservation treatment has revealed a patch of wavy sea beneath the crescent moon in the top left of the painting. Through this metaphor, Ralegh likens the moon goddess Cynthia to the queen and the water to himself (using a pun on his name Walter), signifying his willingness to be controlled by his sovereign as the moon controls the tides.

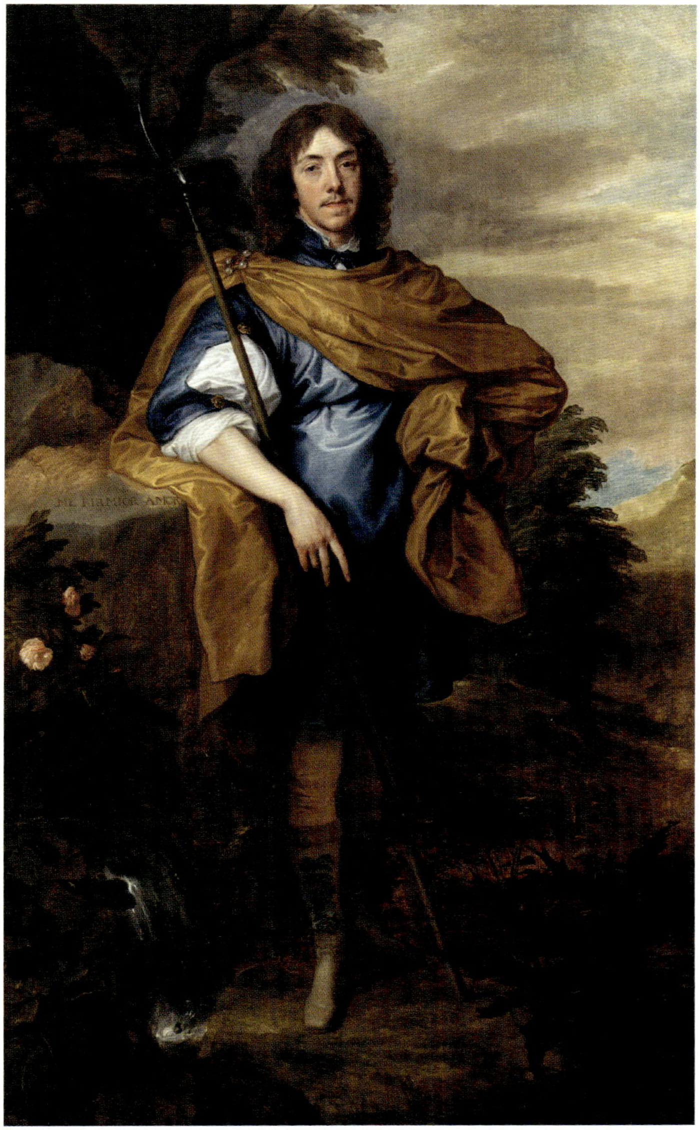

36 **Lord George Stuart, 9th Seigneur of Aubigny** (1618–42)

Sir Anthony van Dyck, *c.*1638

Oil on canvas, 2184 × 1334mm
NPG 5964

Son of the Duke of Lennox, Lord George was brought up in France, inheriting the Seigneury of Aubigny in 1632. The sitter was described by Lord Clarendon in his *History of the Rebellion* as 'a gentleman of great hopes, of a gentle and winning disposition, and of a very clear courage'. He was typical of the young men who flocked to the king's standard, but he was killed at the Battle of Edgehill in 1642, while leading a troop in the Prince of Wales' Regiment of Horse.

His portrait is thought to have been painted by Sir Anthony van Dyck before the English Civil War (1642–51) and may date from 1638, when he secretly married Katherine, daughter of Theophilus Howard, 2nd Earl of Suffolk. Stuart's portrayal here suggests nothing of the political situation that was about to overwhelm him and his family. It shows him in the guise of a shepherd, languidly leaning on a rock in a landscape. The rock behind Stuart is inscribed with the Latin motto *ME FIRMIOR AMOR* (Love is stronger than I am), which probably refers to his secret marriage.

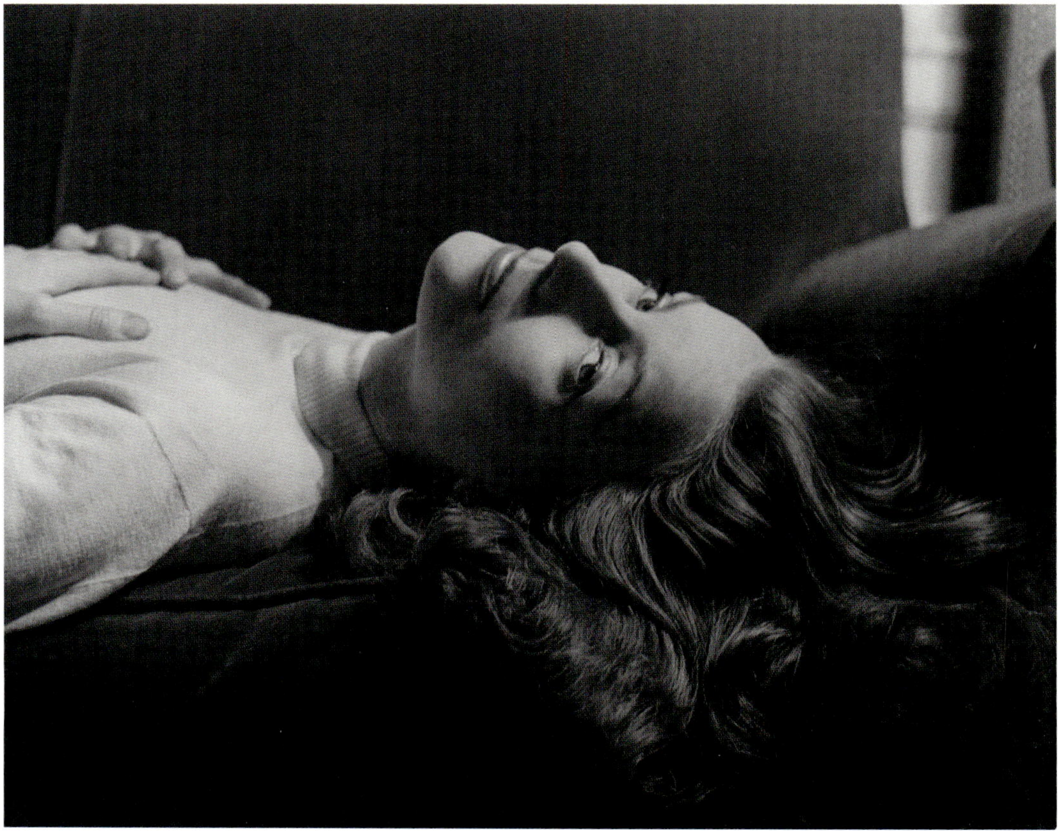

37 **Greta Garbo** (1905–90)
Sir Cecil Beaton, 1946
Gelatin silver print, 243 × 294mm
NPG x40124

38 **Greta Garbo** (1905–90)
Sir Cecil Beaton, 1946
Gelatin silver print, 242 × 293mm
NPG x40128

Born in Stockholm, Sweden, Greta Garbo was one of the greatest and most elusive Hollywood actors of the 1920s and 1930s. Following her success in the silent film *The Saga of Gösta Berling* (1924), she was signed by the Metro-Goldwyn-Mayer studio. She is best remembered for her leading roles in *Queen Christina* (1933) and *Anna Karenina* (1935), and retired after the box-office failure of *Two-Faced Woman* (1941).

The photographer Sir Cecil Beaton had long been fascinated by Garbo before their first meeting in 1932. Although they were both in same-sex relationships at the time, Beaton was left infatuated. When they met again in 1946, their friendship developed into an affair. Beaton went so far as to propose marriage, but Garbo declined. These intimate photographs of her were taken by Beaton during their first photoshoot together at the Hotel Plaza, New York. Garbo, typically reclusive, was said to have agreed to the shoot as she needed a new passport photograph. However, she adopted several poses, reclining on a couch, informal and relaxed, as shown in the photographs here. When published in American *Vogue* in July 1946, the reclining close-up of her face was printed upright – and is reproduced as such here – emphasising her 'lion's mane' hair, as Beaton described it in his diaries. A selection of the photographs, only one of which Garbo had agreed to being reproduced, appeared in print, which soured her friendship with Beaton.

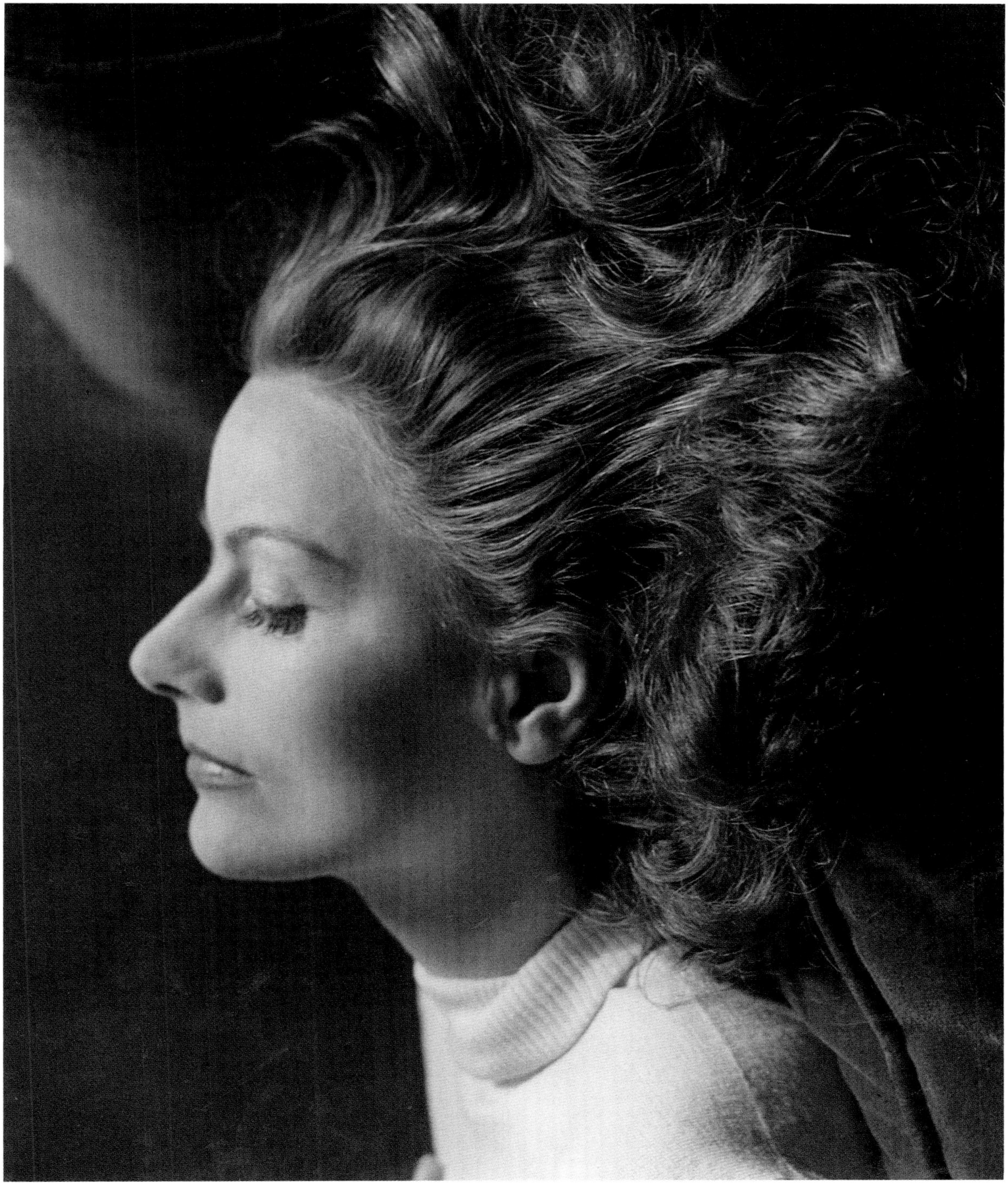

39 Arthur Capel, 1st Baron Capel (1604–49) and Elizabeth, Lady Capel (d.1661) with their children

Cornelius Johnson, *c.*1640

Oil on canvas, 1600 × 2591mm
NPG 4759

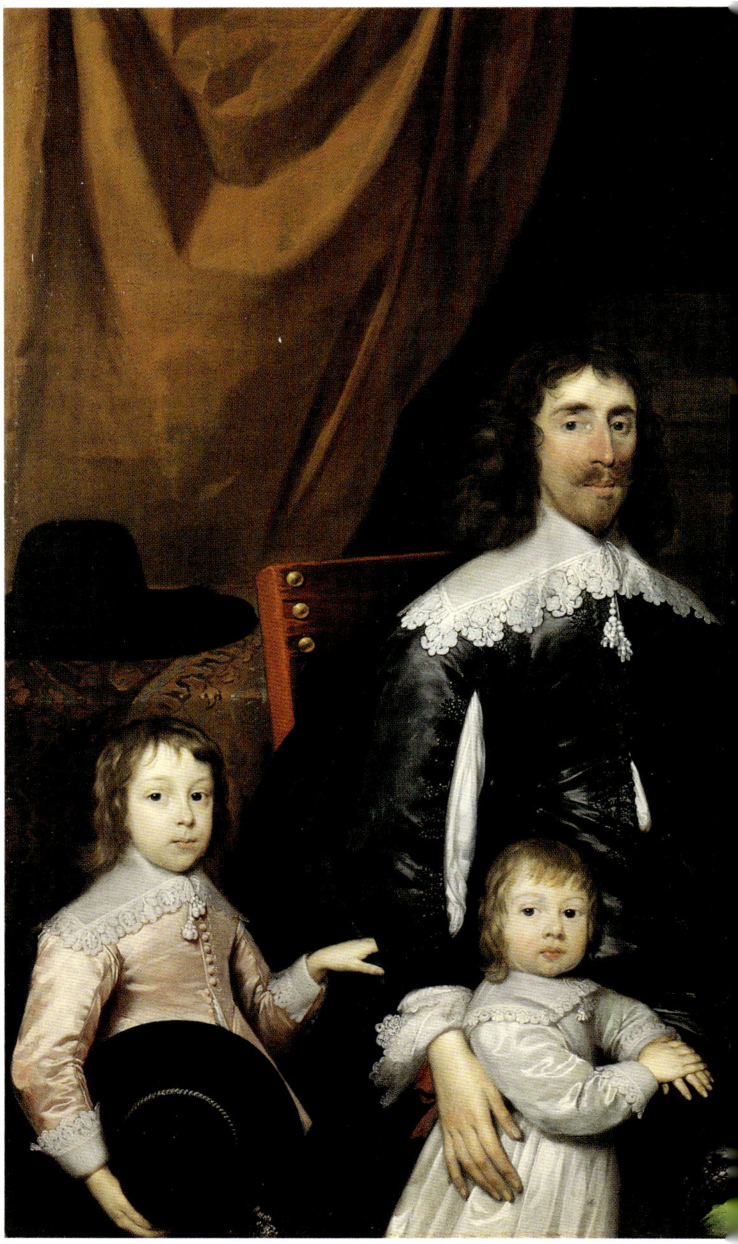

This grand family portrait shows Lord and Lady Capel with five of their nine children – from left, Arthur, later Earl of Essex (1631–83), Henry, later Baron Capel of Tewkesbury (1638–96), Charles (d.1657), Elizabeth, later Countess of Carnarvon (1633–78), and Mary, later Duchess of Beaufort (1630–1715) – at a time when they were enjoying a comfortable life as one of the richest families in England. The gardens that form the backdrop are perhaps those of Little Hadham, the Capels' home. This peaceful scene belies the turbulence that was shortly to overtake the Capels. Initially opposed to Charles I's policies, Lord Capel became a Royalist during the civil wars in reaction to the violence of Parliamentarian views. He was captured and executed shortly after the king himself. His oldest son, Arthur, was later accused of involvement in the Rye House plot of 1683 (a plan to assassinate King Charles II and his brother James, Duke of York) and died in suspicious circumstances while imprisoned in the Tower of London. Henry Capel, however, was a successful politician, who also created a garden at Kew, the beginnings of the Royal Botanic Gardens. His daughter, Elizabeth, later became a talented botanical artist, and his other daughter, Mary, was a distinguished horticulturalist.

The painter Cornelius Johnson, the English-born son of an émigré Netherlandish family, was a fashionable and accomplished artist. This work shows the influence of Anthony van Dyck's painting *Charles I and Henrietta Maria with Their two Eldest Children* (Royal Collection, 1632).

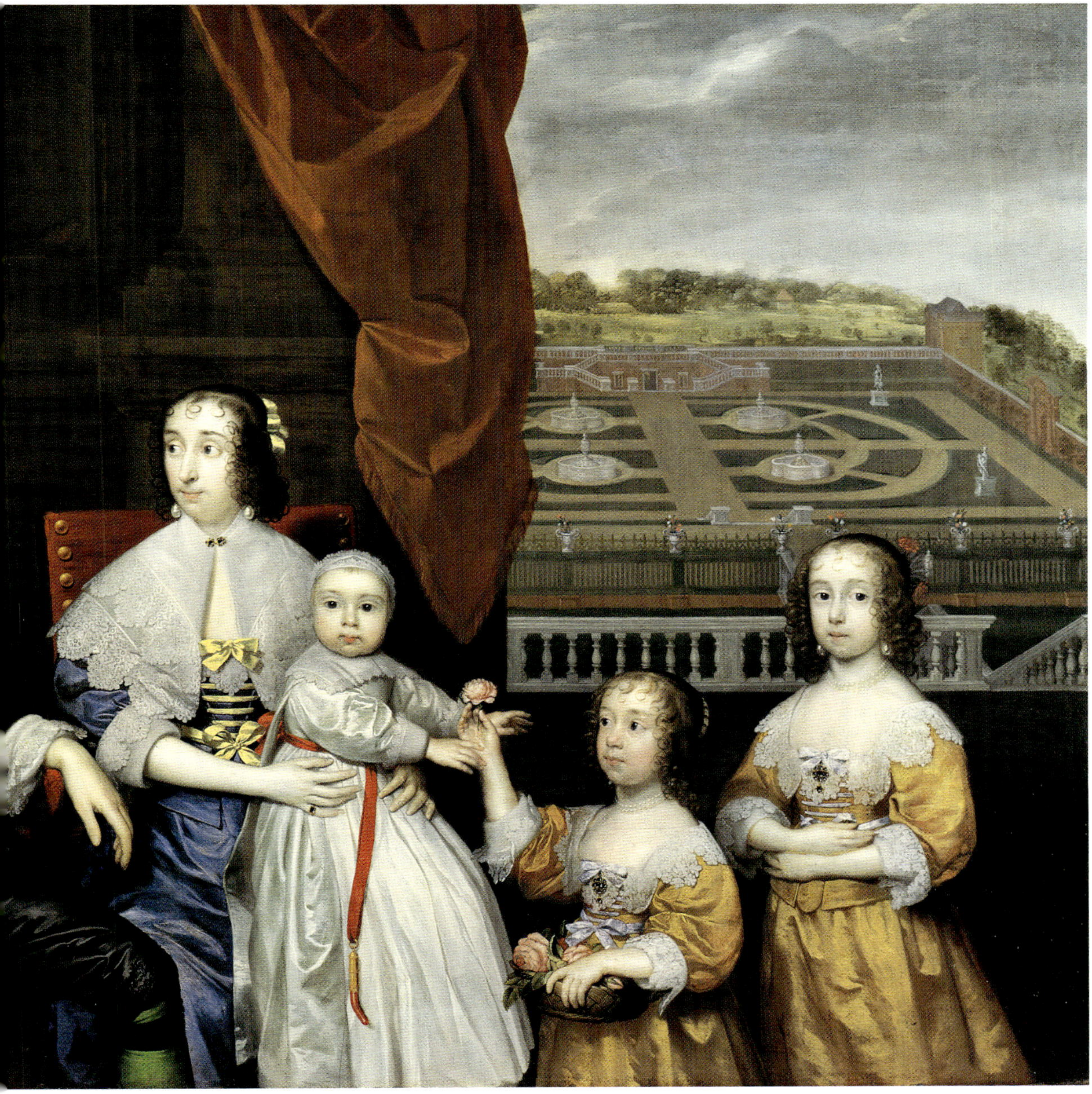

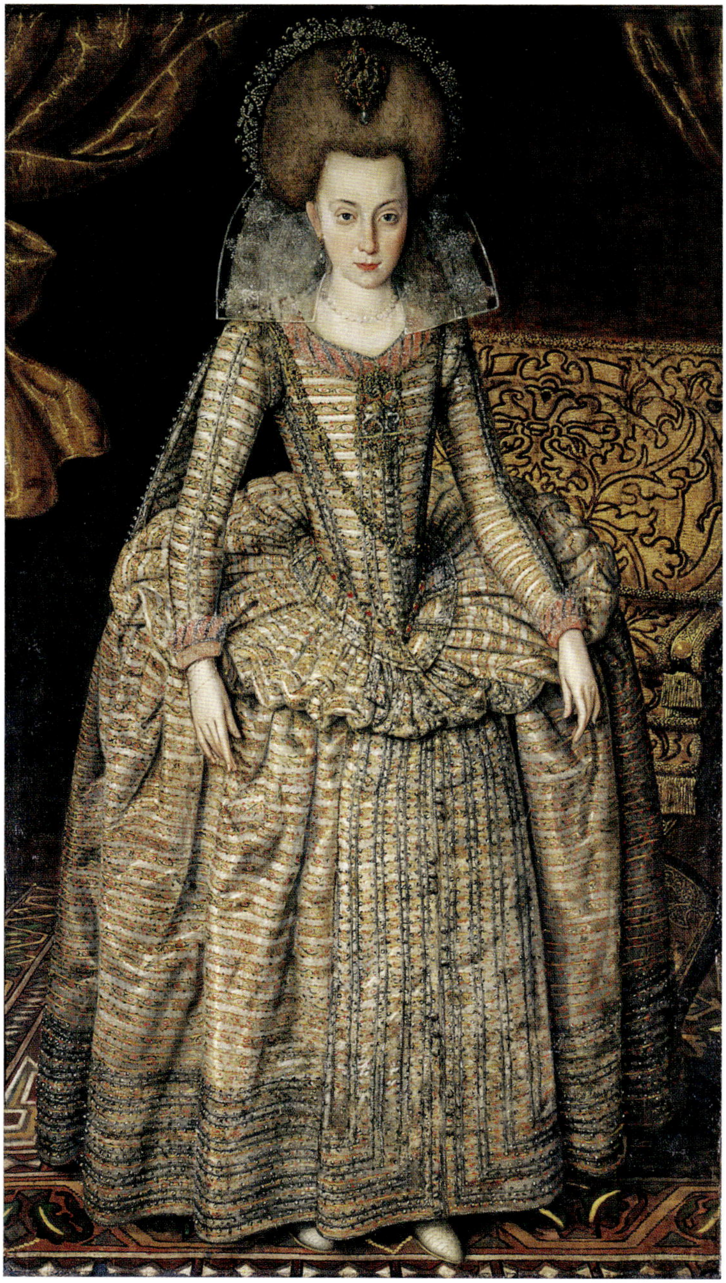

40 **Princess Elizabeth, Queen of Bohemia and Electress Palatine** (1596–1662)
Robert Peake the Elder, c.1610

Oil on canvas, 1713 × 968mm
NPG 6113

When James VI of Scotland ascended the throne of England as James I in 1603, one of the major factors in the optimism felt by the English public was the fact that James, unlike his predecessor Elizabeth I, had a family: an heir, a 'spare' and a marriageable daughter. Elizabeth, named after her godmother Elizabeth I, was a focus for hope and expectation, and an important pawn in the game of international royal marriage negotiations. She was married at the age of sixteen to Frederick, Elector Palatine, a German Protestant prince from Heidelberg. In 1659, Frederick took the disastrous decision to accept the throne of Bohemia, and he and Elizabeth moved to Prague, where they reigned for less than a year before being ousted by the armies of the Roman Catholic Habsburg emperor, Ferdinand II. The rest of Elizabeth's life, much of it as a widow, was lived in exile in The Hague, where she worked hard to keep her plight and that of her children in the minds of her allies, and came to symbolise militant Protestantism as the tragic 'Winter Queen'.

Robert Peake was responsible for much of the decorative painting at court, but also painted numerous portraits of the royal children. Peake's portrait of Elizabeth, aged 14, draws attention to her rich clothing and jewellery, including a ruby and diamond brooch pinned to her hair, and a diamond chain across her chest, advertising her eligibility as a wealthy and beautiful potential bride.

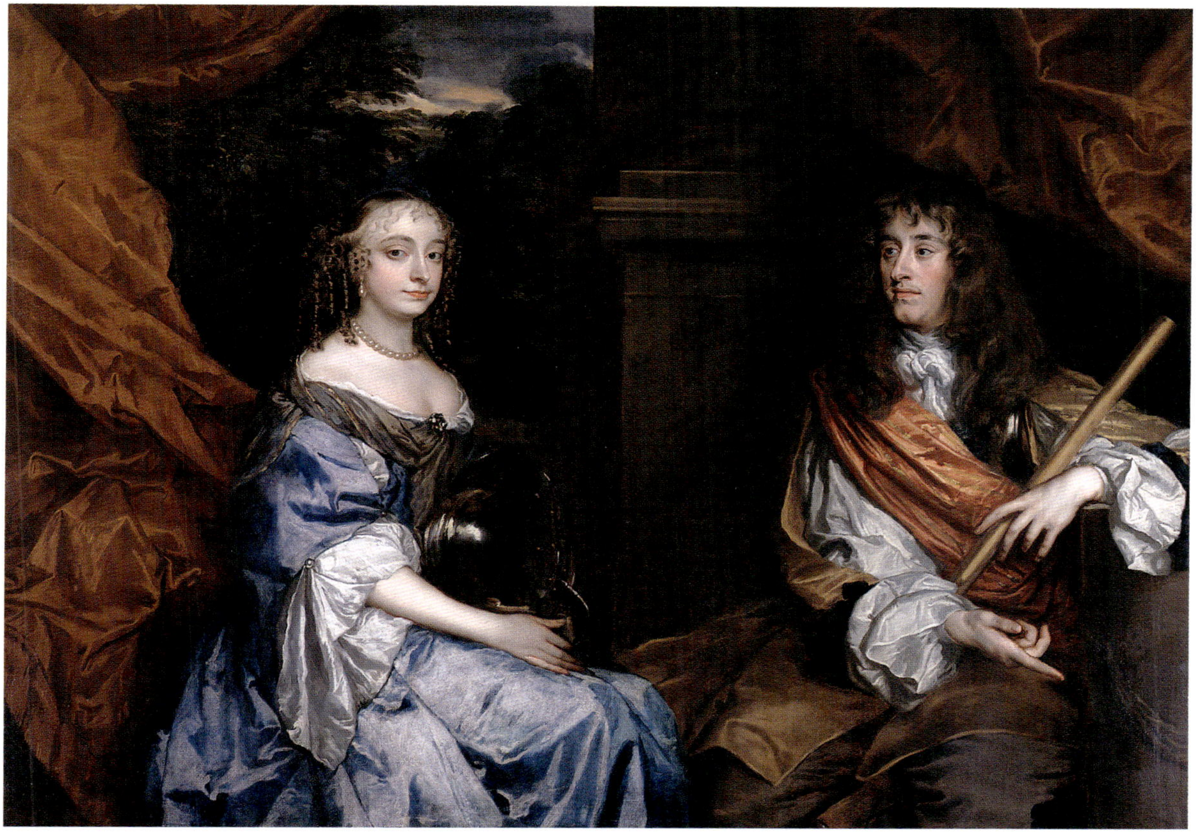

41 Anne Hyde, Duchess of York (1637–71) and King James II (1633–1701)

Sir Peter Lely, c.1661–2

Oil on canvas, 1397 × 1920mm
NPG 5077

Anne Hyde was the daughter of Edward Hyde, Earl of Clarendon, Charles II's most powerful minister at the time of his restoration to the throne in 1660. She and James, Charles's younger brother, had begun a relationship while the court was still in exile on the Continent; Anne became pregnant and James promised to marry her. After the Restoration, however, James's marriage prospects became much better, and a number of attempts were made, first to prevent this marriage to a 'commoner', and then, after it had taken place in secret, to deny that it had happened. Eventually, with the king's support, there was a general reconciliation and the marriage was acknowledged publicly.

It was probably around this time or shortly afterwards that this elegant double portrait was painted by Peter Lely. It is a celebration not just of married love but also of the Stuart family's wealth and military might. Anne was to die young, shortly after the birth of her last child. Both James and Anne were Roman Catholic converts, and James later married an Italian Catholic princess, Mary of Modena. He inherited the throne from his brother in 1685 but was ousted three years later to live in exile for a second time until his death in 1701. However, two of James and Anne's daughters, Mary and Anne, were eventually to become queens of England, though both ruled as Protestants.

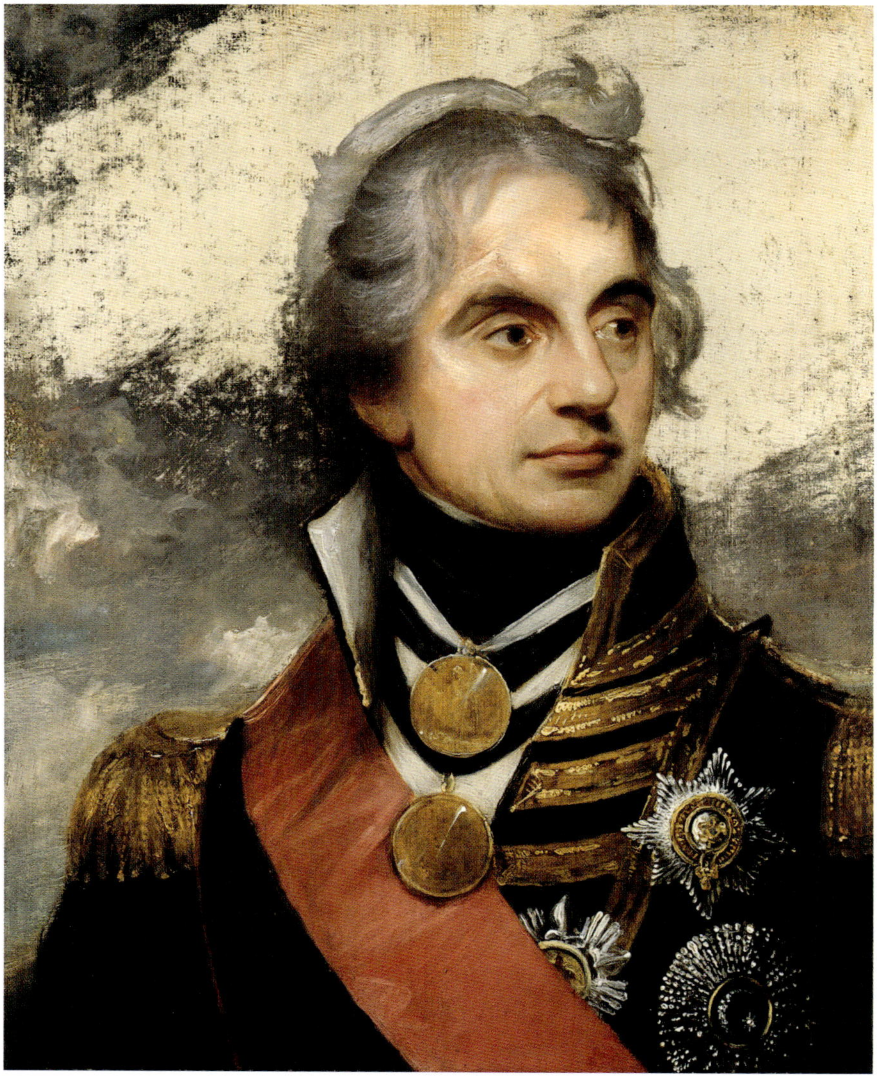

42 **Horatio Nelson** (1758–1805)

Sir William Beechey, 1800

Oil on canvas, 623 × 483mm
NPG 5798

Admiral Lord Nelson remains one of Britain's most illustrious war heroes, and his memorial has pride of place in London's Trafalgar Square. Charismatic, self-confident and vain, he was ever conscious of his public profile. He was also a notorious maverick in battle and prone to insubordination, traits he dubbed 'the Nelson Touch'. In 1793, following the outbreak of war with France, he lost an eye in a successful attack on Corsica, and his right arm in a battle of 1797. Nelson was a masterful tactician leading the British fleet to victory at the Battle of Cape St Vincent (1797) and the Battle of the Nile (1798). While convalescing in Naples, Nelson famously began an affair with Emma, Lady Hamilton. He subsequently destroyed Napoleon's sea power at the Battle of Trafalgar (1805), where he was mortally wounded.

This vivid sketch by William Beechey is a study for a full-length portrait commissioned by the City of Norwich in Norfolk, where Nelson was born. The artist's alteration to the shape of the head is clearly visible, yet the eye colour, which is depicted as brown instead of grey, was not corrected. Nevertheless, it is considered the most faithful likeness of the admiral. Portraits such as Beechey's helped to consolidate Nelson's reputation as a dashing romantic hero, and his relationship with Emma Hamilton has inspired numerous books and films, including *That Hamilton Woman* (1941) starring Vivien Leigh and Laurence Olivier.

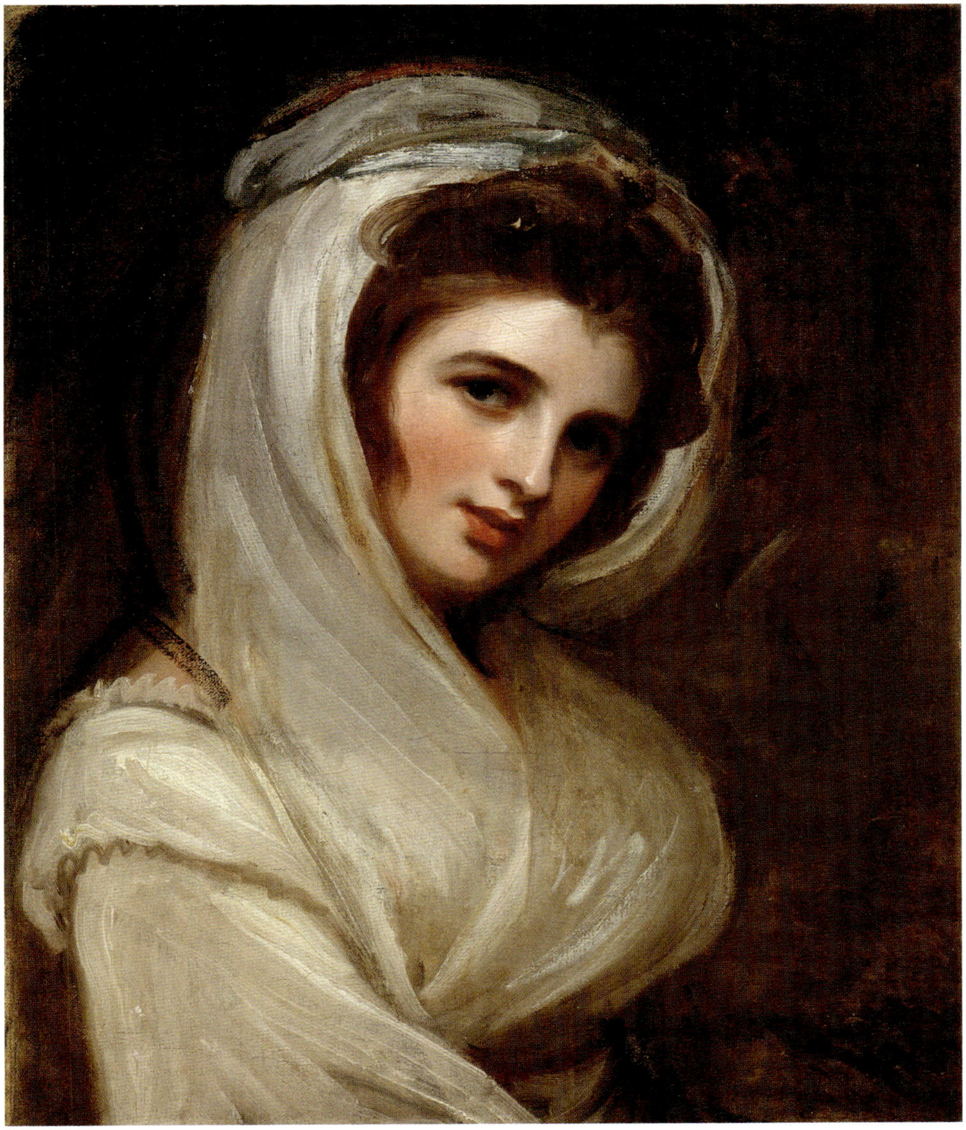

43 **Emma Hamilton** **(*c.*1765–1815)**
George Romney, *c.*1785
Oil on canvas, 623 × 521mm
NPG 4448

Emma, Lady Hamilton, is celebrated as Lord Nelson's mistress. She was also muse to George Romney, who painted her portrait obsessively. From blacksmith stock, she rose to riches in an era not known for its social mobility. An irresistible beauty and one-time dancer at the Georgian venue the Temple of Health, she said in 1791: 'I wish ... to show the world that a pretty woman is not always a fool.' In 1791 she married Sir William Hamilton, British envoy in Naples, where, two years later, she met Horatio Nelson and found enduring love and some sense of equality, since neither had been born wealthy and both were elevated by talent. Her 'Attitudes', a new form of performance art based on the telling of ancient myths in which she struck classical poses using nothing but drapery and lighting to evoke moods and moments from literature, brought her international fame. She became a confidante to the Queen of Naples, and the first woman awarded the Maltese Cross. In 1813, after the deaths of Nelson and Hamilton, her bankruptcy led to her arrest for debt (a pension codicil to Nelson's will having been denied by the government). She died, destitute, two years later in Calais.

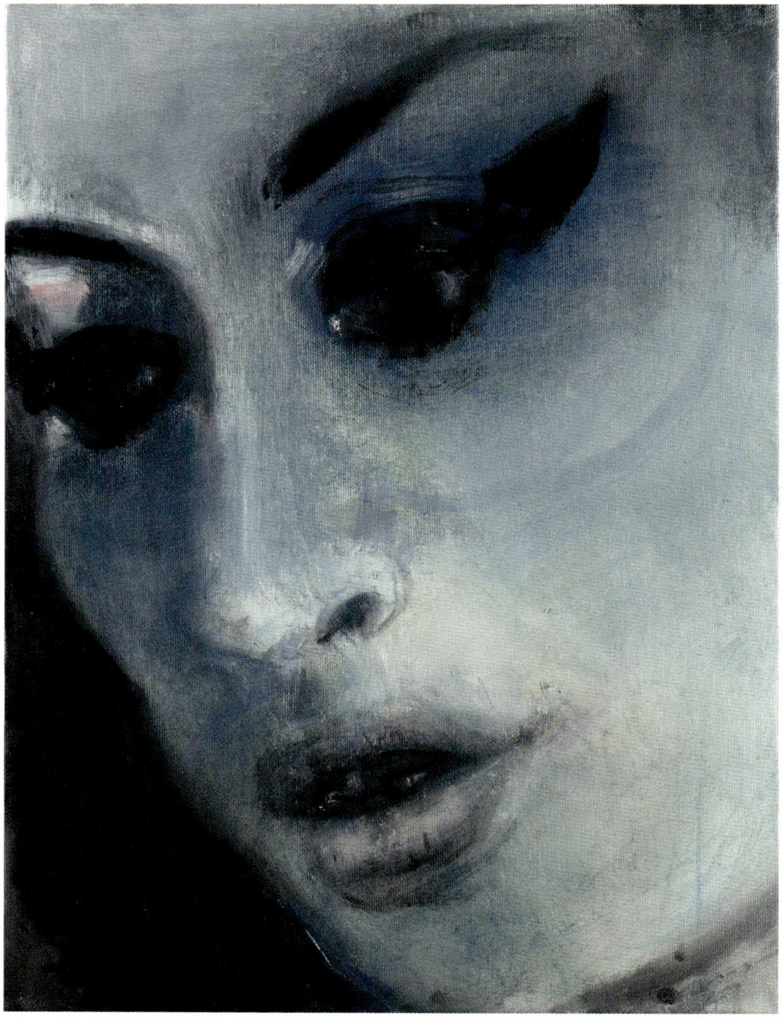

44 **Amy Winehouse** **(1983–2011)**
('Amy-Blue')
Marlene Dumas, 2011
Oil on canvas, 400 × 300mm
NPG 6948

Amy Winehouse was born in north London and trained at the Sylvia Young Theatre School and in 2002 she signed to the Island/Universal record label. Embracing the soulful and candid lyrics of female singers and groups of the 1960s, such as Dinah Washington and The Ronettes, Winehouse's impact on the music industry was a renewed affection for genuine vocal talent in pop. During her career, Winehouse won five Grammys and a Brit award for best female artist. Her internationally acclaimed albums include *Frank* (2003), *Back to Black* (2006) and the posthumously released *Lioness* (2011).

Amsterdam-based, South African artist Marlene Dumas is concerned with issues relating to race, identity and power, and the proliferation of images in contemporary culture. Winehouse's rebellious nature and tumultuous private life inevitably led to media attention, and, like many of Dumas's works, this portrait is derived from a photographic source. Such use of secondary material is key to understanding her work as a reflection of the social and political ideas and obsessions of our time. Her portrait of Winehouse is commemorative, made after the singer's death. It portrays Winehouse at close-crop and simplifies her characteristic features. The translucent blues speak as much of Winehouse's musical influences as of the melancholy details of her life. Dumas has likened the singer's description of being 'given' a voice to the way she herself feels about her own ability to draw.

45 **Leonora Carrington** (1917–2011)

Lee Miller, 1939

Modern gelatin silver print, 253 × 255mm
NPG P1075

Leonora Carrington was an English-born surrealist known for her fantastical paintings and writings that fuse the mundane and magical, animals and humans. The daughter of a Lancashire textile magnate, she met Max Ernst, the German dada and surrealist artist, in 1937 at a dinner party to celebrate the opening of his first major exhibition in London. According to the hostess, Ursula Goldfinger, Ernst and Carrington exchanged intense gazes across the dinner table. They eloped to Paris a few months later when Carrington was 19 years old and Ernst 45. In 1938 they moved to an eighteenth-century farmhouse in the village of Saint-Martin-d'Ardèche in the south of France, which became a focal point for the couple's creative collaborations. Together they sculpted hybrid creatures out of stone, and Ernst produced paintings and collages to accompany Carrington's writings.

This photograph is from a series taken by the American photographer Lee Miller while she was staying with her partner, Roland Penrose, at Carrington and Ernst's house in Saint-Martin-d'Ardèche. The house had become a centre of surrealist gatherings in the months before the outbreak of the Second World War. The idyll came to an end, though, when Ernst was imprisoned by the Vichy government as an 'enemy alien' shortly after war broke out. He and Carrington were briefly reunited, but Ernst was arrested again and returned to the concentration camp at Les Milles in May 1940. Carrington fled to Spain, where she suffered a breakdown and was incarcerated for six months under horrific conditions in a sanatorium. Although the pair met again by chance in a Lisbon market in May 1941, they never rekindled their relationship. Carrington eventually moved to Mexico, and divided her time between there and the USA until her death in 2011.

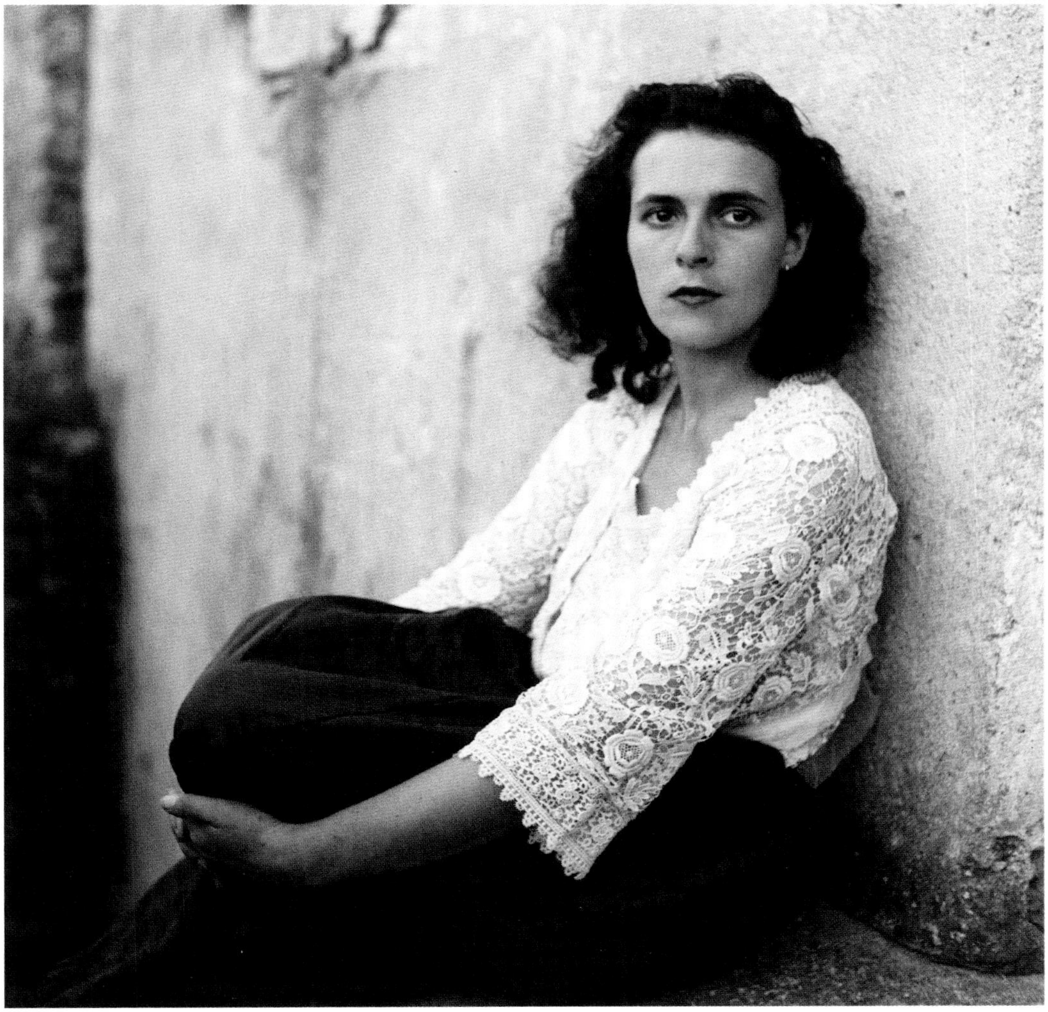

46 **Kate Moss** **(b.1974)**

Mario Sorrenti, 1993

Inkjet print, 1000 × 850mm
NPG P1276

Kate Moss is one of the most successful models in the fashion industry. Born in Croydon, London, and talent spotted at the age of fourteen, she appeared on the cover of *The Face* magazine in 1990 and British *Vogue* in 1993, both photographs by Corinne Day. Moss has subsequently appeared on over 300 magazine covers and in major advertising campaigns internationally. She was Model of the Year at the British Fashion Awards in 2006, and received a Special Recognition award in 2013 in honour of her contribution to fashion.

This photograph was taken for an advertising campaign for the Calvin Klein perfume Obsession. Sorrenti and Moss met in 1991 when they were both modelling. They fell in love and moved in together. Inspired by Moss, Sorrenti developed a fascination with photographing her. His photography was brought to the attention of fashion designer Calvin Klein, who sent the couple to the British Virgin Islands for ten days to shoot his new campaign. The unaffected, make-up free beauty of the resulting monochrome images propelled the 19-year-old Moss to supermodel fame and initiated Sorrenti's successful career as a fashion photographer.

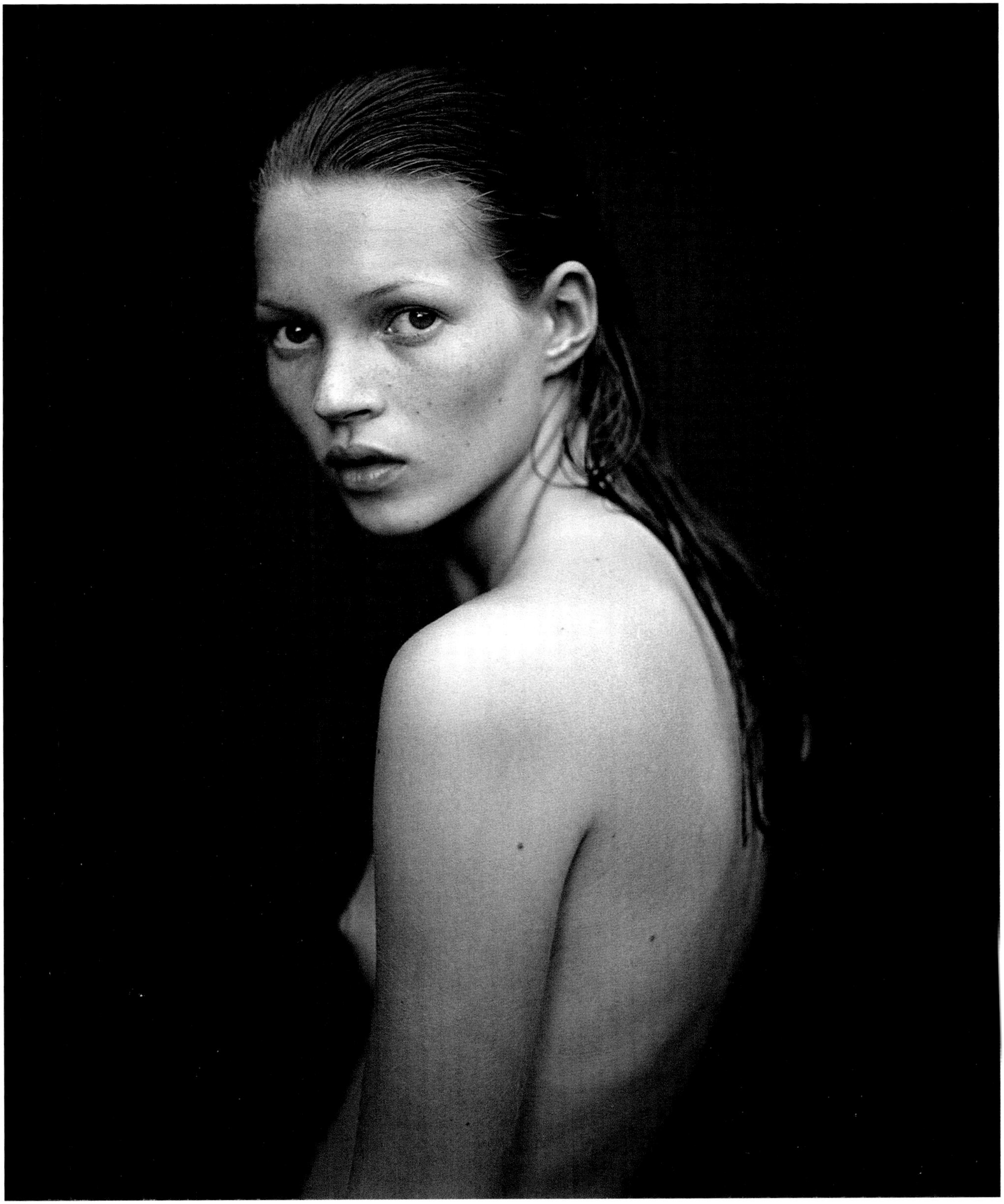

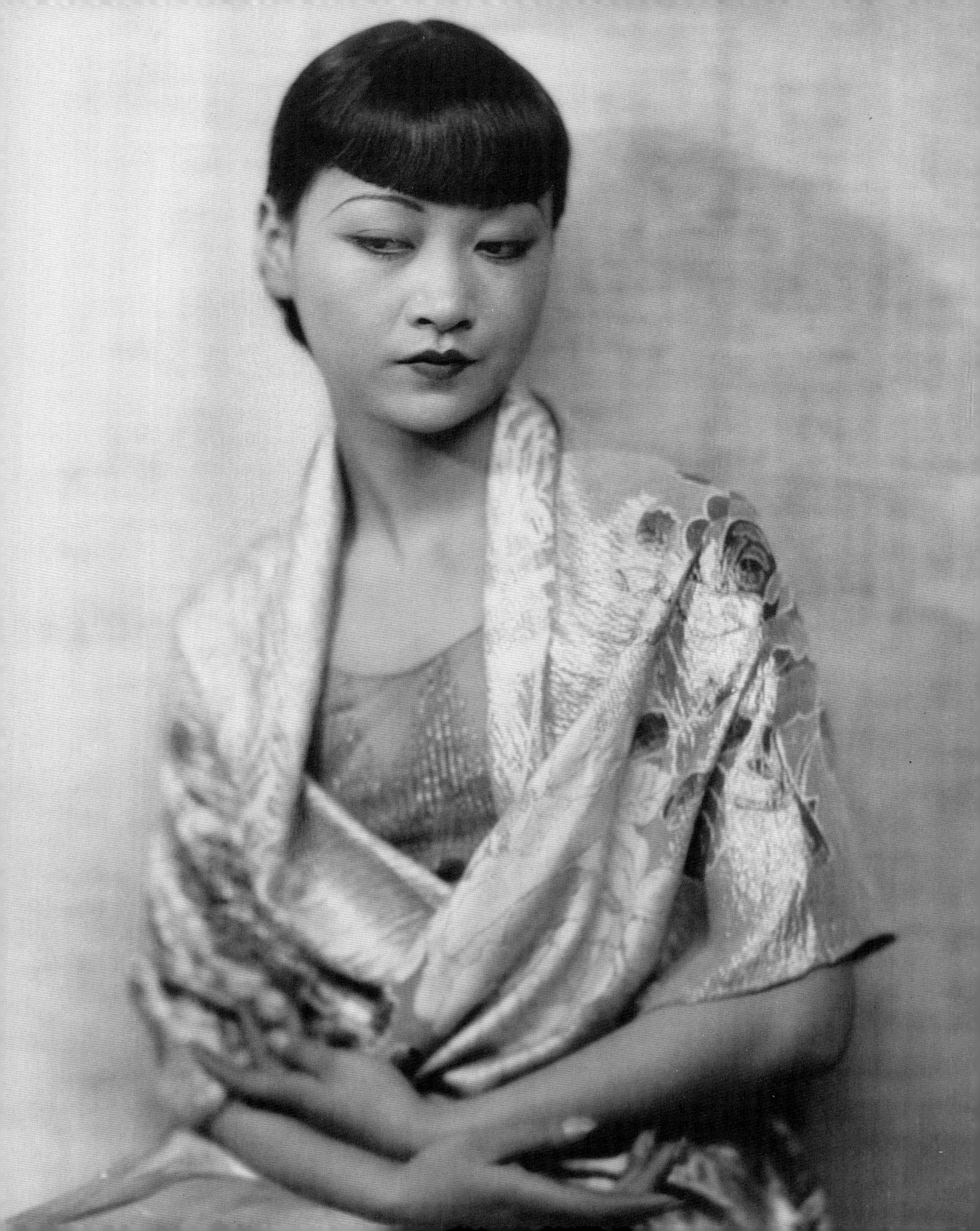

Identity

Portraiture is inextricably linked to notions of identity. Viewing a portrait naturally sparks questions about the sitter's identity. At the most basic level this relates to who they are, or were, and can develop into more complex considerations about the values and beliefs that are projected through the artwork. The experience of viewing a portrait involves reflection about what it is that makes the sitter distinct from us and what we share in common.

This section introduces various types of identity and different approaches to their visual representation. Although painted 500 years ago, the incredible technique of Anthonis Mor seems to dissolve time and create a palpable sense of the living presence of Sir Henry Lee (see p.84), while the symbolism of his costume declares his loyalty and devotion to Queen Elizabeth I.

A sitter's professional identity is often indicated by artists through the use of props, for example Thomas Gainsborough's portrait of Karl Friedrich Abel (see p.87) includes his viola da gamba as an extension of his musical personality. A collaboration between Ayuba Suleiman Diallo (see p.85) and the painter William Hoare produced the first known British portrait of a freed slave. Through Diallo's self-fashioning, viewers are drawn to the red Quran that he wears proudly around his neck affirming his religious identity.

However, sometimes a portrait can reveal a different, less-known side of a person's identity. For example, Walter Sickert's informal painting of the iconic British prime minister Winston Churchill (see p.90) depicts the sitter not in a political context but instead as a willing art student, poised and engaged to learn from an experienced artist.

The fluidity of gender identities across time is explored in Thomas Stewart's portrait of the eighteenth-century fencing instructor, Chevalier d'Éon (see p.82), and Charles Buchel's portrait of the writer Radclyffe Hall (see p.83), in which her lesbian identity and defiance of convention are proclaimed by her masculine dress. The musician David Bowie (see pp.96–7) is an icon of contemporary notions of identity due to his continually evolving stage personae and his playful relationship with gender stereotypes.

DETAIL **Anna May Wong, 1929**

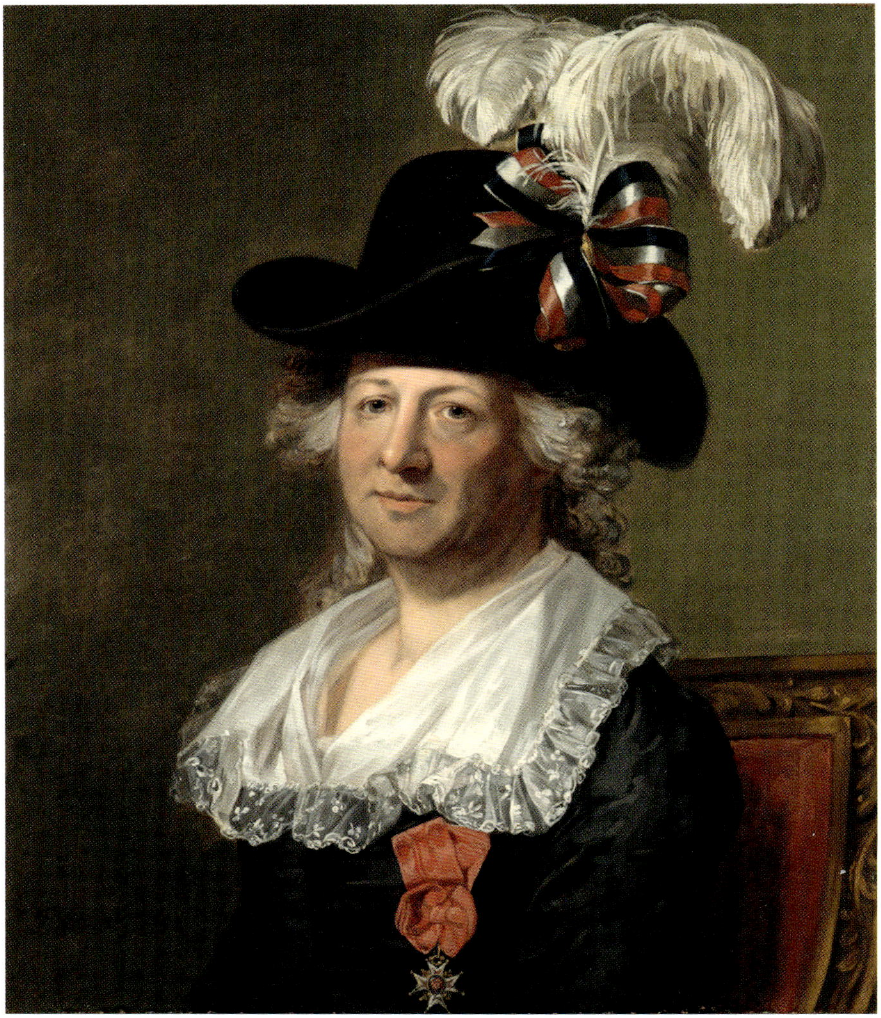

47 Chevalier d'Éon (1728–1810)
Thomas Stewart,
after Jean Laurent Mosnier, 1792
Oil on canvas, 765 × 640mm
NPG 6937

This painting of the celebrated French soldier, diplomat and fencer Chevalier d'Éon (Charles Geneviève Louis Auguste André Timothée d'Éon de Beaumont) is the earliest portrait in the Collection of a person who is known to have presented as a man and as a woman in public life. There was widespread and demeaning contemporary curiosity about d'Éon's gender identity, a subject on which d'Éon refused to speak openly; eighteenth-century society did not technically permit any deviation from strict binary oppositions between male and female. D'Éon first came to England as a diplomat, playing a key role in peace negotiations that ended the Seven Years War (1756–63) between France and Britain. Some years later, d'Éon was exiled from France for taking part in a spy scandal to sell French state secrets to the British. D'Éon returned to England in 1785, and commenced living openly as a woman and working, to great acclaim, as a professional fencer. While fighting, d'Éon often wore a black dress, like the one in this portrait, and the Croix de St Louis medal, France's military order of chivalry, also depicted.

This portrait by Thomas Stewart is a contemporary copy of an original portrait painted by the French artist Jean-Laurent Mosnier. The Mosnier painting had been exhibited at the Royal Academy in 1791, where, according to the *Public Advertiser* dated 23 March 1792, it was received with 'general satisfaction' by the public. D'Éon sports a large tricolour cockade, showing allegiance to the new revolutionary government in France, from whom d'Éon was trying to extract a state pension.

48 **Radclyffe Hall** (1880–1943)

Charles Buchel, 1918

Oil on canvas, 914 × 711mm
NPG 4347

The writer and poet Radclyffe Hall is best known today for her semi-autobiographical novel *The Well of Loneliness*, which invoked public outrage following its publication in 1928 for its candid and sympathetic depiction of a lesbian relationship. Despite protestations from Vera Brittain, Arnold Bennett, T.S. Eliot and Virginia Woolf, the publication was banned in Britain. In a letter of thanks to one supporter, Hall explained: 'I wrote the book in order to help a very much misunderstood ... section of society.'

A woman of independent means, Hall had first published several volumes of verse before turning to novels from 1924. *Adam's Breed* (1926) was awarded two prestigious literary awards – the James Tait Black Memorial Prize (1926) and the Prix Femina Vie Heureuse (1927). The ban on *The Well of Loneliness* was overturned in 1949, six years after Hall's death. Her life, like her writing, was ground-breaking and controversial. Preferring to be known as 'John' rather than her given name, Marguerite, she wore masculine clothes and, at a time when male homosexual behaviour was illegal, she lived openly with the singer Mabel Veronica Batten and later with the sculptor Una, Lady Troubridge, who bequeathed this painting to the National Portrait Gallery.

This portrait precedes the publication of her first book, *The Forge* (1924), by several years. Hall cultivated the masculine appearance captured in this portrait by Charles Buchel, by pinning back her hair and wearing a grey silk cravat, monocle and well-cut jacket. However, Hall's dress was not unique among progressive and intellectual women, who, since the late nineteenth century, had increasingly incorporated elements of the masculine wardrobe into their own as being more practical and professional.

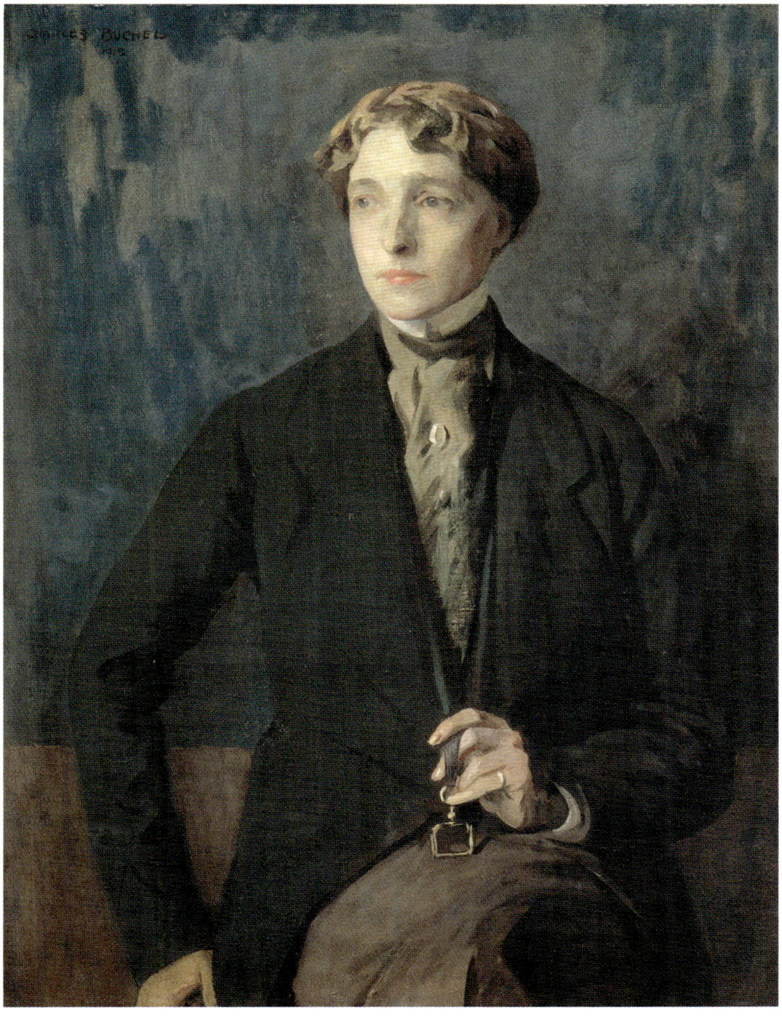

49 **Sir Henry Lee** (1533–1611)
Anthonis Mor, 1568

Oil on panel, 641 × 533mm
NPG 2095

Kentish-born Henry Lee was educated by his uncle, the poet Sir Thomas Wyatt, and entered royal service at the age of fourteen. As his epitaph recorded, he served five monarchs over the course of his long career and 'kept himself right and steady in many dangerous shocks and utter turns of state'. He achieved his greatest renown at the court of Elizabeth I, serving as Master of the Armoury and devising the annual Accession Day tilts on 17 November in her honour. These elaborate celebrations became the most important Elizabethan court festival, and created an environment in which the court could compete for the queen's favour.

This portrait was painted in Antwerp in 1568 while Lee was travelling in Europe. The painting is rich in clues and symbols about the sitter's identity. He wears the queen's colours of black and white, and his sleeves are decorated with armillary spheres (symbols of celestial harmony) and lovers' knots, which were personal emblems of Elizabeth and probably refer to his role as her champion. The significance of his gesture is unclear, but it also appears in a portrait of Edward, 3rd Baron Windsor, who accompanied Lee on his travels. The gesture, in addition to the ring tied around his arm in the manner of a chivalric favour, may indicate an offer of love and devotion, either to the queen, a friend or a lover. The artist Anthonis Mor was one of the most esteemed portraitists working in Europe; he had returned to the Netherlands in 1561, after being appointed principal court painter to Philip II of Spain in London in December 1554.

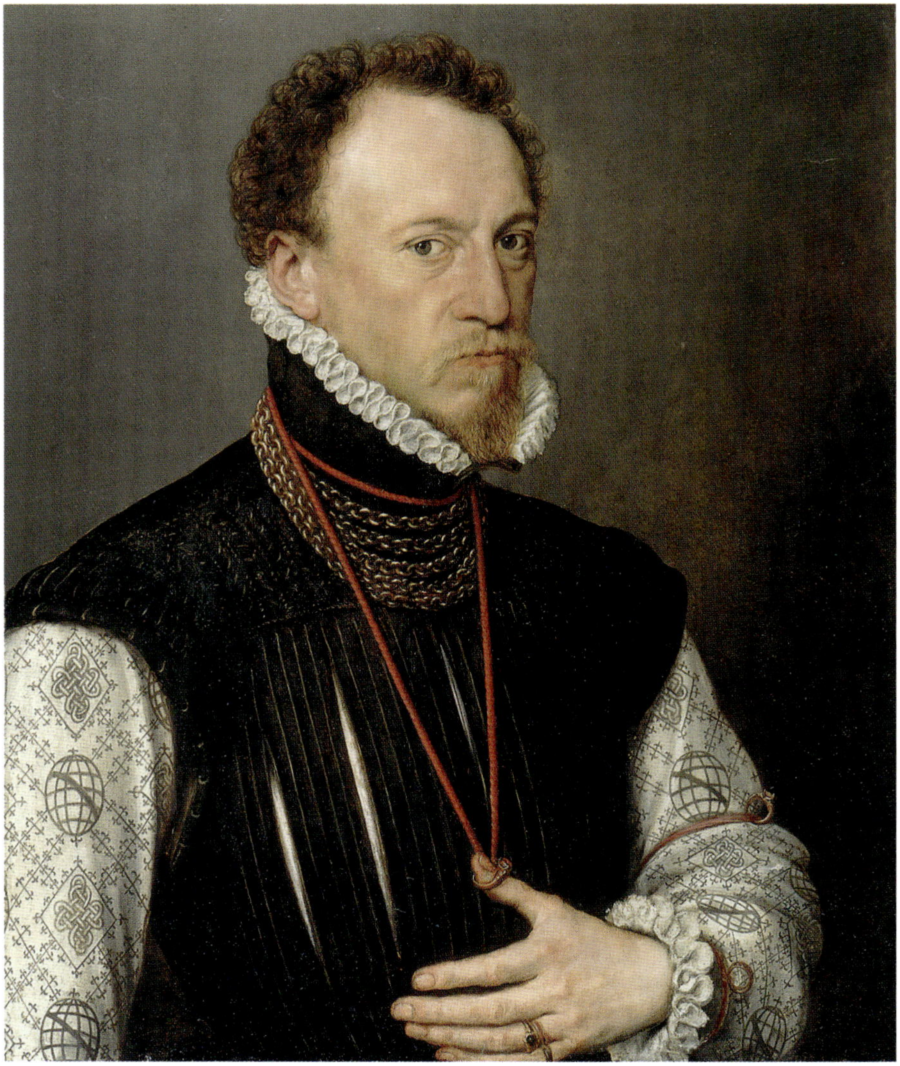

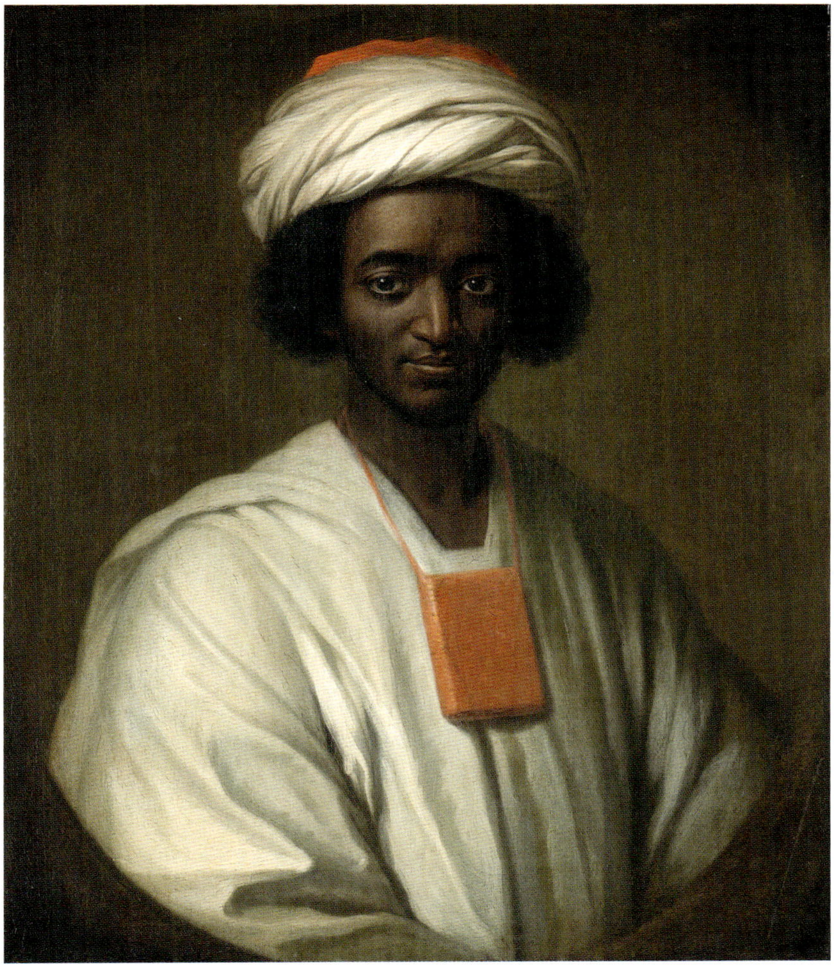

50 Ayuba Suleiman Diallo (Job ben Solomon) (1701–73)

William Hoare, 1733

Oil on canvas, 762 × 635mm
NPG L245

Ayuba Suleiman Diallo was an educated man from a wealthy family of Muslim clerics in the Senegal/Gambia region of West Africa, whose family traded commodities and slaves. In 1730, on his return from a trip to sell slaves, he was captured by enemies and sold to the same European representative of the Royal African Company with whom he had recently traded. His attempts to secure his release were unsuccessful, and he was transported to America, where he was sold to a plantation owner. By his own enterprise, and assisted by several strokes of good fortune, Diallo was brought to London in 1733. Recognised as a deeply pious and educated man, in England Diallo mixed with high and intellectual society, was introduced at court and was eventually bought out of slavery by public subscription. His elite status and education allowed him to attain his freedom and return home in 1734, making him one of the very few victims of the transatlantic slave trade to return to Africa. Through the publication of his memoirs in 1734, Diallo had an important and lasting impact on Britain's understanding of West African culture, black identity and Islam. In the early years of the nineteenth century, advocates of the abolition of slavery cited Diallo as a key figure in asserting the moral rights and humanity of Africans.

William Hoare's compelling portrait of Diallo is the earliest known British oil portrait of a freed slave, and the first to honour an African subject as an individual and an equal. It was painted at the time when there was a new interest in Islamic culture and faith in Britain, and provides a fascinating insight into the eighteenth-century response to other peoples and religions. Diallo's West African identity and Islamic faith are expressed through the use of costume and the Quran he wears around his neck.

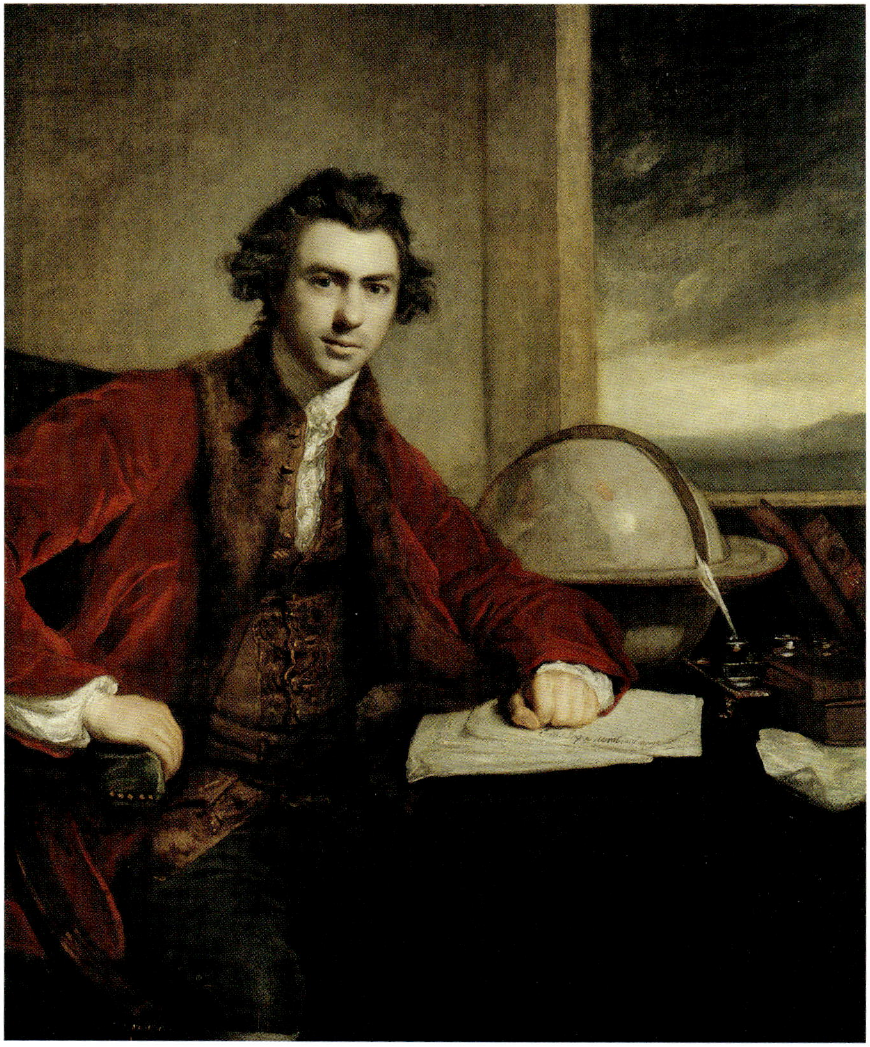

51 **Sir Joseph Banks** (1743–1820)
Sir Joshua Reynolds, 1771–3
Oil on canvas, 1270 × 1015mm
NPG 5868

This portrait of Joseph Banks by Joshua Reynolds was painted on Banks's return to England, to a rapturous welcome, having participated in Captain James Cook's successful Pacific voyage on the *Endeavour* (1768–71). Reynolds's portrait alludes to Banks's identity as an explorer through the globe on the table, while the inscription on the letter, a quotation from Horace, translates as 'tomorrow we will set out again upon the vast sea'.

Banks had developed his scientific expertise on an earlier expedition to Labrador and Newfoundland in 1766. The *Endeavour* voyage to Tahiti, New Zealand and Australia gave him an unparalleled opportunity to study local plants, wildlife and people. He made a unique natural history collection, learned Tahitian and participated in local traditions, including being tattooed. On his return to England in 1771, he was introduced to George III, who became a close friend and supporter. Cook's second expedition of 1772–5 could not accommodate Banks's entourage; instead Banks organised a voyage to explore the natural history of Iceland. In Britain he held positions of great scientific influence and advised the government on the establishment of the Royal Botanic Gardens at Kew and the first British colonies in Australia. Banks was elected president of the Royal Society in 1778. In recent decades, Banks's legacy has been the subject of re-evaluation in light of the exploitation of indigenous people during the *Endeavour* voyage, and his active support for British colonial expansion.

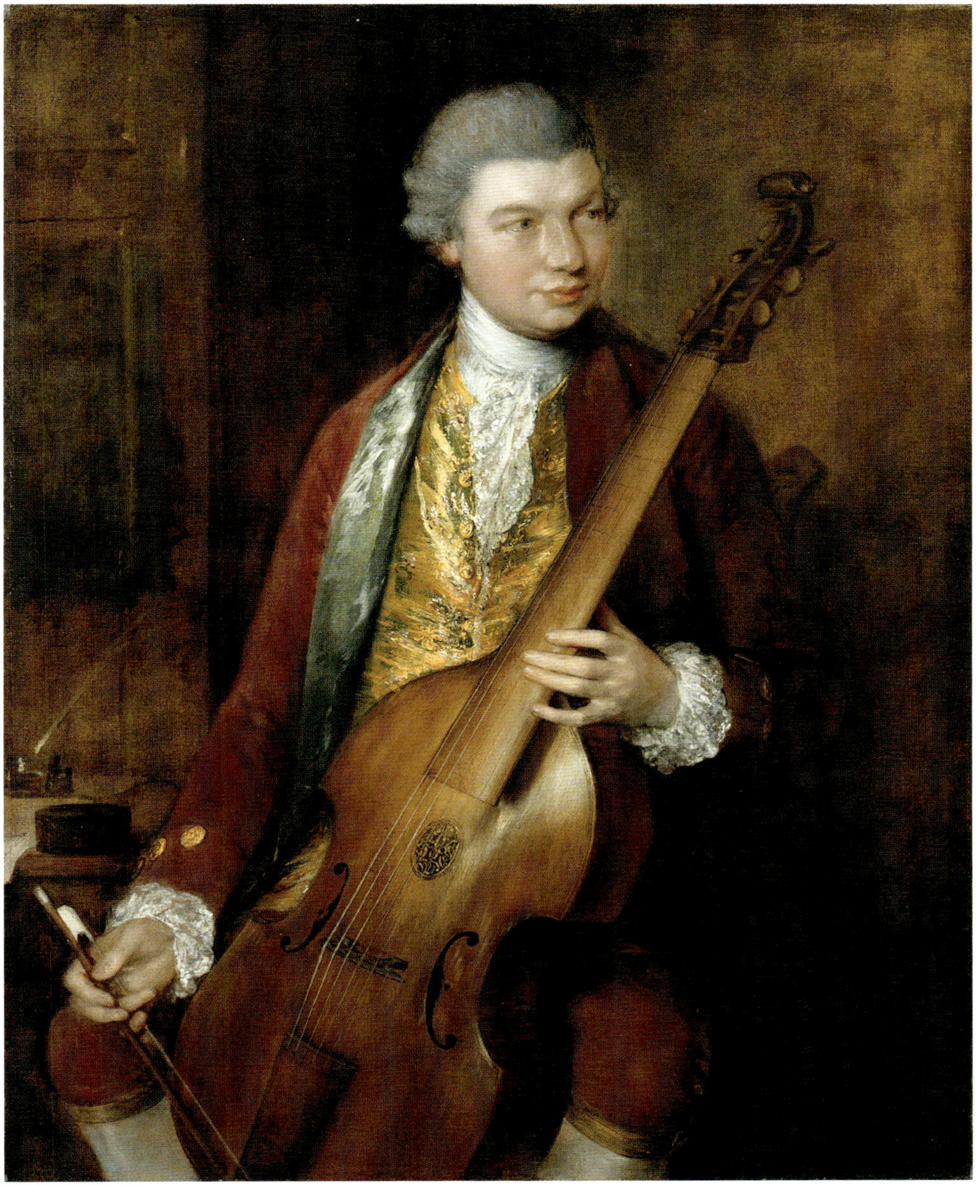

52 **Karl Friedrich Abel** (1723–87)
Thomas Gainsborough, *c.*1765
Oil on canvas, 1267 × 1013mm
NPG 5947

One of the last of the great viola da gamba virtuosi, the German musician Karl Friedrich Abel arrived in London in 1759. He became famous for the subscription concerts that he organised with Johann Christian Bach at the Hanover Square Rooms.

This portrait celebrates Abel's identity as a musician. He and the artist Thomas Gainsborough were close friends who shared a passion for the viola da gamba and a love of life. Gainsborough became a skilful performer on the instrument and his careful portrayal of the underhand grip of the bow reflects his understanding of it. In return for his teaching, Abel received some paintings and many drawings by his friend. On Abel's death, Gainsborough said, 'I shall never cease looking up to heaven the little while I have to stay behind – in hopes of getting one more glance of the man I loved from the moment I heard him touch the string.'

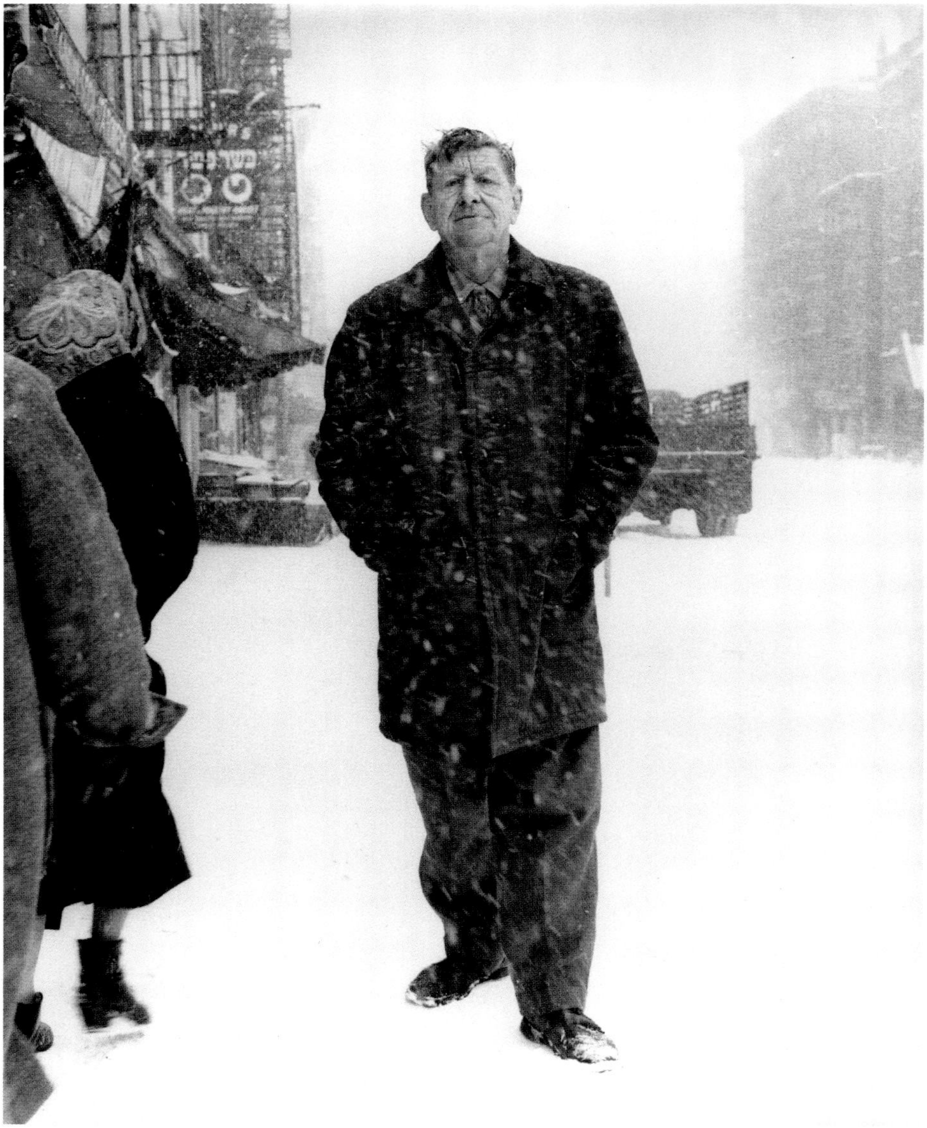

53 W.H. Auden (1907–73)
Richard Avedon, 1960
Gelatin silver print, 600 × 483mm
NPG P614

The third son of a doctor and a missionary nurse, Wystan Hugh Auden grew up in Solihull and described his early advantages as 'good genes and good education'. He is best known for his poems of the 1930s and 1940s – including *Poems* (1930), *Look, Stranger!* (1936) and *For the Time Being* (1944) – and for his collaborations with Christopher Isherwood on *The Dog Beneath the Skin* (1935), *The Ascent of F6* (1936) and *On the Frontier* (1938). He travelled widely, including visiting Berlin in 1928, where he explored the gay subculture that flourished in Weimar Germany, and to Spain in 1937 to fight for the Republican cause. He frequently wrote about gay love at a time when homosexuality was still criminalised in Britain.

In the late 1950s Auden returned to England, where he had been elected professor of poetry at Oxford. Despite residual hostility in his home country caused by his wartime move to America, his three annual lectures were highly successful and published in *The Dyer's Hand* (1962). Auden continued to spend his winters in New York, and this portrait by the celebrated American photographer Richard Avedon was taken near his apartment in St Mark's Place, New York.

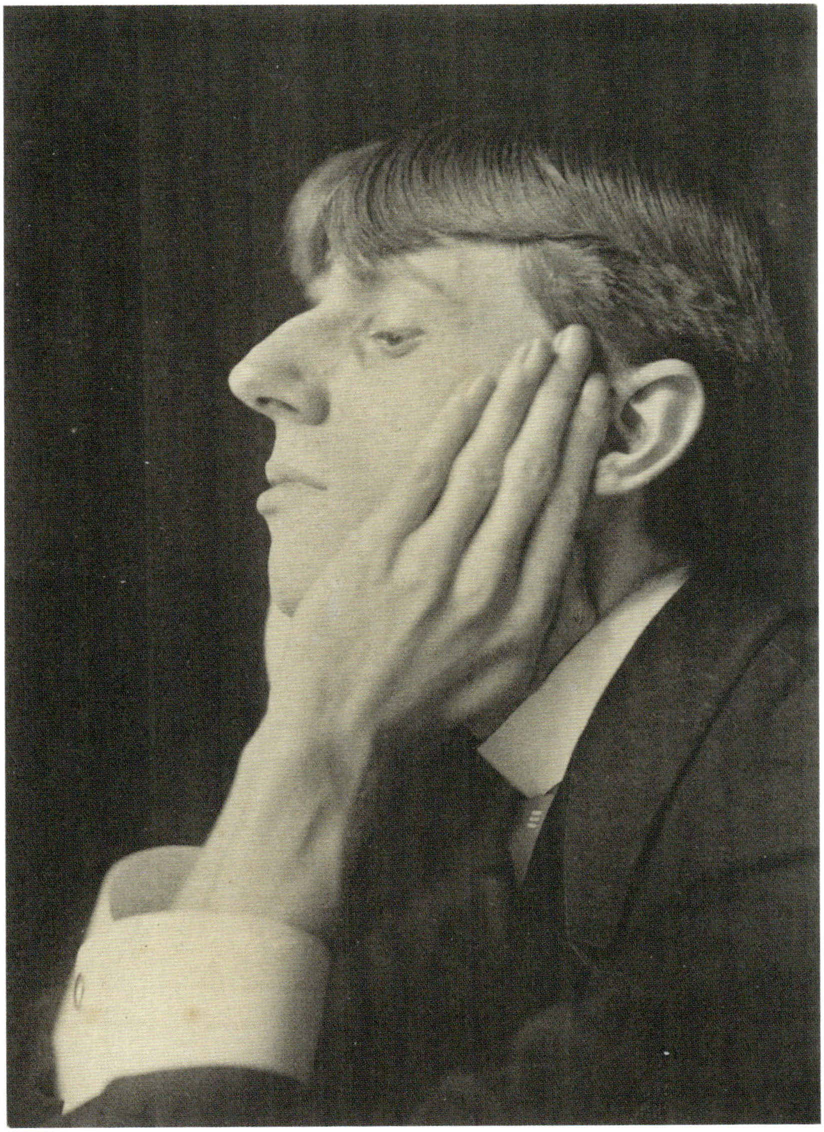

54 **Aubrey Beardsley** **(1872–98)**
Frederick Henry Evans, *c.*1894
Platinum print, 136 × 97mm
NPG P114

In a short life of intense and fevered activity, Aubrey Beardsley produced many brilliant, original and highly finished black-and-white drawings. He was an aesthete of elegance and charm, and a witty conversationalist. His frequently morbid and erotic illustrations for the fashionable magazines the *Yellow Book* and the *Savoy*, and his responses to Alexander Pope's *Rape of the Lock* and Oscar Wilde's *Salome*, made him a cult figure of the decadent movement. The exploration of sexual liberation and gender fluidity in his work has made him an iconic figure within the history of queer identity.

A recommendation by Frederick Henry Evans facilitated Beardsley's career as a full-time illustrator, and their friendship resulted in this defining portrait. Beardsley adopted the pose when his friend jested that his face was like a 'gargoyle'. Beardsley wrote to Evans on 20 August 1894: 'I think the photos are splendid; couldn't be better.' Evans experimented with the platinum process; matt and dense, it was favoured by members of the leading art photographers' group, the Linked Ring.

55 **Sir Winston Churchill** (1874–1965)

Walter Sickert, 1927

Oil on canvas, 457 × 305mm
NPG 4438

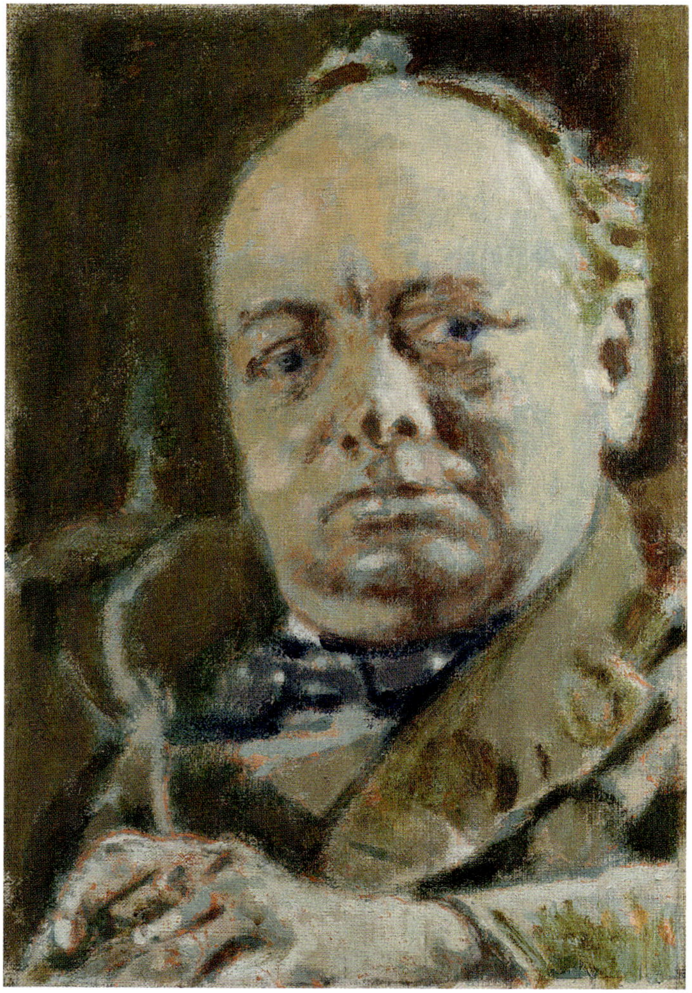

Sir Winston Churchill achieved iconic status for leading Britain in the Allied victory over Nazi Germany in the Second World War. He is instantly recognisable, usually holding a cane and wreathed in cigar smoke. Churchill's background was one of great privilege: born at Blenheim Palace, Oxfordshire, into a wealthy, aristocratic family, he served in the army before becoming a Member of Parliament in 1900, and was appointed First Lord of the Admiralty in 1911. Over the next two decades, his career was less assured; in fact, following the failure of the Dardanelles expedition in 1915, he was forced to resign. He returned to ministerial office in 1917 after a period of active service, and, as Chancellor of the Exchequer, returned Britain to the gold standard, which led to the General Strike of 1926. As an imperialist, he opposed his party's policy of self-government for India, and resigned again in 1931. Churchill consistently opposed appeasement with Hitler, and challenged Neville Chamberlain's leadership in 1940, succeeding him as prime minister until 1945. Voted out of office in the first post-war general election, he returned to power in 1951, aged nearly 77, and led the country until 1955. While his achievements as a wartime leader are widely celebrated, it has been argued that his cabinet's policy failures exacerbated the 1943 Bengal famine.

The painting shown here was undertaken when Churchill was Chancellor of the Exchequer. At the time, Walter Sickert was giving Churchill painting lessons at the latter's house, Chartwell in Kent. He may have had sittings for this work, but Sickert often worked straight from photographs. The informality of the portrait reveals a different side to Churchill's personality – a willing student rather than a formidable statesman. In a letter of 26 September 1927 to his wife, Clementine, who had introduced him to Sickert, he wrote: 'Sickert arrived on Friday night and we worked very hard at various paintings and had many discussions … I see my way to paint far better pictures than I ever thought possible before. He is really giving me a new lease of life as a painter.' However, Churchill himself disliked the portrait and gave it away soon after it had been presented to him.

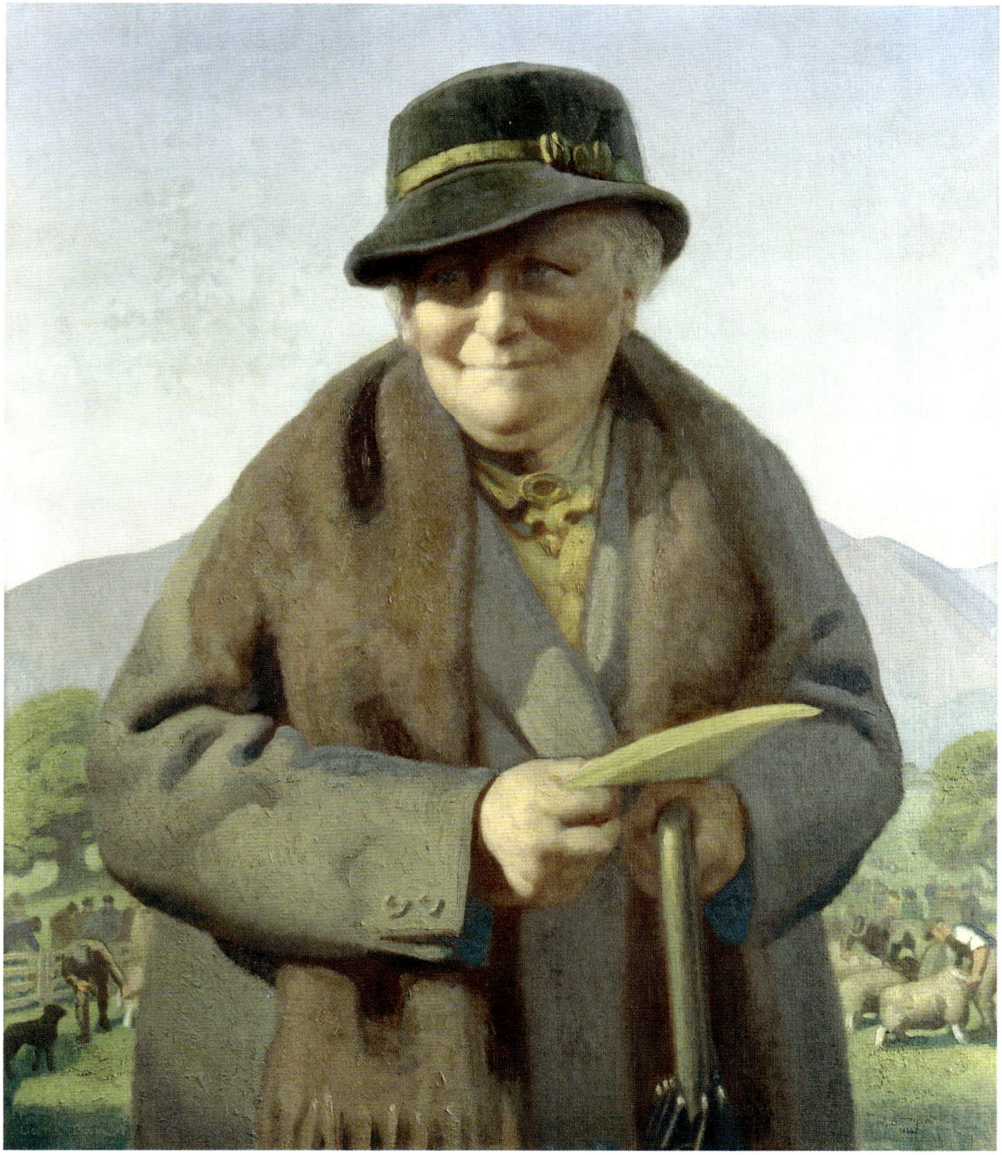

56 **Beatrix Potter** **(1866–1943)**
Delmar Banner, 1938
Oil on canvas, 749 × 622mm
NPG 3635

Beatrix Potter was a writer, artist and conservationist. Informally educated, she spent hours drawing in the Natural History Museum. Her children's stories, which she wrote and illustrated, began as letters to a child. The anthropomorphic characters of her tales – including Peter Rabbit, Squirrel Nutkin, Jemima Puddle-Duck and Tom Kitten – display an unsentimental observation of human nature. They have achieved international recognition, continuously published by Frederick Warne & Co., and the characters have been reproduced in ceramic, animated film and ballet.

Potter farmed in the Lake District and was passionate about preserving the landscape and culture. Indeed, in contrast to her international fame as a children's author, Potter spent more of her life farming than writing. This portrait by her neighbour Delmar Banner celebrates her Cumbrian farming identity by showing her as a respected breeder and judge of Herdwick sheep at an agricultural show. Potter married her solicitor, William Heelis, in 1913, and later bequeathed her 4,000 acres of land to the National Trust.

57 **Harry Belafonte** (b.1927)
Dorothy Wilding, 1954

Chlorobromide print, 281 × 236mm
NPG x4386

Harry Belafonte is a Grammy award-winning singer who popularised calypso, a style of Afro-Caribbean music, with an international audience. He rose to fame in the 1950s, releasing his album *Calypso* (1956), the first LP by a solo artist to sell over one million copies. He also starred in several films, including the successful musical *Carmen Jones* (1954), and Broadway shows such as *3 for Tonight* (1954). Besides calypso, Belafonte is well known for other musical genres, including blues, folk and gospel, and has released thirty studio albums and eight live albums. A supporter of the civil rights movement in the United States, he was a friend and confidant of Martin Luther King Jr, and has continued his social activism in a number of causes, including the Anti-Apartheid Movement, and working for UNICEF as a goodwill ambassador.

The portrait photographer Dorothy Wilding shot several photographs of the young Belafonte in her New York studio in February 1954, including this brooding and pensive image. It was a moment of rising stardom for the singer, yet he has since written in his autobiography *My Song: A Memoir of Art, Race and Defiance* (2011) that at the time he was grappling with his dual heritage: 'My racial identity confused me still; I was black, yes, but West Indian, playing to white audiences – a cultural hybrid, in between.'

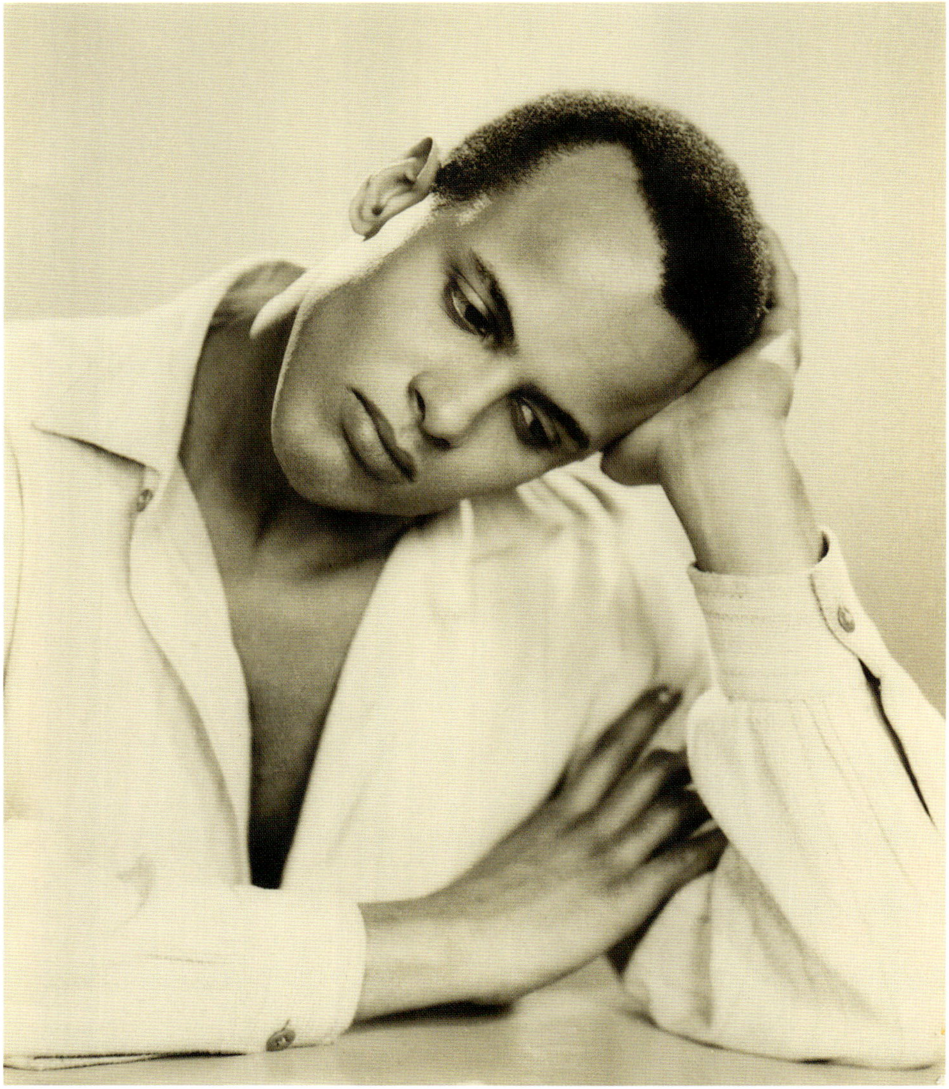

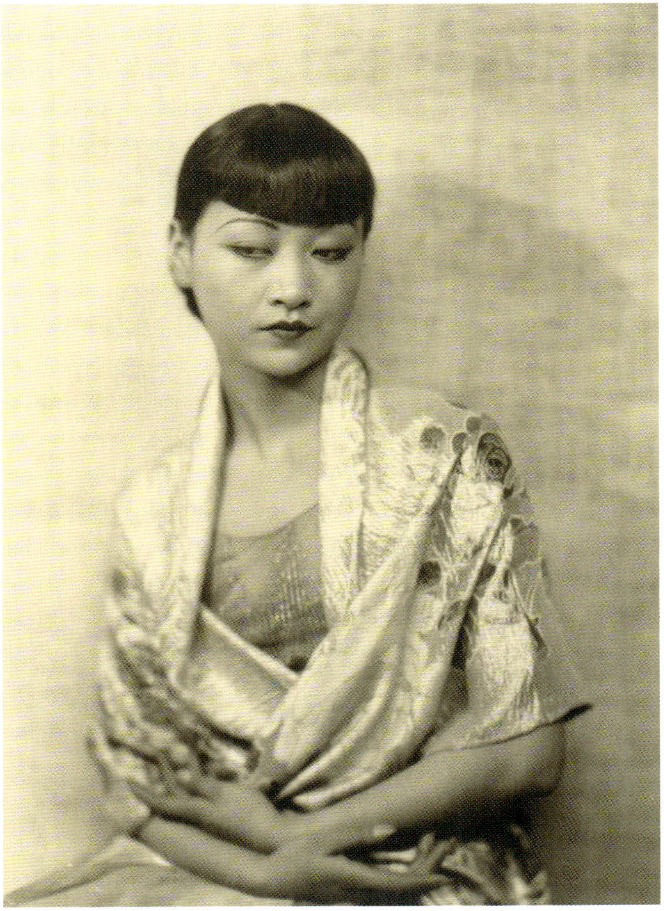

58 **Anna May Wong (1905–61)**
Dorothy Wilding, 1929
Chlorobromide print, 418 × 295mm
(image size)
NPG x26341

The Chinese-American actor Anna May Wong, born in Los Angeles, was a silent-era idol, one of the first and, for a time, the only woman of Chinese descent to work in Hollywood in an era when non-Asian actors customarily took Asian roles. With *The Toll of the Sea* (1922), a barely modified version of the Madam Butterfly plot and her first leading role, she became an overnight sensation. Two years later in *The Thief of Bagdad* (1924), a Douglas Fairbanks Jr swashbuckler, she all but outshone her co-star, and a year later, in *Peter Pan*, she starred as Tiger Lily. Wong left Hollywood temporarily for Europe in 1928, as she was tired of the stereotypical, timeworn roles on offer. She remarked later: 'Why is it the screen Chinese is nearly always the villain? And so crude a villain – murderous, treacherous, a snake in the grass. We are not like that. How should we be, with a civilisation that is so many, many times older than that of the West?' In Europe she exuded Hollywood star power and was not short of work. In London she was treated as a fashion icon in the making, with a universal allure and distinctive sense of style. But the films – or at least Hollywood cinema – ultimately let her down. Despite her pioneering example and outspokenness, Asian roles began to return to white actors, and she was subjected to racism throughout her career due to her Chinese identity, including not being able to share an on-screen kiss with a white actor.

She appeared in over sixty films, and is best known for her starring roles alongside Marlene Dietrich in Joseph von Sternberg's *Shanghai Express* (1932) and in the classic British silent melodrama *Piccadilly*, released in 1929 – the year the leading British society photographer Dorothy Wilding took this portrait. In her autobiography, *In Pursuit of Perfection* (1958), Wilding recalled: 'Anna May Wong ... had the first long red fingernails I had ever seen. When I lifted her hands to "drape" them, they were so fragile that one felt one was holding the most delicate snowdrops. She was the softest and gentlest creature one can imagine.'

59 Anne Brontë (1820–49), Emily Brontë (1818–48) and Charlotte Brontë (1816–55)

Patrick Branwell Brontë, *c.*1834

Oil on canvas, 902 × 746mm
NPG 1725

This is the only surviving group portrait of the English novelists, Anne, Emily and Charlotte Brontë, painted by their brother Branwell, aged 17. Their most well-known novels include Anne's *Agnes Grey*, Emily's *Wuthering Heights* and Charlotte's *Jane Eyre*, all first published in 1847 under their respective pseudonyms, Acton, Ellis and Currer Bell. The portrait was thought to have been lost until it was discovered folded up on top of a cupboard by the second wife of the Reverend A.B. Nicholls, Charlotte Brontë's widower, in 1914. The barely discernible male figure in the middle, previously concealed by a painted pillar that has become slightly transparent with age, is almost certainly a self-portrait of Branwell that he subsequently painted out of the composition. Following the portrait's acquisition, the National Portrait Gallery made the highly unusual decision not to restore it, but to retain the fold marks and paint losses – evidence of the neglect it had suffered that has proved integral to the portrait's enduring appeal. The portrait's apparent shortcomings as a work of art, described as 'not much better than sign-painting' by Elizabeth Gaskell in her *Life of Charlotte Brontë* (1857), can be attributed to the relative youth and inexperience of its artist and also its unfinished state. This has not diminished its power to fascinate generations of visitors. Branwell died of bronchitis in 1848, rapidly followed by Emily and Anne, both of whom had contracted tuberculosis. Charlotte died in March 1855, weakened by excessive morning sickness in the early stages of pregnancy.

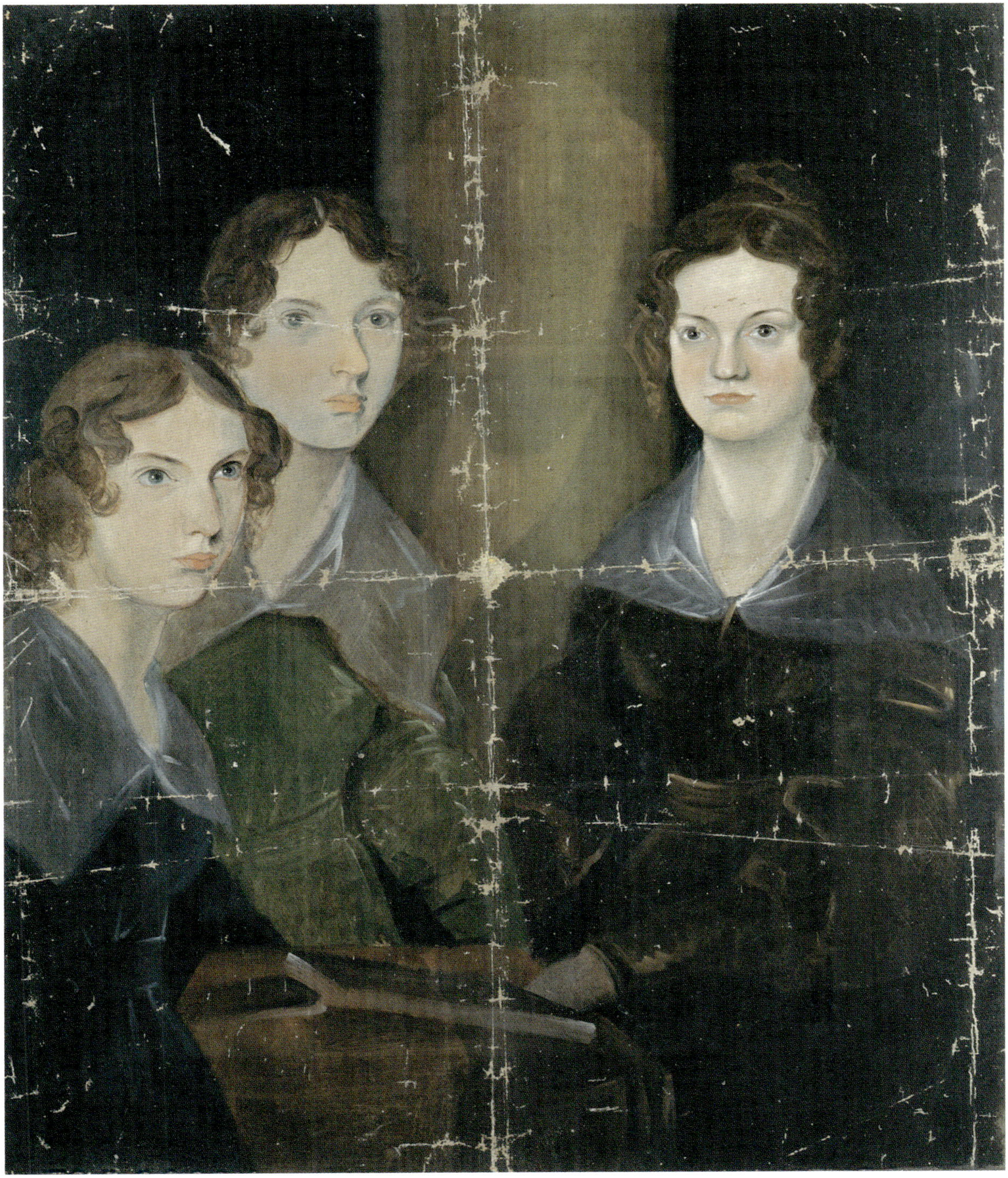

60 David Bowie (1947–2016)

Brian Duffy, 1973

Chromogenic print, 197 × 197mm (image size)
NPG x137463

Born David Robert Jones in Brixton, south London, singer-songwriter David Bowie gained recognition with his single 'Space Oddity' in 1969, the release of which coincided with the first moon landing. He subsequently achieved international fame with his rock albums *The Rise and Fall of Ziggy Stardust and the Spiders from Mars* (1972) and *Aladdin Sane* (1973). Bowie's music career spanned more than four decades, with his last album, *Blackstar,* released two days before his death in 2016. A musical and cultural icon, he pioneered an experimental approach to identity, which revolved around the regular reinvention of his stage personae, such as Ziggy Stardust and the Thin White Duke. His 1970 album *The Man Who Sold the World* provoked controversy because of his androgynous appearance on the cover with long hair and wearing a dress.

Renowned for his distinctive make-up, futuristic costumes and theatrical performances, Bowie appeared as one of his flamboyant stage alter-egos for the cover of his sixth album, *Aladdin Sane*. Taken in Brian Duffy's north London studio, a similar pose to the one below, showing Bowie with his eyes closed, was used for the final cover. It has become one of the most recognisable and celebrated of pop images. Brian Duffy, a fashion, music and advertising photographer who came to prominence during the 1960s, is considered, along with David Bailey and Terence Donovan, to have defined the era. He also photographed Bowie for the covers of his albums *Lodger* (1979) and *Scary Monsters (and Super Creeps)* (1980).

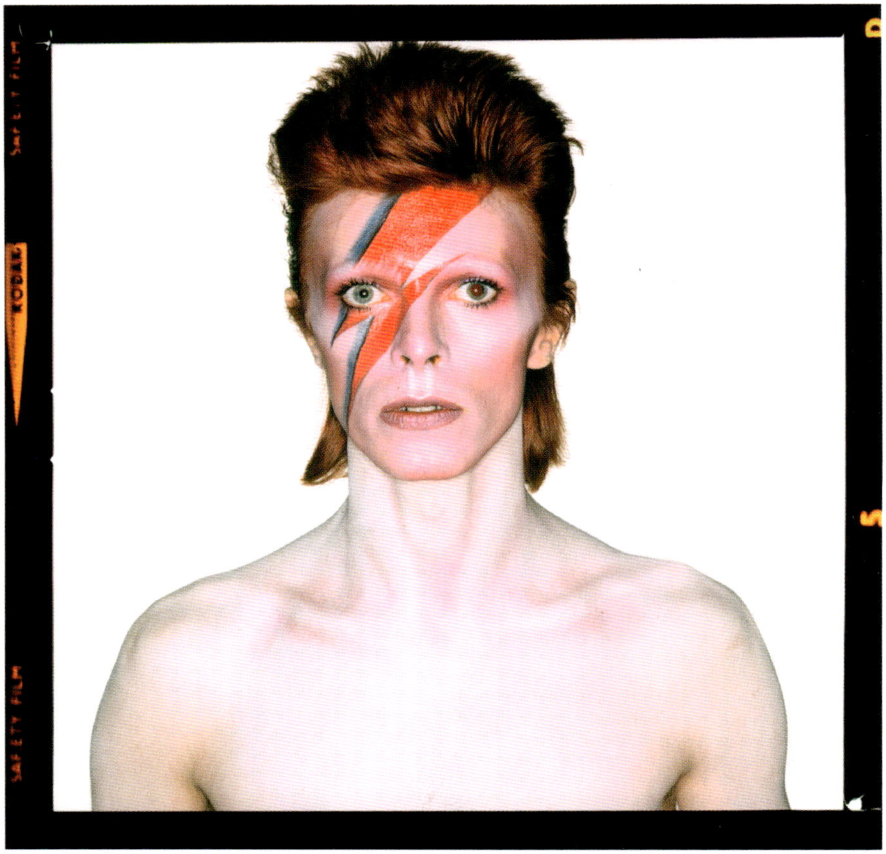

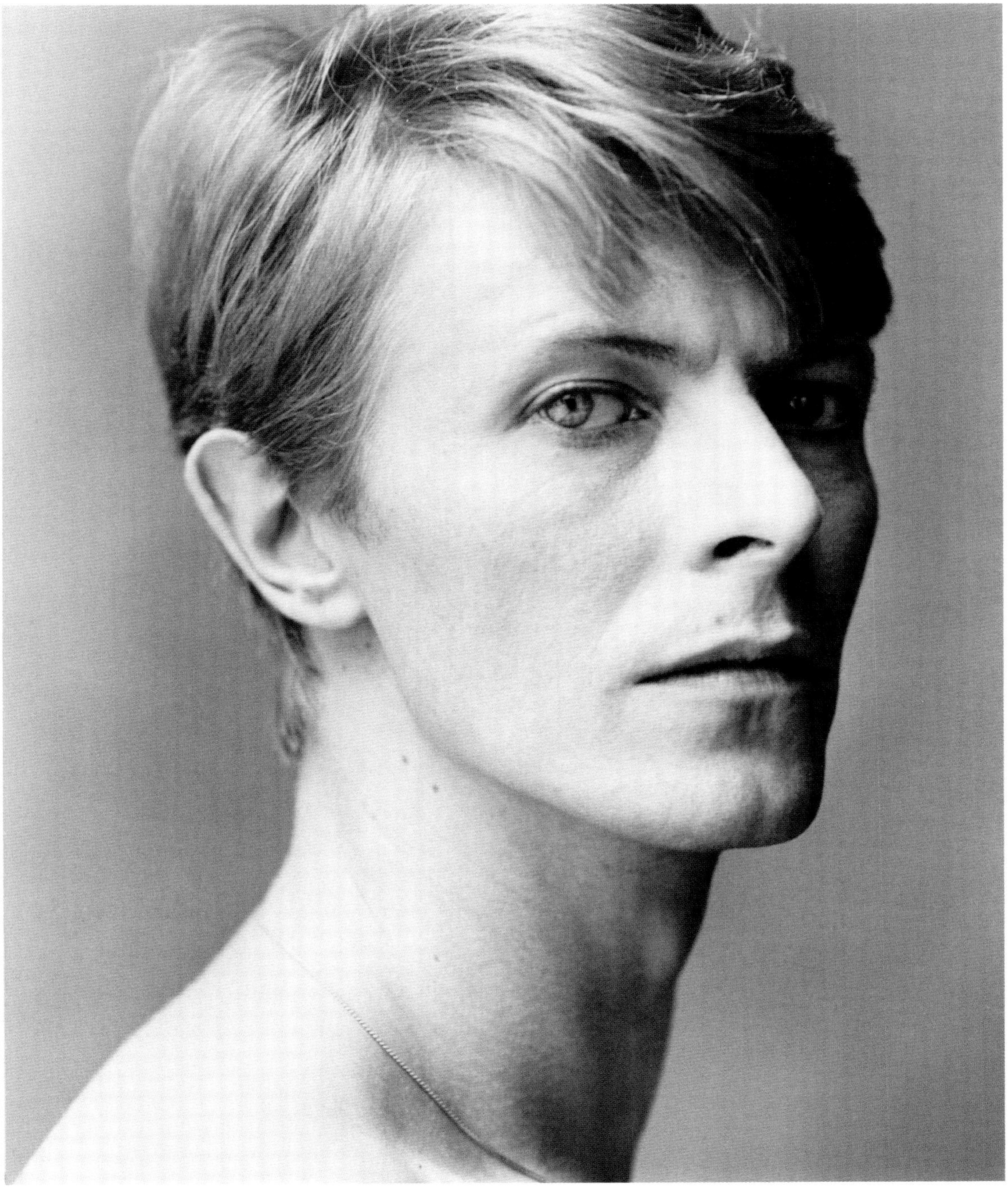

61 **David Bowie** (1947–2016)
Lord Snowdon, 1978
Gelatin silver print, 362 × 297mm
NPG P1855

Lord Snowdon's portrait of David Bowie, with its sensitive handling of light, shade, pose and framing, celebrates the musician's androgynous elegance. It was first published in the September 1978 issue of British *Vogue*, and Jonathan Mantle wrote in the accompanying interview: 'The ambiguity and mystery of his image have much to do with his ability to keep at least one jump ahead of his audience.'

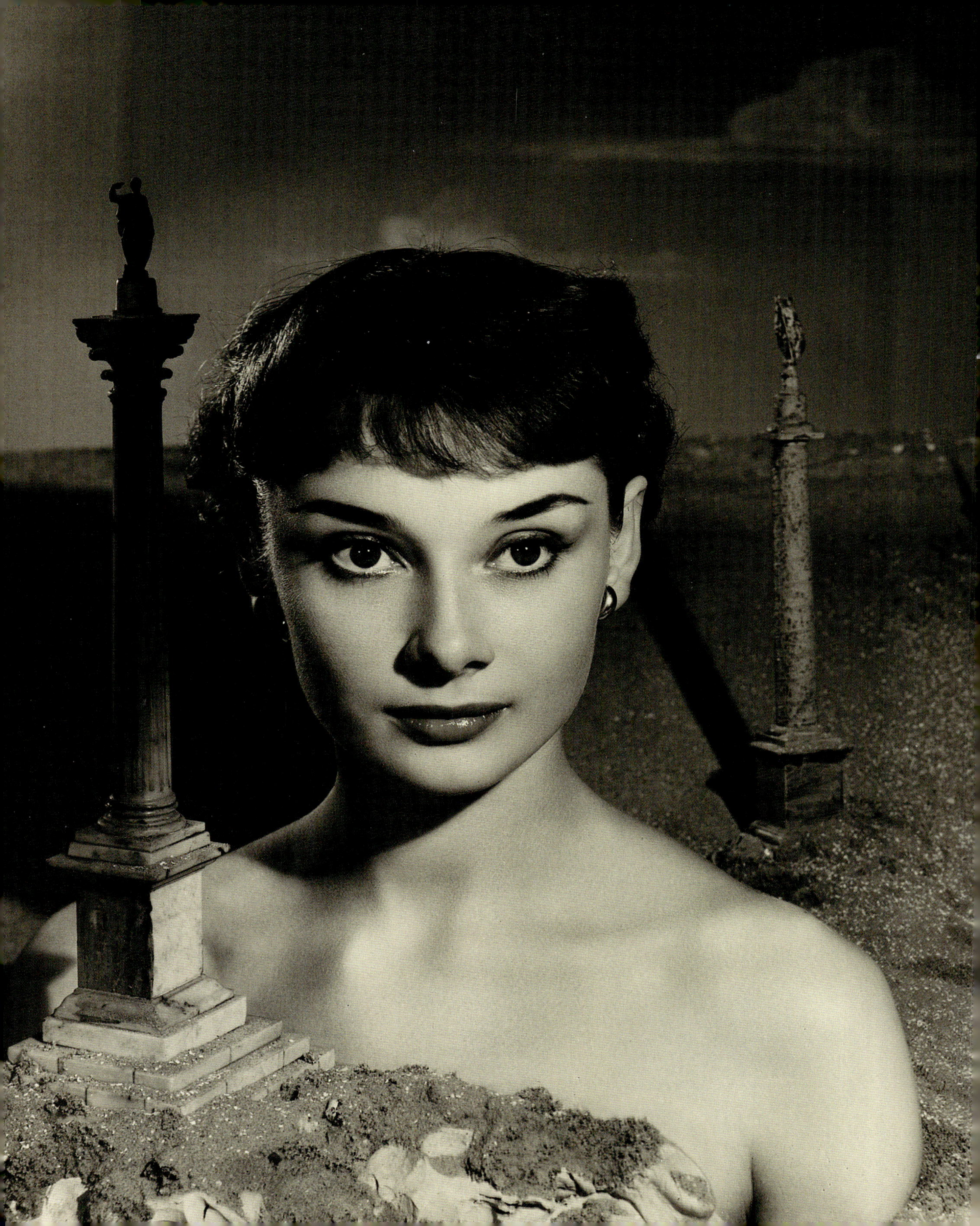

Innovation

From the earliest civilisations, people have sought out means of creating an enduring record of their existence. Portraits that focus on a sitter's facial characteristics have been one response to this human need. This section concentrates on the creative ways in which artists have responded to the limitations imposed by the genre, challenged its traditions and expanded its possibilities.

The relationship between portraiture and illusionism, the precise replication of physical appearances, has led to remarkable innovations. In the sixteenth century, artists such as Hans Eworth utilised oil paint to realistically reproduce the appearance of fabrics and accessories. His portrait of Lord and Lady Dacre (see p.100) uses minute brushstrokes to recreate the glint of jewels and texture of fur, silk and flesh with great precision. The viscosity of oil paint was exploited to the full by Sir Peter Paul Rubens, whose mastery of the medium gives his portrait of the Earl of Arundel an exceptional vivacity (see p.101). An equivalent mastery of his material enabled the French sculptor Auguste Rodin to achieve a remarkable degree of animation in his sculptures, as in his bronze head of William Ernest Henley (see p.104).

The invention of photography profoundly expanded the possibilities of portraiture by providing a reasonably straightforward and effective way of creating a likeness. An early exponent of the new art form was the writer Lewis Carroll, who in 1858 made a series of photographs of Alice Liddell (see pp.106–7), the inspiration behind his famous story *Alice's Adventures in Wonderland*. Carroll would later influence the twentieth-century art movement surrealism, which was innovatively applied to photography in a series of theatrical and often amusing photographs by Angus McBean (see pp.108–9).

To some extent, photography freed portrait artists in other media from the need to create precise illusionistic likenesses. A notable example is Patrick Heron's experimentation with abstraction and cubism in his portrait of T.S. Eliot (see p.111). Andy Warhol's silkscreen prints combine a photographic record of appearance with exaggerated colour to emphasise the glossy facade of his subjects (see p.113). Warhol's simplification of the face to its essential elements is taken to an extreme in Michael Craig-Martin's portrait of the architect Dame Zaha Hadid (see p.112). Computer software animates the frontally posed, head-and-shoulders portrait with an ever-changing combination of bold colours. This marriage of tradition, new concepts and new technology points towards exciting avenues for further innovation within the always-evolving art of portraiture.

DETAIL **Audrey Hepburn, 1950**

5

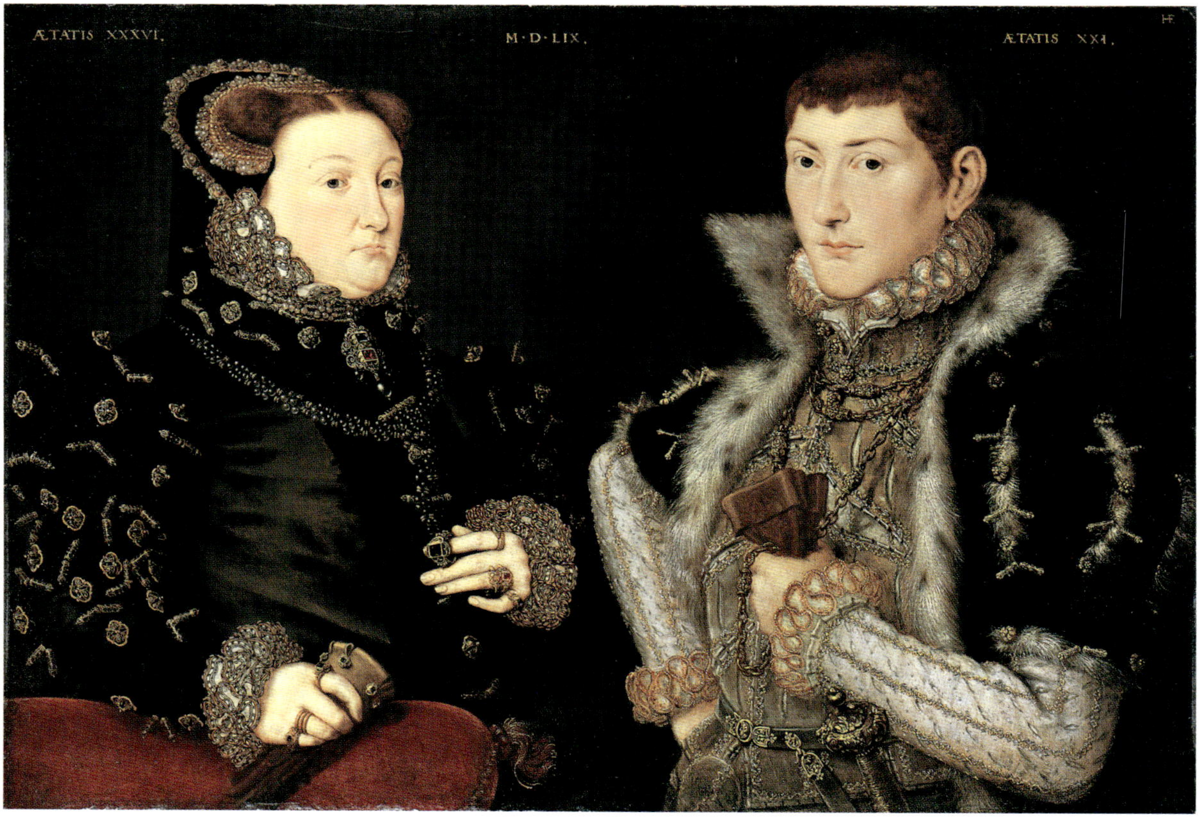

62 Mary Neville, Lady Dacre (1524–c.1576) and Gregory Fiennes, 10th Baron Dacre (1539–94)

Hans Eworth, 1559

Oil on panel, 500 × 714mm

NPG 6855

This unusual and highly accomplished double portrait of mother and son was probably painted to commemorate the restoration of the Dacre family fortune. Mary Neville was the widow of Thomas Fiennes, 9th Baron Dacre, who had been executed in 1541 for his part in a poaching incident in which a man had been killed. His titles and honours were forfeit, and Lady Dacre, who subsequently married twice, was forced to campaign for their restoration to her son; this was finally granted during the first year of Queen Elizabeth I's reign. Intriguingly, it is Lady Dacre who is shown in the act of putting on a ring, which was often used to demonstrate the assumption of dynastic power; she also occupies the position on the left of the composition, which was usually taken by the husband in double portraits that commemorated marital union.

This portrait is signed in monogram by the painter Hans Eworth, one of the most distinguished Netherlandish artists to work in England in the mid-sixteenth century. His exquisite handling of oil paint enabled him to create paintings with a greater sense of realism than most of his English contemporaries. Indeed, the most innovative and influential artists working in England during the sixteenth century tended to be artists who had trained on the Continent, such as Hans Holbein the Younger and Hans Eworth.

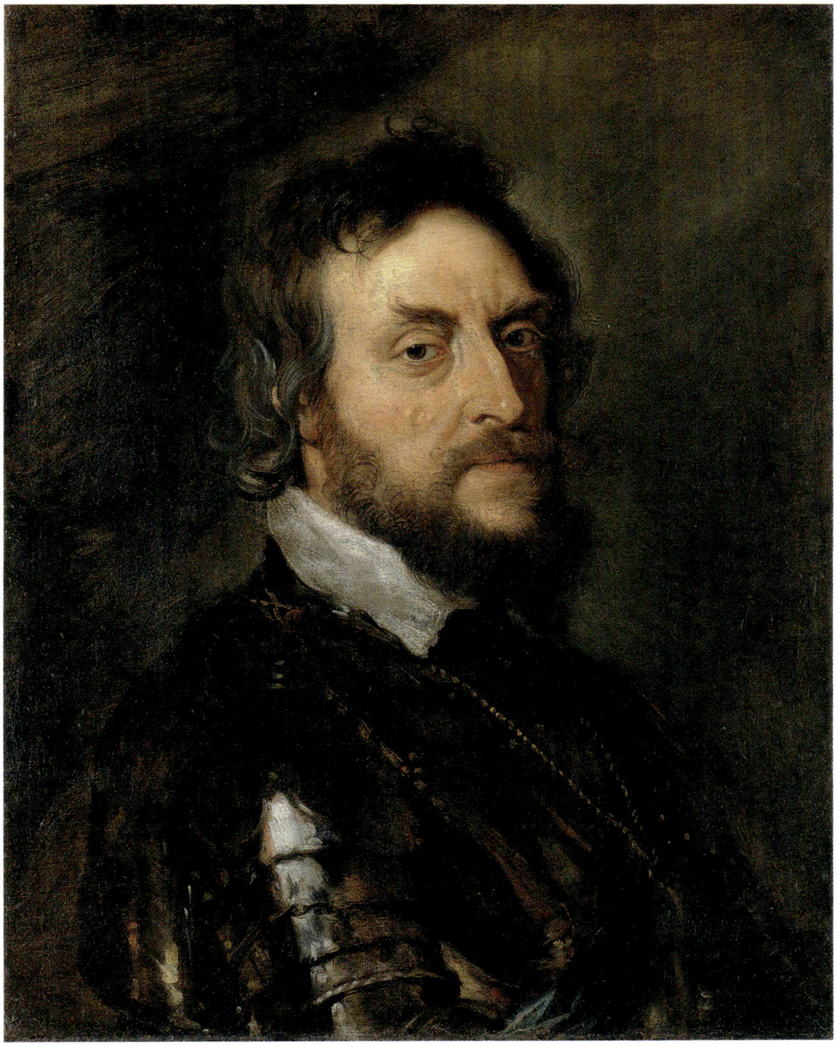

63 Thomas Howard, 14th Earl of Arundel (1585–1646)

Sir Peter Paul Rubens, 1629

Oil on canvas, 606 × 533mm
NPG 2391

This outstanding portrait represents the most influential connoisseur of his age, Thomas Howard, Earl of Arundel. He was heir to one of the great noble families in England, but at the time of his birth it had fallen into disrepute because of his father's involvement in Catholic plots against Queen Elizabeth I. The Arundel title was restored by King James I, and Howard rose to become one of King Charles I's most trusted courtiers. His impact on English art was considerable; he owned the first major collection of classical antiquities in London, and fostered the careers of the architect and theatre designer Inigo Jones and the artists Wenceslaus Hollar and Sir Anthony van Dyck.

This portrait was painted in 1629, when the Flemish painter Peter Paul Rubens was in London on a diplomatic mission. It was also during this visit that Rubens began work on the monumental ceiling paintings for the Banqueting House, Whitehall. Rubens admired Arundel's collections and, according to a letter to Arundel from his secretary, called him 'one of the four evangelists, and a patron of our art'. The portrait here focuses on the sitter's imposing and dignified character. He wears the sash of the Order of the Garter and a gleaming suit of armour, befitting his status as Earl Marshal. The vitality and dynamism of Rubens's technique astounded English patrons, and his brief presence in London paved the way for his most talented protégé, Anthony van Dyck, to be appointed court painter to King Charles I in 1632.

64 Charles Vane-Stewart, 3rd Marquess of Londonderry (1778–1854)

Sir Thomas Lawrence, 1812

Oil on canvas, 1435 × 1180mm
NPG 6171

The general and diplomat Charles Vane-Stewart was one of the foremost participants in the Napoleonic Wars and its political aftermath. As a dashing cavalry officer, Stewart acted as Adjutant-General for Arthur Wellesley, 1st Duke of Wellington, from 1809 to 1812, distinguishing himself at the battles of Douro, Talavera and Badajoz. As ambassador to Vienna from 1814 to 1823, he assisted his half-brother, Lord Castlereagh, and afterwards helped Wellington in the peace negotiations.

Thomas Lawrence was born in Bristol, England, in 1769 and first came to public attention as a self-taught child prodigy drawing portraits at his father's inn in Devizes. Establishing himself in London aged 18, he painted portraits that brilliantly captured the glamour of the age with dazzling brushwork and innovative use of colour. Succeeding Sir Joshua Reynolds as Britain's pre-eminent portrait painter, he was knighted in 1815 and served as president of the Royal Academy from 1820 until his death in 1830.

Stewart was a long-term supporter and close friend of Lawrence, presenting him to the Prince Regent, and helped broker the prince's commission to paint the allied leaders who defeated Napoleon. In this painting Lawrence has created the ultimate romantic military icon: a dashing cavalry officer depicted with brilliance and swagger in his hussar uniform and wearing the Peninsular Medal he was awarded after the Battle of Talavera in 1809. Its martial vitality anticipated the heroic air of the celebrated series of allied commanders Lawrence was to paint for the Waterloo Chamber at Windsor from 1814. The portrait here was celebrated by Lawrence's contemporaries and is regarded as an icon of British military portraiture.

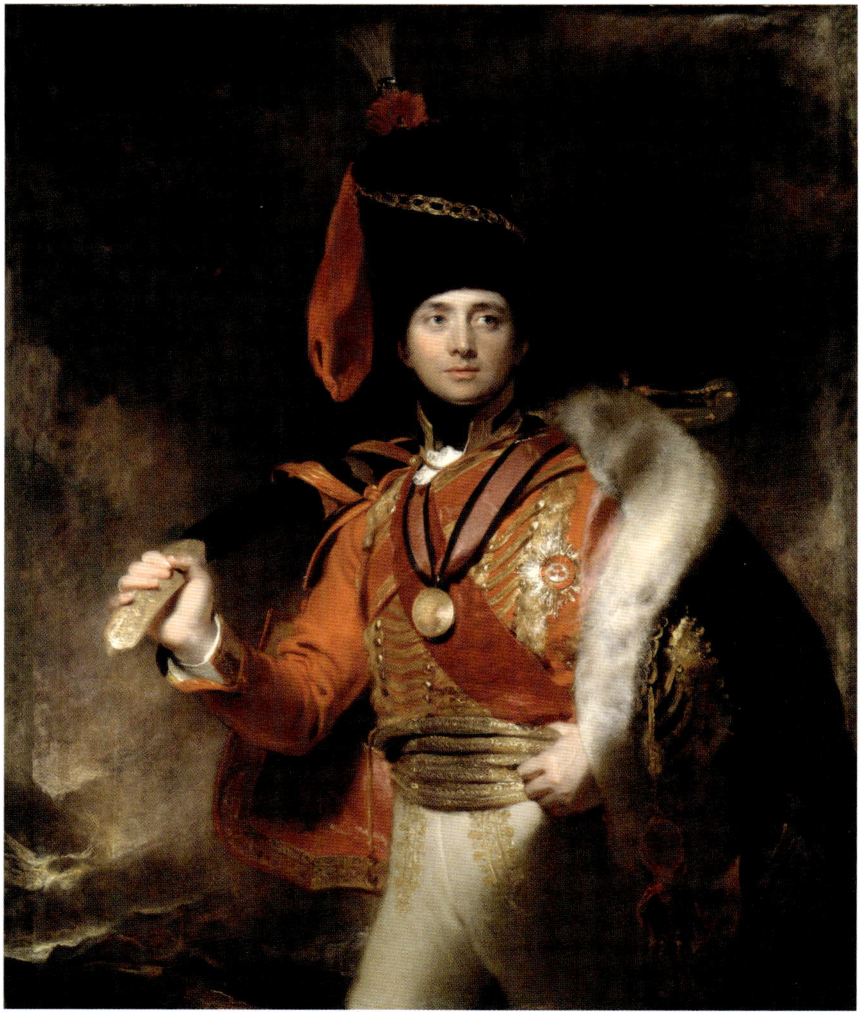

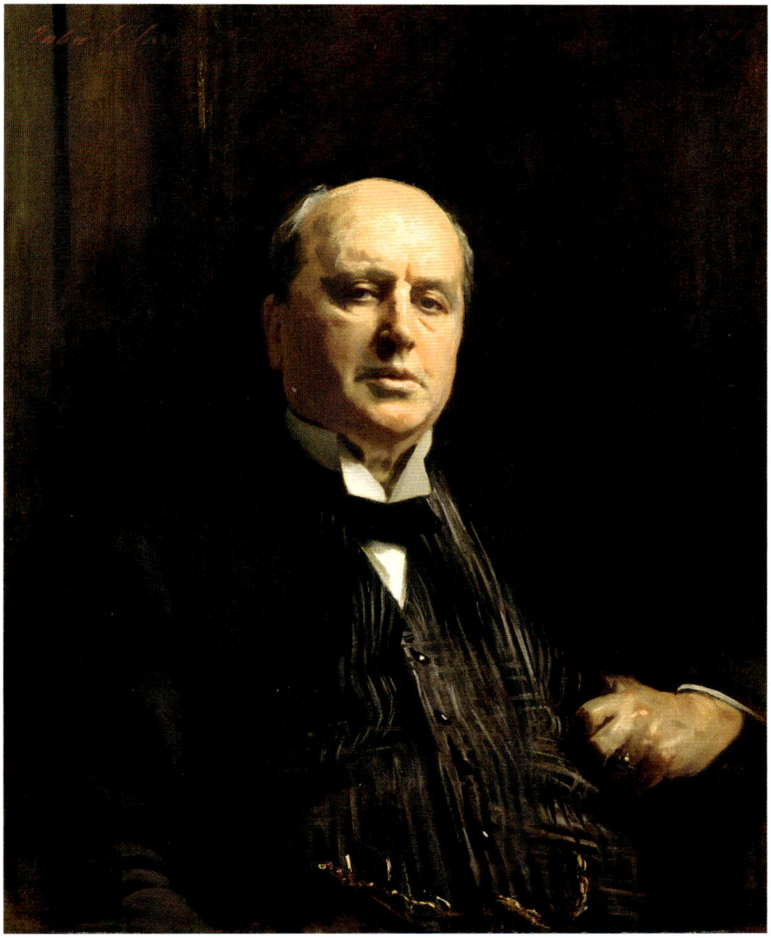

65 **Henry James** **(1843–1916)**
John Singer Sargent, 1913
Oil on canvas, 851 × 673mm
NPG 1767

The American-born author Henry James is especially remembered for his novels that explore the conflict between American and European attitudes, such as *Washington Square* (1880), *The Portrait of a Lady* (1881) and *The Golden Bowl* (1904). His compatriot John Singer Sargent was born in Florence to American expatriates. He studied painting in Italy and France, and in 1884 caused a sensation at the Paris Salon with his painting of Madame Gautreau, which critics found aesthetically offensive with its indifference to conventions of pose, modelling and treatment of space, yet today is considered to be a masterpiece. The scandal persuaded Sargent to move to England, where he established himself as the leading portrait painter of his generation, with paintings of remarkable technical virtuosity, vitality and glamour.

The painter and playwright Walford Graham Robertson, who knew both men, described John Singer Sargent and Henry James as true friends in his publication *Time Was: Reminiscences* (1931): 'They understood each other perfectly and their points of view were in many ways identical.' This closeness perhaps explains the difficulty that Sargent found in executing an effective likeness of the novelist. He had portrayed James three times previously, but remained dissatisfied with his efforts. The plan for the 1913 portrait was initiated by the American writer Edith Wharton, who petitioned James's friends in England to subscribe to the commission in celebration of his seventieth birthday. By this date Sargent was uncomfortable with portrait painting, having largely ceased the practice, and nervous about painting his friend. Both sitter and artist were, however, immensely pleased with the result. The portrait achieved notoriety whilst on display at the Royal Academy in 1914 because on 4 May it was attacked by Mrs Mary Wood, a militant suffragette, who slashed the picture three times with a small hatchet before being restrained. Although it was fully restored by the artist, the tears in the canvas can still be discerned.

66 **William Ernest Henley** (1849–1903)

Auguste Rodin, 1884–6

Bronze head, 394mm high
NPG 1697

William Ernest Henley was a British poet, dramatist and critic. Disabled from the age of twelve, he suffered from tuberculosis of the bone, which resulted in the amputation of his left leg below the knee. Henley edited various magazines and occupied a prominent place during the *fin de siècle* and wrote prolifically on literature and art. A friend and collaborator of the author Robert Louis Stevenson, he was the inspiration for the character of Long John Silver in the children's adventure classic *Treasure Island* (1883). Stevenson admitted that 'it was the sight of your maimed strength and masterfulness that begot John Silver in *Treasure Island*'.

The portrait bust was a dominant form of sculpture during the nineteenth century. Considered particularly suitable for statesmen, busts were often commissioned to dignify public spaces and architecture, and are included in roundels on the exterior of the National Portrait Gallery building. The format was reinvigorated at the end of the century by Rodin, and his bust of Henley was made as a token of friendship. During his editorship of the *Magazine of Art*, Henley helped to popularise Rodin's work in Britain. The dynamic modelling of the original clay is evident in the richly textured bronze cast, resulting in an expressive rather than an idealised portrait.

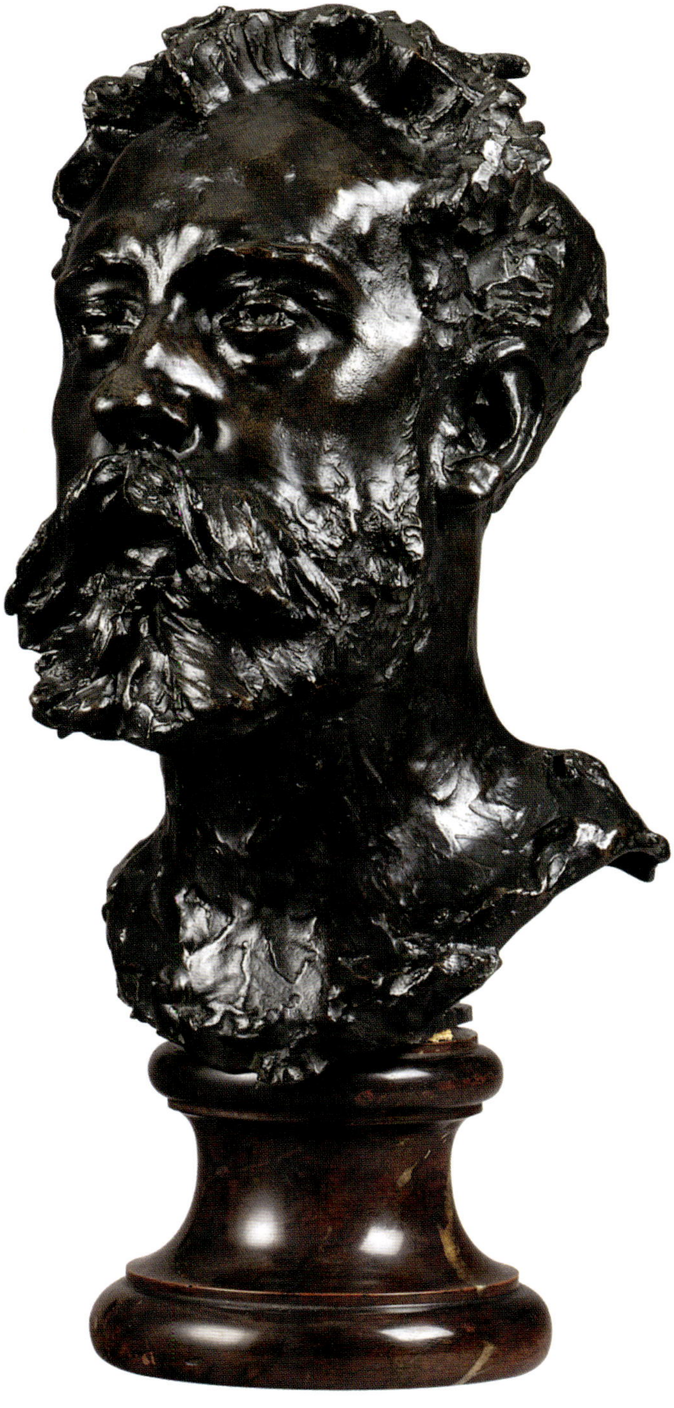

67 **Sir Osbert Sitwell** (1892–1969)
Frank Dobson, 1994, based on a work of 1922
Bronze head, 520 × 190mm
NPG 6321

An author of poetry, fiction, biography and travel writing, Sir Osbert Sitwell joined the army in 1911 and served throughout the First World War. Although the majority of his poetry is light and satiric, his early poems, such as 'The Winstonburg Line' (1919), are pacifist in tone. Sitwell was a supporter of the avant-garde poets Ezra Pound and T. S. Eliot, and a patron of the young composer William Walton, writing the libretto for his oratorio *Belshazzar's Feast* in 1926. Sitwell is now best known for his five-volume autobiography *Left-Hand, Right Hand* (1944–50).

Influenced by Constantin Brancusi and Henri Gaudier-Brzeska, Frank Dobson pioneered a modernist response to portrait sculpture in Britain. This thoughtful and slightly cubist bust of Sitwell was the result of a commission from the sitter in 1921. The striking polished bronze statue was cast from the original plaster, which is also in the National Portrait Gallery Collection. Sitwell went for sittings in Dobson's house in Manresa Road, Chelsea, almost every day for a period of three months in late 1921 and early 1922, just at the time when he, his sister Edith and their lodger, William Walton, were planning the avant-garde musical entertainment *Façade*. Dobson became involved by designing the backdrop for the first public performance of *Façade*, which took place at the Aeolian Hall, London, in 1923.

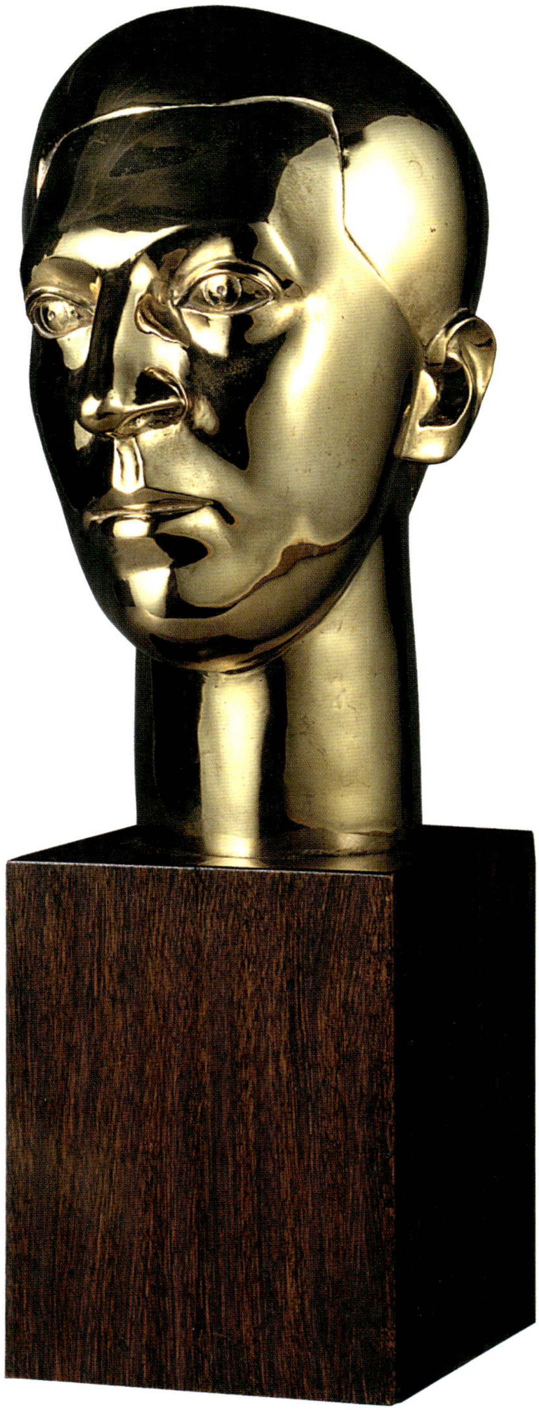

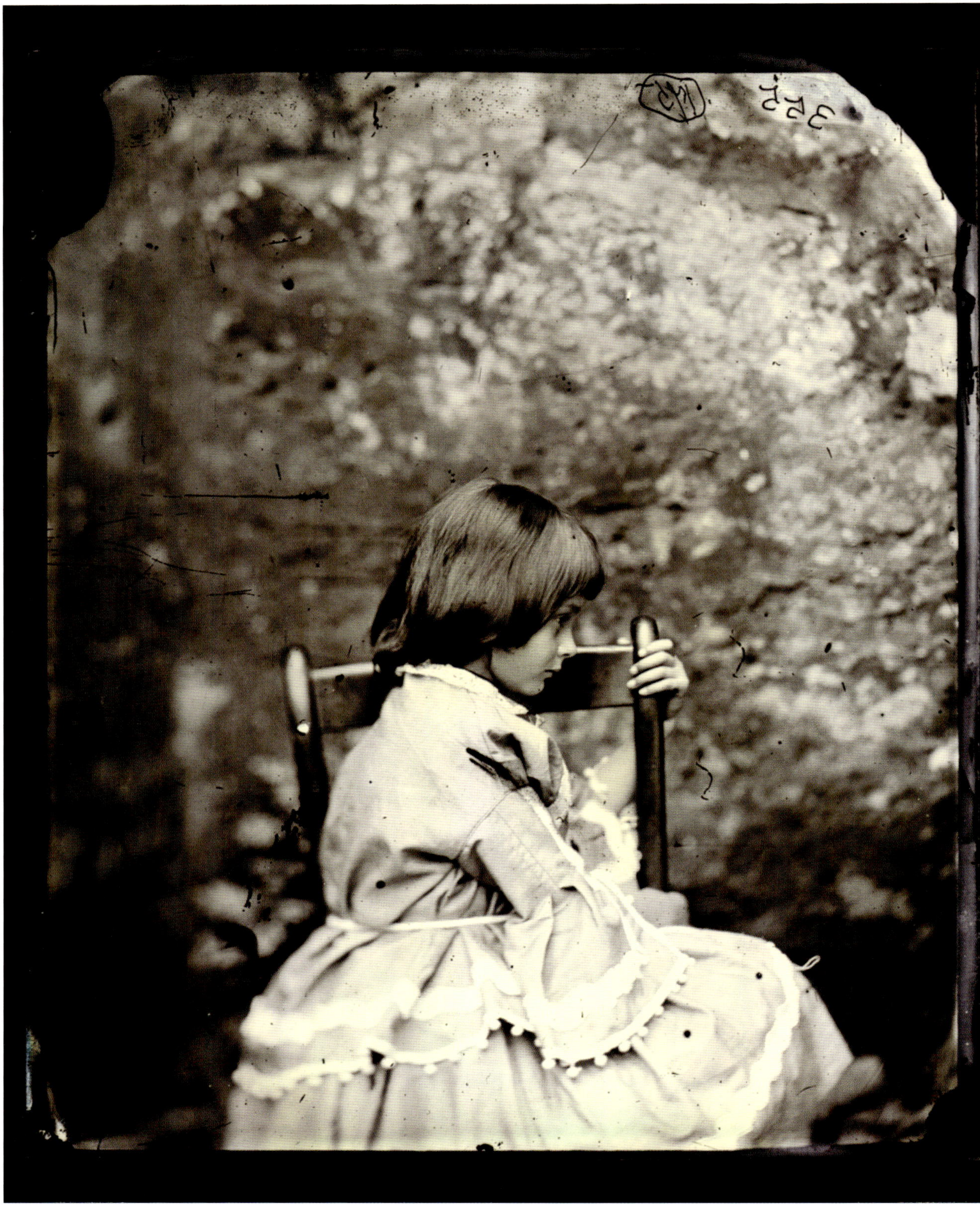

68 Alice Liddell (1852–1934)

Lewis Carroll, 1858

Modern albumen print, 152 × 127mm
NPG x200147

Lewis Carroll was the pen name of Charles Lutwidge Dodgson. He was an academic who lived his entire adult life in Christ Church, Oxford, even as his alter ego became a world-famous children's author. In addition to writing, lecturing and publishing scholarly books on mathematics, he was a pioneering amateur photographer. The innovation of photography revolutionised the ability of non-artistically trained people to make portraits. According to his diaries, Carroll took his first photographs on 1 May 1856 with his new Ottewill folding box camera. He mastered the wet-collodion photographic process, which enabled him to make multiple prints from a negative. This photograph shows Alice Liddell, the daughter of the dean of Christ Church and the inspiration for Carroll's most famous literary work.

The Liddell family moved from London to Oxford in 1856, and soon afterwards befriended Carroll. He became a regular visitor, playing croquet with the children, telling them stories and taking them on picnics by the river Isis, and he used Alice and her younger sister Edith as subjects for his photography. On one of their picnics in 1862, he created the story of *Alice in Wonderland*. Alice, aged 10, asked him to write it down for her; this he did, drawing his own illustrations, in a notebook that now resides in the British Library. It was published in 1865 as *Alice's Adventures in Wonderland,* and its sequel, *Through the Looking-Glass and What Alice Found There*, appeared in 1871.

69 **Audrey Hepburn** (1929 – 93)

Angus McBean, 1950

Gelatin silver print, 495 × 380mm (uneven)
NPG P1295

One of the most photographed actors of her generation, Audrey Hepburn appeared in dance, theatre and television productions, and over thirty films. Along with many other accolades, she received three Best Actress awards from the British Academy of Film and Television Arts and was nominated five times for Academy Awards, winning once for her performance in *Roman Holiday* (1953). She possessed a determined work ethic and a distinct vision for her public identity, yet was always self-deprecating about her talents in published interviews. Recognised around the world as a fashion icon, Hepburn had a legendary style that appeared simple, achievable and sometimes androgynous, yet it was unfailingly sophisticated. Such apparently chameleonic qualities enabled Hepburn to respond to and push against the gender expectations of her time, both through her film career and her carefully crafted image.

This photograph of the then-unknown Hepburn was originally used as an advertisement for Crookes Lacto-Calamine lotion in 1951. With its clever use of props, including antique miniature classical columns, and bizarre juxtapositions of scale, the portrait creates a fantastical tableau. Hepburn's bare head and shoulders emerge out of the sand like McBean's celebrated pre-war photographs of actors commissioned by *The Sketch*, which were inspired by the surrealist art of the era. Asked to find a 'new face', Angus McBean remembered Hepburn's distinctive beauty from the previous year, when he had photographed the stars of the London theatrical revue *Sauce Tartare*. The advertising campaign was hugely successful, appearing in fashion magazines, such as *Vogue* and *Tatler*. Hepburn made her Broadway debut in the title role of *Gigi* in the same year.

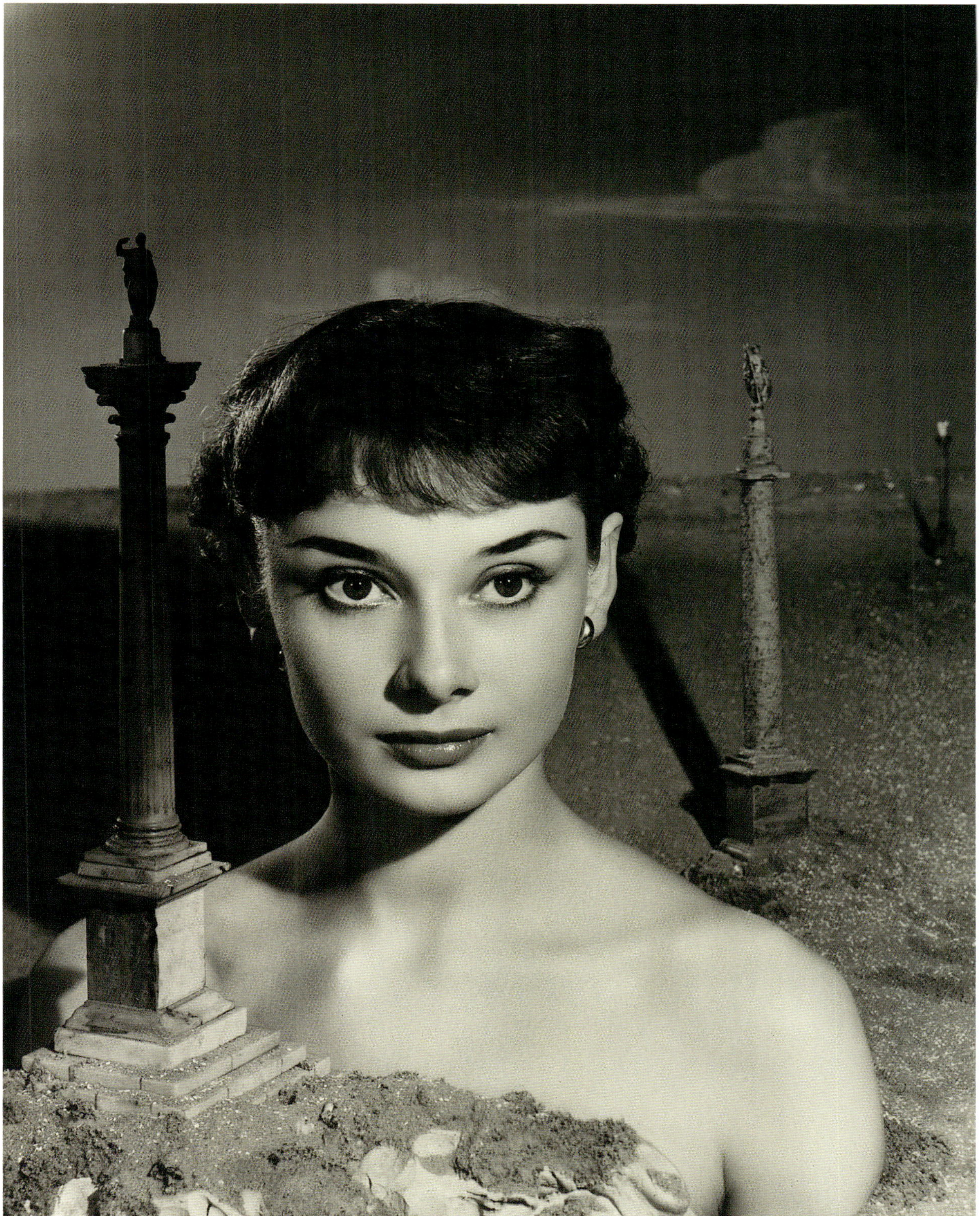

70 **Dame Darcey Bussell** (b.1969)

Allen Jones, 1994

Oil on canvas, 1829 × 1521mm
NPG 6252

In 1989 Darcey Bussell became the youngest ever principal dancer at the Royal Ballet, and went on to become one of the most highly acclaimed British ballerinas of her generation. She performed in *The Prince of the Pagodas* as Princess Rose, a role she created as the last muse of choreographer Sir Kenneth MacMillan. Bussell established herself as a dancer of artistic significance in MacMillan's *Manon* in 1992. During her ballet career she performed all the major roles in the classical repertoire, including Aurora in *The Sleeping Beauty* and Odette/Odile in *Swan Lake*, with companies including the Kirov Ballet and New York City Ballet. After retiring in 2002, she appeared as a judge on the BBC series *Strictly Come Dancing*.

The portrait shown here was commissioned from the artist Allen Jones in 1994, at a time when Bussell's popularity was helping to revive the fortunes of the Royal Ballet at Covent Garden. Jones had risen to prominence in the 1960s, and his highly sexualised depictions of women often proved controversial. Bussell posed over seven evenings at the artist's studio, following a day's rehearsal at the Royal Ballet. She admired the physicality of Jones's depiction, and the sense that she was 'going somewhere'. Bussell's pose *en pointe* can be compared with Jones's images of women wearing stiletto heels; the unnatural posing of the figure which occurs in both fascinated the artist. His use of simplified form and bold colour are characteristic of pop art, the art movement that invigorated culture in the mid-twentieth century and to which he was affiliated. The portrait's distinct colour changes from yellow at the top to pink and violet at the bottom follow the Bauhaus colour wheel theory, which likens the colour spectrum 'to the entire world'.

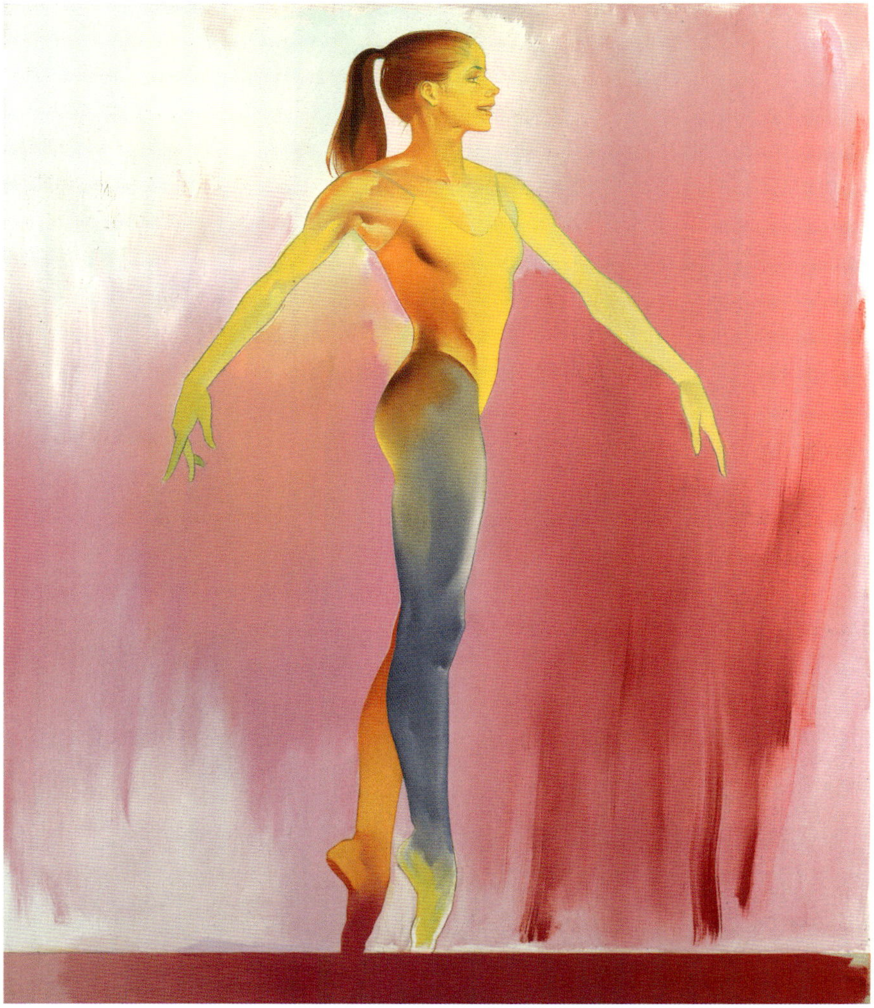

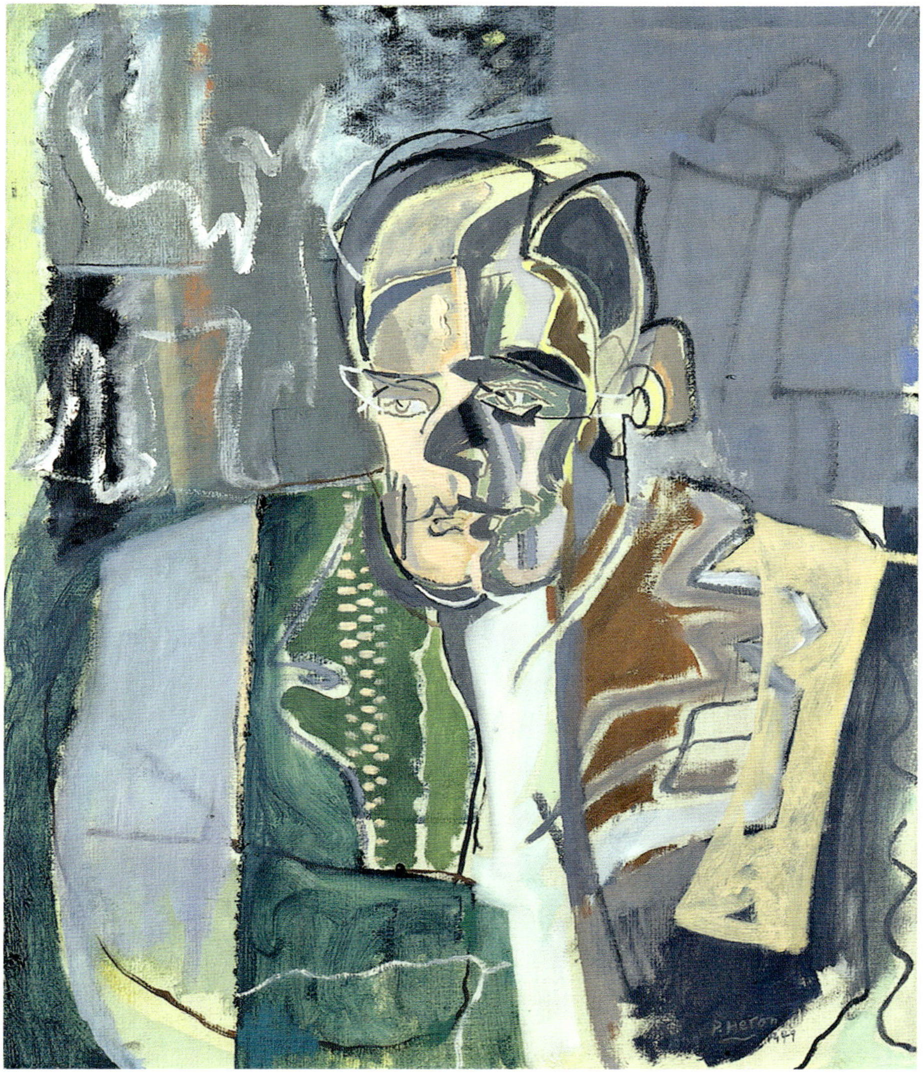

71 **T.S. Eliot (1888–1965)**

Patrick Heron, 1949

Oil on canvas, 762 × 629mm
NPG 4467

T.S. Eliot is one of the twentieth century's greatest poets. The genesis of this portrait by Patrick Heron was a drawing made from life on 4 March 1947. Two months earlier, the young, relatively unknown painter had written to Eliot, then already widely celebrated and on the cusp of being awarded the Nobel Prize for literature, asking whether he would be willing to sit for a portrait. Encouraged by a positive response, Heron visited Eliot in his office at the publishers Faber & Faber, where he was a director. An electricity crisis meant that there was no heating, so Eliot awaited his visitor wearing a blue overcoat, references to which can be seen in the completed painting. Observing the writer of *The Waste Land* (1922) and *Four Quartets* (1943), both landmarks in modern literature, Heron recalled 'finding myself looking into the grey eye of this greatest of living writers, and feeling that I was looking into the most conscious eye in the universe'. At that time, Heron's art was influenced by Pablo Picasso, Georges Braque, Pierre Bonnard and Henri Matisse, and their example is evident. Subsequent drawings from life and related experimental studies, underpinned a progressively abstracted image that distils only the essentials of Eliot's appearance. This drew on observation but eventually, according to the artist, was made 'from memory very slowly, after a period of nearly three years'. Heron references cubism by incorporating two views of the subject, one full face and the other in profile.

72 **Dame Zaha Hadid** (1950–2016)

Sir Michael Craig-Martin, 2008

Wall mounted LCD screen with integrated software, 1257 × 749mm
NPG 6840

Dame Zaha Hadid was an Iraqi-British architect and founder of Zaha Hadid Architects. Sometimes referred to as the 'queen of the curve', her work is characterised by multiple perspective points and fragmented geometry, designed to evoke the chaos of modern life. Her buildings can be seen all over the world, and her most renowned projects include the London Aquatics Centre (built for the 2012 Olympic Games), the Rosenthal Center for Contemporary Art in Cincinnati and the Guangzhou Opera House in China. In 2004, Hadid became the first woman to receive the prestigious Pritzker Architecture Prize. She won the RIBA Stirling Prize in 2010 and 2011 for the MAXXI (National Museum of Twenty-First Century Art), Rome, and the Evelyn Grace Academy, London, respectively. In 2016, she became the first individual female recipient of the Royal Gold Medal, awarded annually since 1848 by the Royal Institute of British Architects.

This portrait marks a new departure for British conceptual artist Sir Michael Craig-Martin. It consists of a LCD monitor that hangs on a wall like a painting and displays a line drawing of Zaha Hadid wearing an Issey Miyake jacket. While the linear drawing is fixed, the intense colours in the portrait and its background slowly but constantly change. These changes are controlled by computer software, which makes random choices. There are so many variables that no one will ever see precisely the same image twice. Just as Hadid used computer-aided design to show the fluid nature of her spaces, her own likeness is appropriately realised as a computer portrait in a state of perpetual flux.

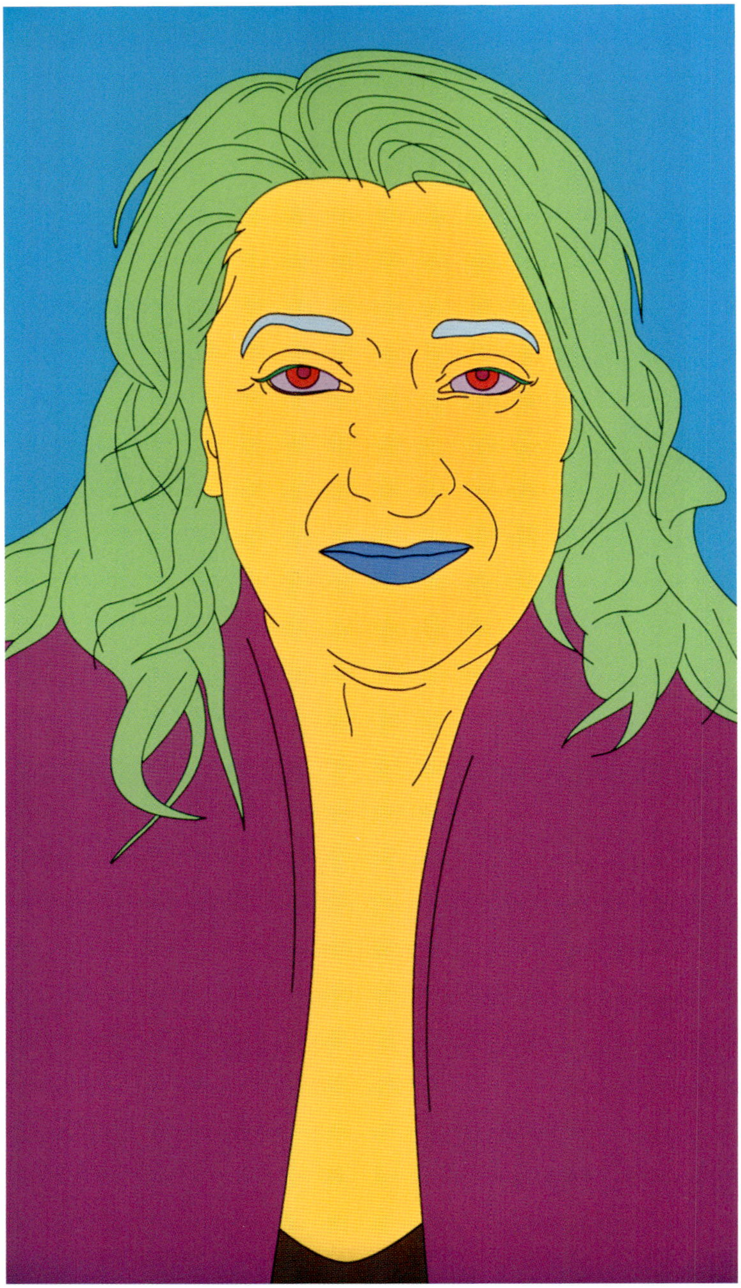

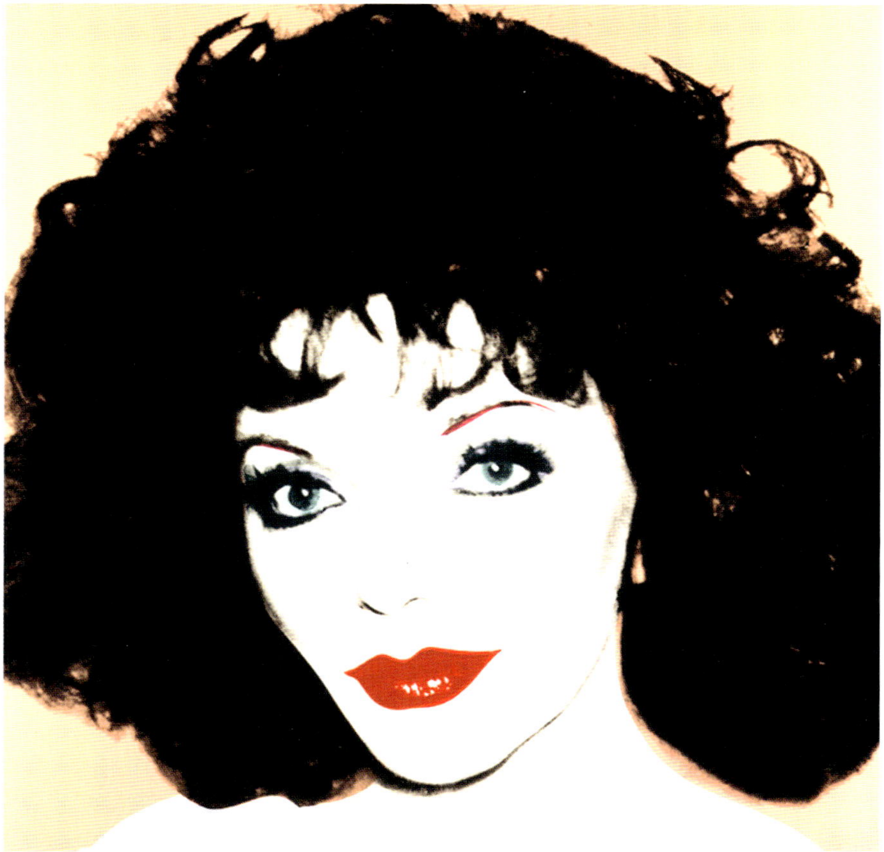

73 **Dame Joan Collins** (b.1933)
Andy Warhol, 1985
Silkscreen ink on synthetic polymer paint on canvas, 1016 × 1016mm
NPG 6257

Dame Joan Collins is the daughter of theatrical agent Joe Collins and sister of the novelist Jackie Collins. She trained at RADA, made her stage debut in *A Doll's House* (1946) and her film debut in *Lady Godiva Rides Again* (1951). She moved to the United States, where her Hollywood debut was in *Land of the Pharaohs* (1955). In 1981 she enjoyed critical and popular success in the role of Alexis Carrington Colby in the television series *Dynasty*. In 2015 Collins was a made a dame for her lifetime contribution to charity work.

Andy Warhol had a radical vision for what art could be in an age of immense social, political and technological change. Born and educated in Pittsburgh, he later moved to New York where he had his first solo show in 1952. In 1960 he began to paint from mass-produced images and consumer goods, such as Campbell's soup cans. At his studio, known as the Factory, his assistants mass-produced these images using silkscreen printing, a technique previously reserved for commercial production. In the 1960s Warhol was at the centre of the pop art movement, making experimental films, painting portraits of celebrities, producing a record by the Velvet Underground and founding the magazine *Interview*. In 1968 he was shot, bringing the Factory era to an end. A major retrospective of his work was held at Tate Modern, London, in 2020.

Made at the height of Collins's *Dynasty* fame from a Polaroid photograph taken by Warhol, this silkscreen print combined the camera flash with heightened colours to simplify her features to the bare essentials. Warhol liked the process of silkscreen printing onto canvas as it removed evidence of the artist's hand in favour of a mass-produced 'assembly-line effect', as he described it in his 1980 memoir *POPism*. The boldness and flatness of Warhol's portrait reveals and revels in the superficial glamour of the age.

74 Queen Elizabeth II (b.1926) ('Equanimity')

Chris Levine; Rob Munday, 2012

Lenticular print on lightbox, 795 × 595mm
NPG 6936

Although Princess Elizabeth came to the throne aged just 25, she had been preparing for the role since the abdication of her uncle King Edward VIII, and brought to it a belief in public service, becoming patron of over 600 charities and organisations. Elizabeth II has ruled longer than any monarch in British history, the record having previously been held by Queen Victoria, but she has less immediate power over her subjects than her predecessors. In an age of mass media, Elizabeth II has led her life more publicly than any monarch before her, and is one of the most recognised people in the world. As such, she has become a subject of fascination for artists, ranging from Andy Warhol to Lucian Freud, who have been intrigued by the ubiquity of her public persona.

Ontario-born Chris Levine studied graphic design at Chelsea School of Art and computer graphics at Central Saint Martins School of Art. His practice as a light artist incorporates photography, lasers, holography and stage design. Made by Levine with holographer Rob Munday, *Equanimity* was commissioned by the island of Jersey in 2004 to commemorate their 800-year allegiance to the Crown. Two sittings took place and over 10,000 images were made to create the three-dimensional portrait. Levine picked out the Queen's outfit, including the Diamond Diadem, made in 1820 for King George IV and worn by the Queen in the procession to her coronation. *Equanimity* is the first holographic portrait of the Queen. Unlike a photograph, which takes up only a tiny fraction of a second, the holographic stereogram is constructed from a sequence of still photographic images shot from different angles, and captures a prolonged moment in the Queen's life, contributing to the sense of vividness in the work. Levine has said, 'I'm not a portrait artist in the conventional sense ... yet I hope my sensibility for visual expression and innovation in the use of light validates why I was commissioned to do this work.'

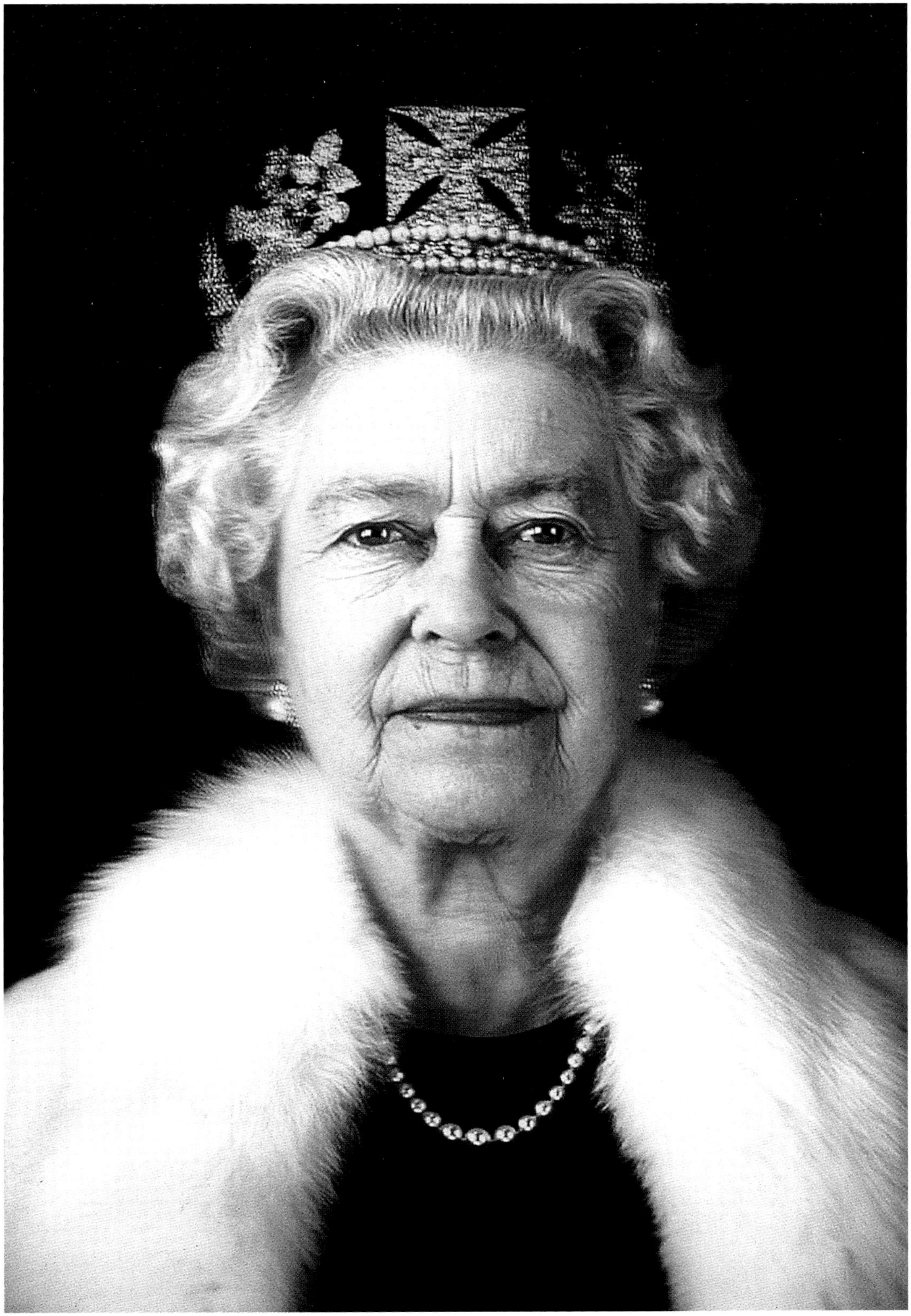

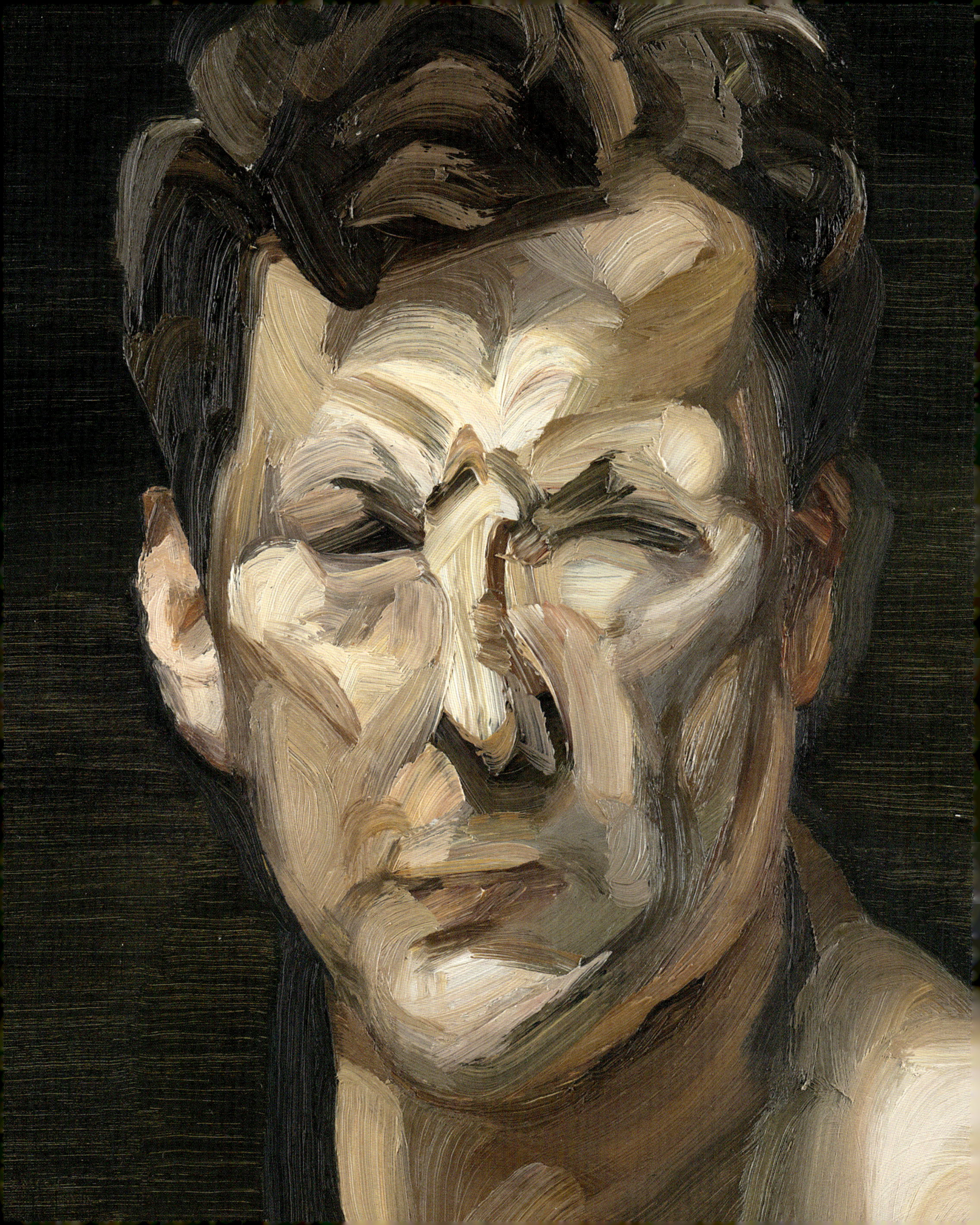

Self-Portrait

Self-portraits are often an artist's most personal legacy, and a variety of motivations lie behind their creation. They can serve the practical purpose of improving an artist's technique, the professional objective of demonstrating their skill, or they can meet more personal needs, such as self-reflection, self-analysis and self-expression. They allow us to gain an insight into not only how artists see themselves, or at least how they wish to be seen, but also how they seek to position themselves in relation to their work and wider society.

The selection of self-portraits in this section span a 400-year period, but all share a strong sense of visual and conceptual concentration. Painted at the outset of his career, Sir Joshua Reynolds presents himself in the act of painting and shielding his eyes in a manner that is tempting to interpret as the young artist looking towards his glittering future success (see p. 122). By contrast, Tracey Emin's bronze sculpture (see p. 130) has an elegiac tone; entitled *Death Mask*, it anticipates an inevitable future in which Emin will be outlived by her art.

The projection of professional identity and social standing is a common feature of self-portraits. Some artists, such as David Hockney, have chosen to present themselves in the studio engaged in the act of making art (see p. 127). Others, like Sir Anthony van Dyck and Gluck (see pp. 118–19 and pp. 124–5), avoid obvious allusions to their profession to focus attention on their elevated status through a confident pose. Angelica Kauffmann plays with the real and imaginary in her self-portrait (see p. 120). Her classicising costume and the tools of her trade would have reminded eighteenth-century viewers of the female personification of painting. The gesture of her left hand and her direct gaze indicate that this is no allegory, and assert Kauffmann's pride at being the author of her own portrait.

The artistic identities of Lucian Freud (see p. 128) and Barbara Hepworth (see p. 123) are powerfully articulated by their distinctive mark-making – Freud's in oil and Hepworth's in pencil. Their expressive styles draw attention to the action of their hands as they have formulated their portraits. Their distinctive personal touch creates an analogy between their work and themselves. Grayson Perry brings a conceptual brilliance to his self-portrait *Map of Days* (see p. 131). Rather than representing his physical appearance, the work takes the form of a map of a walled city in which can be found a delineation of the life events, experiences and emotions that make up his sense of self.

DETAIL **Lucian Freud, 1963**

6

75 **Sir Anthony van Dyck** (1599–1641)

Self-portrait, c.1640

Oil on canvas, 560 × 460mm (oval)
NPG 6987

Anthony van Dyck was by far the most influential painter to have worked in Britain during the seventeenth century, and arguably the most influential portrait painter ever to work in the country. Flemish by birth, he found patronage in a number of European cities, but his longest stay was in England, which he made his home from the beginning of his second visit in 1632 until his death in 1641. Van Dyck decisively turned British portraiture away from the stiff, intricately detailed, formal approach of Tudor and Jacobean painting, developing a distinctive fluid, shimmering style that was to dominate portraiture in Britain right up until the early years of the twentieth century. He was knighted by Charles I on his arrival in England, and appointed Principal Painter to the King; he achieved a status that marked him out as the first British 'celebrity' painter.

Van Dyck's self-portrait is probably the last, and arguably the finest, of his seven known self-portraits. Artists had produced self-portraits in Britain before this time, but few such works are known. The evidence suggests that they were usually produced as likenesses for close friends, or as a means of the artist making a personal artistic, emotional or social statement. The seventeenth century saw a gradual increase in this form of portraiture in Britain as artists began to be regarded – and began to regard themselves – as important creative individuals. Van Dyck stands at the beginning of this change. As far as we know, no artist working in Britain before this had executed so many self-portraits. Van Dyck's repeated re-examination of his features and representation of himself in the context of different iconography reflects a new concern with the painter's identity as a man and as an artist, a concern shared by various of his contemporaries working in the Low Countries, most notably Rembrandt.

This is one of three known self-portraits painted by van Dyck during his time in Britain. He shows himself fashionably dressed but apparently in the act of painting, the line of his arm suggesting his hand raised in the process of applying paint to a canvas. The marked contrast between the broad, rapid, confident handling of the costume and the high level of finish in the face may suggest that the costume is unfinished, or it may be that this self-portrait is simply more experimental than his grand commissioned portraits.

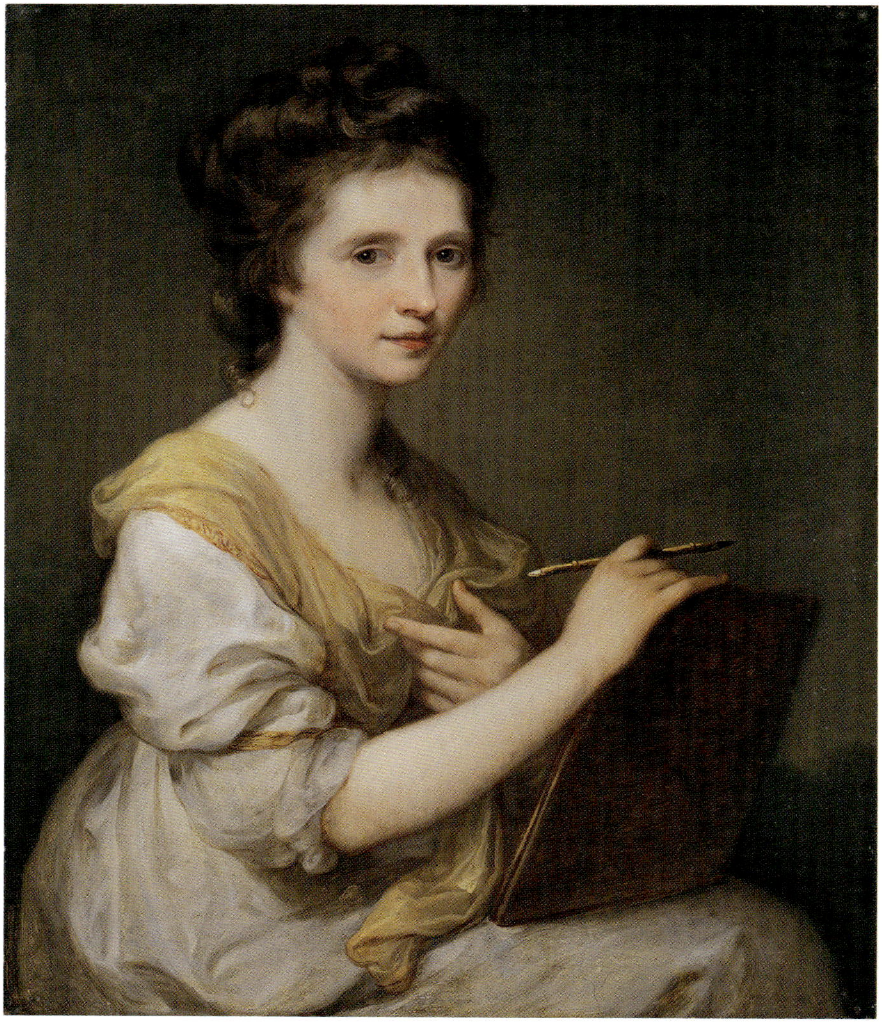

76 Angelica Kauffmann (1741–1807)

Self-portrait, c.1770–5

Oil on canvas, 737 × 610mm
NPG 430

Swiss neoclassical painter Angelica Kauffmann, alongside the flower painter Mary Moser, was one of the two female founder-members of the Royal Academy of Arts, London, in 1768. She achieved this when women were generally marginalised from the visual arts. Kauffmann's father, Johann Joseph Kauffmann, was an artist who guided his daughter's precocious talent. She spent time in Italy, specialising in history and portrait painting, and joining the Accademia di San Luca, Rome, in 1764. Her portrait of the German art historian Johann Joachim Winckelmann of 1764 brought her international attention. In London, between 1766 and 1781, she enjoyed continuing patronage and support from, among other notables, King George III and Sir Joshua Reynolds, then Britain's most influential painter and first president of the RA. However, Kauffmann's trailblazing was tempered by the way she and Moser were depicted in Johan Zoffany's *The Academicians of the Royal Academy* (1771–2). Unlike the men, who are shown in person, the women feature only as portraits hanging on the wall, reflecting the fact that they were not allowed inside life-drawing classes, which that painting illustrates.

Kauffmann painted a number of self-portraits that celebrated her identity as an artist. She shows herself here with the tools of her trade. The positioning of her arms appears to modestly shield her body, but her gaze is confidently directed towards the viewer. Kauffmann thus addressed any potential criticism by asserting that her professional achievements were completely compatible with the beauty and virtue expected of a lady.

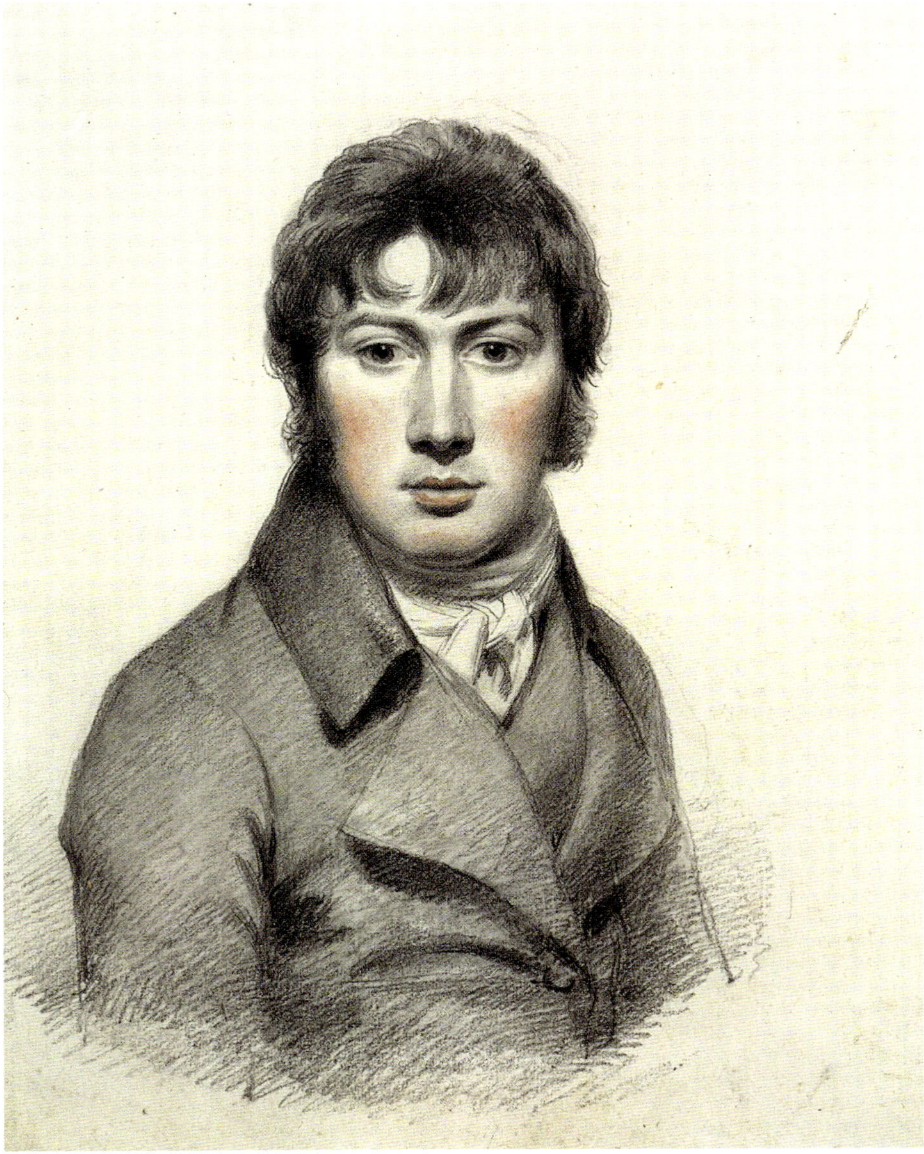

77 **John Constable** (1776–1837)

Self-portrait, *c.*1799–1804

Pencil and black chalk heightened with white and red chalk, 248 × 194mm
NPG 901

Celebrated as one of England's greatest and most progressive landscape artists, John Constable drew lifelong inspiration from his native Suffolk. In 1802 he declared that 'natural peinture' – or landscape – could rival history painting. He made hundreds of outdoor oil sketches, which capture the changing skies with near scientific precision; these helped him bring an immediacy and authenticity to exhibition works developed in the studio. Although Constable met with little contemporary success at home, his painting *The Hay Wain* (1821) did receive a gold medal at the 1824 Paris Salon.

Constable's sensitivity and his slightly melancholy disposition can be easily detected in the intensity of this self-portrait, drawn perhaps shortly after the time he entered the Royal Academy Schools, London, in 1799 or a few years later. The costume he wears is modest and unpretentious: a high-collared woollen coat over a waistcoat, and the simplest white linen cravat.

78 **Sir Joshua Reynolds** (1723–92)

Self-portrait, *c.*1747–9

Oil on canvas, 635 × 743mm
NPG 41

The artist Joshua Reynolds was the leading portrait painter in eighteenth-century Britain, and the first president of the Royal Academy of Arts. In his attempt to elevate the status of portraiture, he borrowed from classical antiquity and the Old Masters to invest his portraits with moral and heroic symbolism in a style known as the 'grand manner'. Although a prolific self-portraitist, he usually presented himself as a gentleman, or 'man of letters', in keeping with his attempts to raise the social status of the arts. This early painting is unique, however, in depicting him at work, clothes loosened, and displaying the tools of his trade: a canvas, palette and brushes. Painted just before he left for a formative trip to Italy, this portrait conveys Reynolds's confidence in his talent and ambition for the future. The use of chiaroscuro (strong contrast of light and dark) indicate his lifelong appreciation of Rembrandt, the most revered master of self-portraiture. The pose and lighting reflect the young artist's eagerness to showcase his versatility and inventiveness. His contemporary and chief rival Thomas Gainsborough allegedly once exclaimed: 'Damn him, how various he is!'

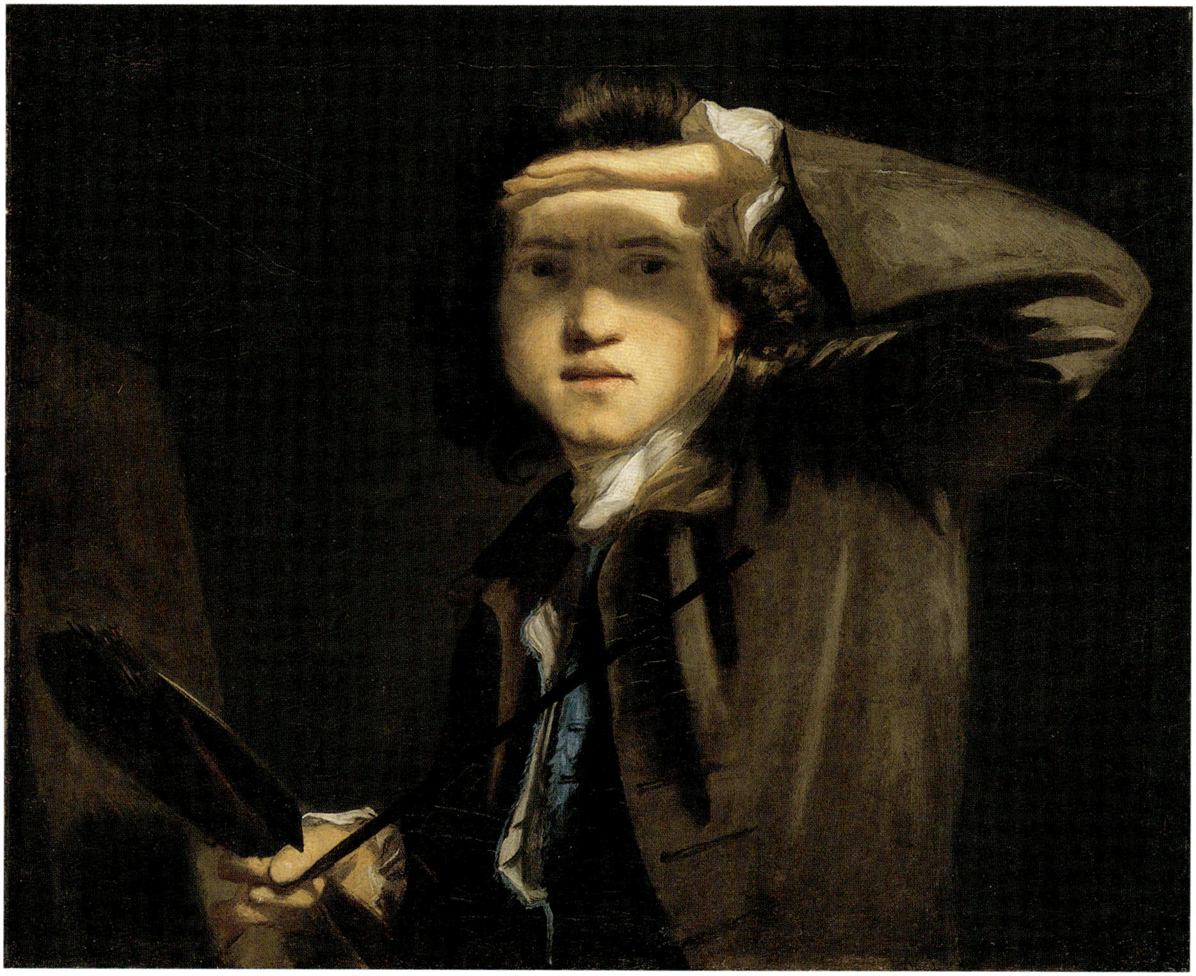

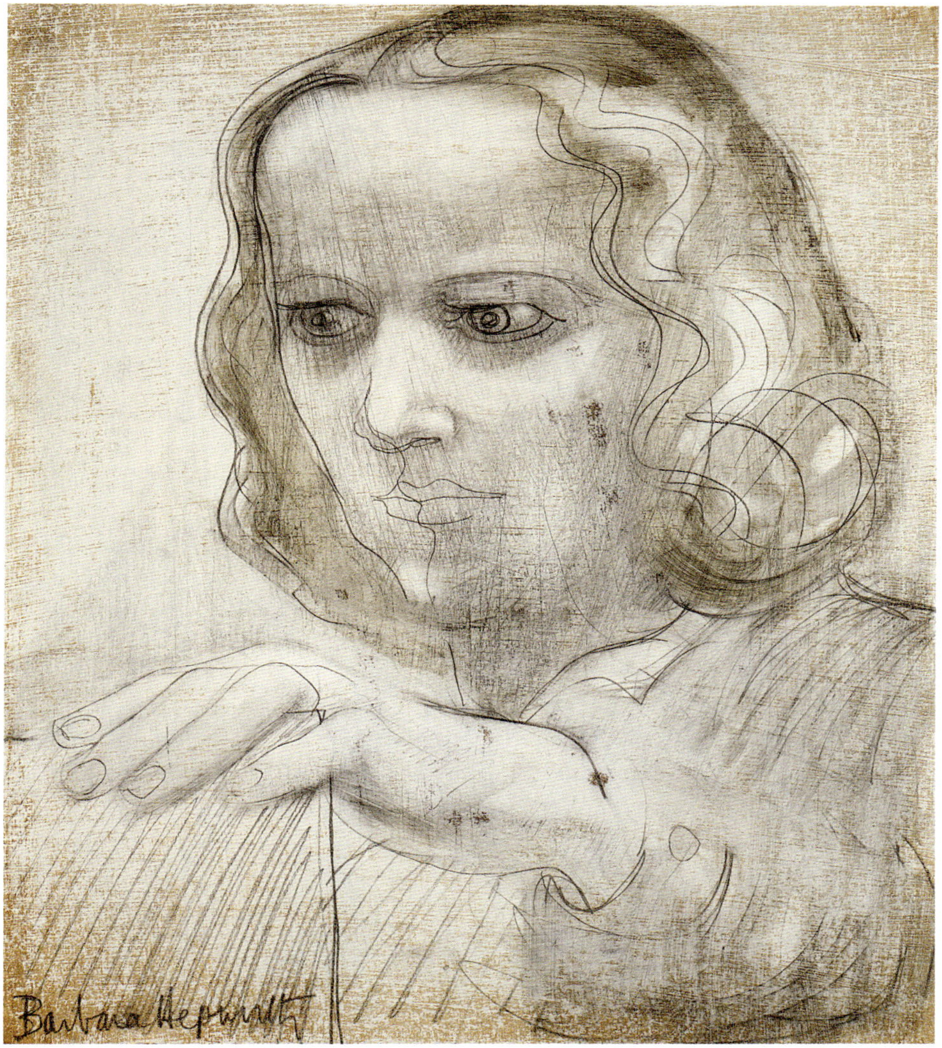

79 Dame Barbara Hepworth (1903–75)

Self-portrait, 1950

Oil and pencil on board, 305 × 267mm
NPG 5919

Barbara Hepworth was born in Wakefield, Yorkshire, where her father was a civil engineer. She won a scholarship to Leeds School of Art in 1919 and there met fellow student Henry Moore. She won another scholarship to the Royal College of Art, where Sir William Rothenstein was principal. She left with a diploma in 1924 and then travelled with a scholarship to Tuscany. In Italy she married the sculptor John Skeaping, and they returned to England in November 1926. In 1931 Hepworth joined the Seven and Five Society, whose members included Moore and Ben Nicholson, to whom Hepworth was married between 1933 and 1951. Her large sculptures were part of the British modern movement (she was especially known for her subtle use of the hole) and with them she achieved international recognition. Her work is represented in more than 100 collections throughout the world, and her studio in St Ives, Cornwall, is now a museum. Hepworth believed that 'there is a whole range of formal perception belonging to feminine experience. So many ideas spring from an inside response to form.'

The board on which Hepworth has drawn this self-portrait has a thin coating of gesso. Into this she has made brisk pencil marks indicating her hand holding the board – a classic method of self-portrayal. The surface texture is full of scratches and indentations, giving it a three-dimensional quality. In places, the white is rubbed down, and orange paint glows around the edges. The whole is a vivid, confident sketch: lively, vigorous, informal but in control.

80 **Gluck** (1895–1978)

Self-portrait, 1942

Oil on canvas, 306 × 254mm
NPG 6462

Born Hannah Gluckstein into the family that founded the Lyons catering empire, Gluck attended classes at St John's Wood School of Art, London, from 1913 to 1916, and then spent time at the artists' colony at Lamorna, Cornwall. It was there that she met Laura Knight, whose studio she later bought; Ella Naper, whom she also painted; and Alfred Munnings, who sketched her portrait. She consistently broke gender norms, and by 1918 took on the genderless name Gluck ('no prefix, suffix or quotes', as she asserted), wore masculine clothes, cut her hair short and smoked a pipe. In 1936 Gluck painted a double profile portrait to commemorate her 'marriage' to the writer and socialite Nesta Obermer. The work, with its overt lesbianism, would have been considered provocative and subversive at a time when female relationships were censured. The painting was later used on the cover of a 1983 edition of Radclyffe Hall's seminal novel, *The Well of Loneliness* (1928), about a lesbian relationship. Gluck designed and patented the 'Gluck Frame' and, in the 1950s, successfully campaigned for better quality oil paints in England.

Although this self-portrait of 1942 is small in scale, as was much of Gluck's work, it has tremendous presence. The artist's expression is simultaneously haughty and confident, yet somehow sad and weary. The only real source of colour is a patterned kerchief, and the rest of the palette uses muted, neutral tones. The artist's rigorous personality is implied by the focus on the head and the lack of flattery regarding her furrowed brow and clearly delineated lips.

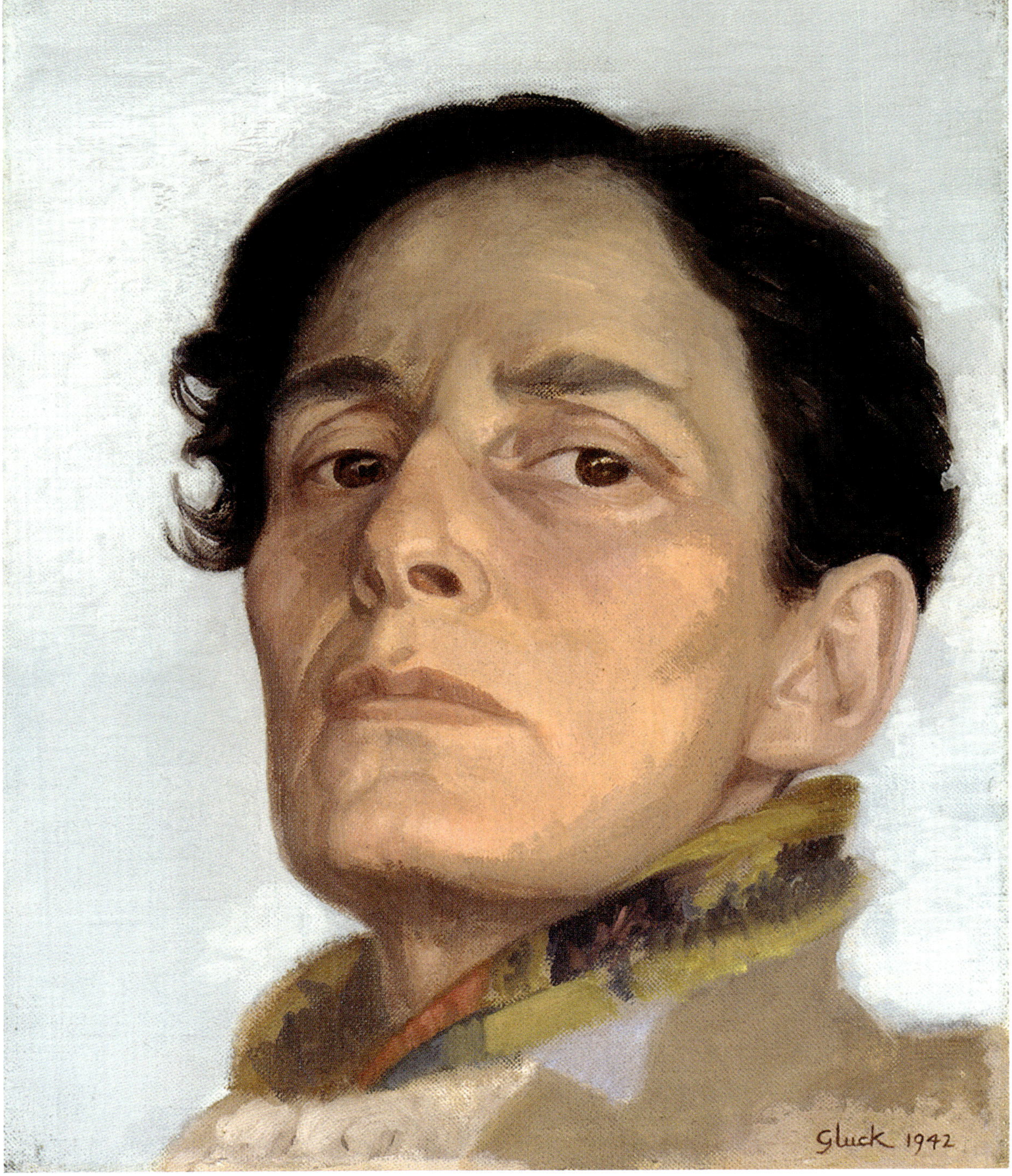
Gluck 1942

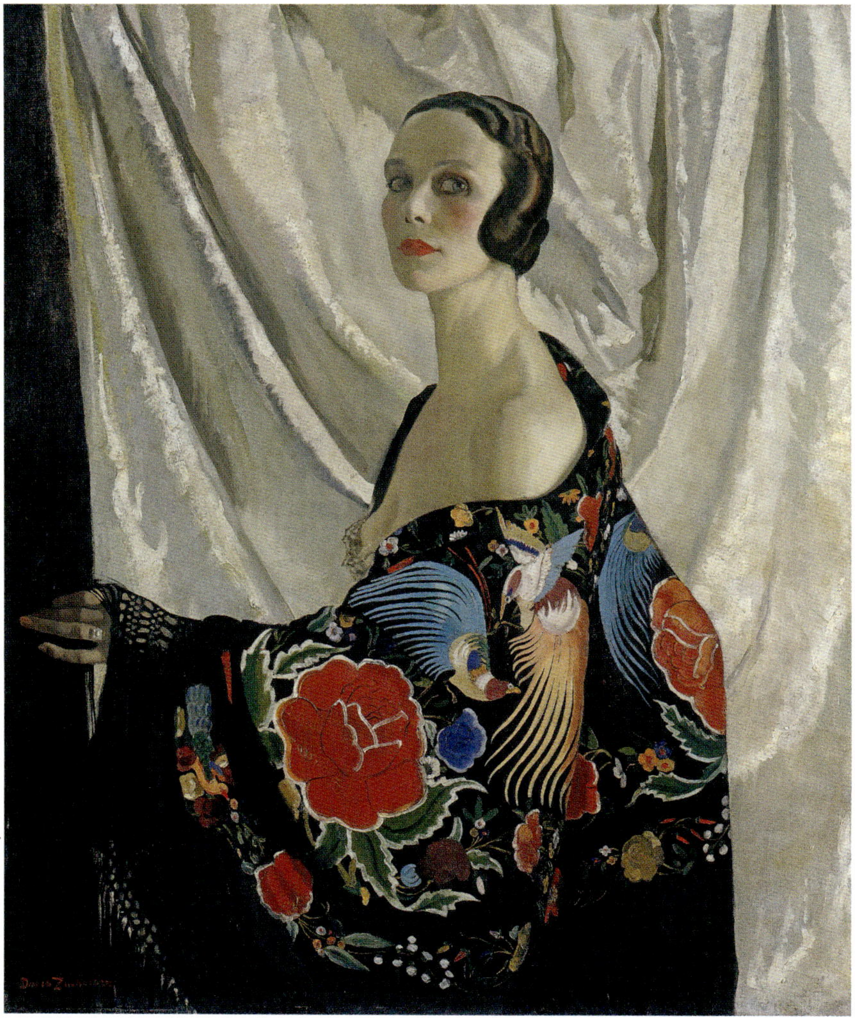

81 **Doris Zinkeisen** (1897–1991)

Self-portrait, exhibited 1929

Oil on canvas, 1072 × 866mm
NPG 6487

Doris Zinkeisen was born in Gareloch, Argyllshire. Her father's family were originally from Bohemia and had settled in Scotland 200 years previously. Doris attended Harrow School of Art and won a scholarship to the Royal Academy. On leaving the Academy, she went to work in stage design for the actor-manager Sir Nigel Playfair, who also wanted her to sing, but she was adamant that she should remain 'behind the scenes'. She designed costumes and sets for Old Vic Theatre productions (also creating Sir Laurence Olivier's make-up for the 1955 film *Richard III*). She painted the mural for the Verandah Grill on the *Queen Mary* ocean liner in 1936, and in 1938 she wrote *Designing for the Stage*. During the Second World War, she was commissioned by the War Artists Advisory Committee and in April 1945 was one of the first artists to enter the Nazi concentration camp Bergen-Belsen, where she stayed for three days. Two of the paintings she made there can be seen in the Imperial War Museum, London.

Her talent as a costume designer for the stage is perhaps indicated in this theatrical self-portrait, where the prominent make-up of the period is stressed. The heavily embroidered Chinese shawl draped off her shoulders lends a provocative air. She seems about to leave the set, pulling aside the black curtain with a hand half-covered by the black edging of the shawl. The portrait was painted mostly in her hotel bedroom in Sydney, Australia, while she was on a world tour. It was exhibited at the Royal Academy in 1929 under her married name, Mrs Grahame Johnstone, both ironically denying her connection with the creation of the image and asserting her social position.

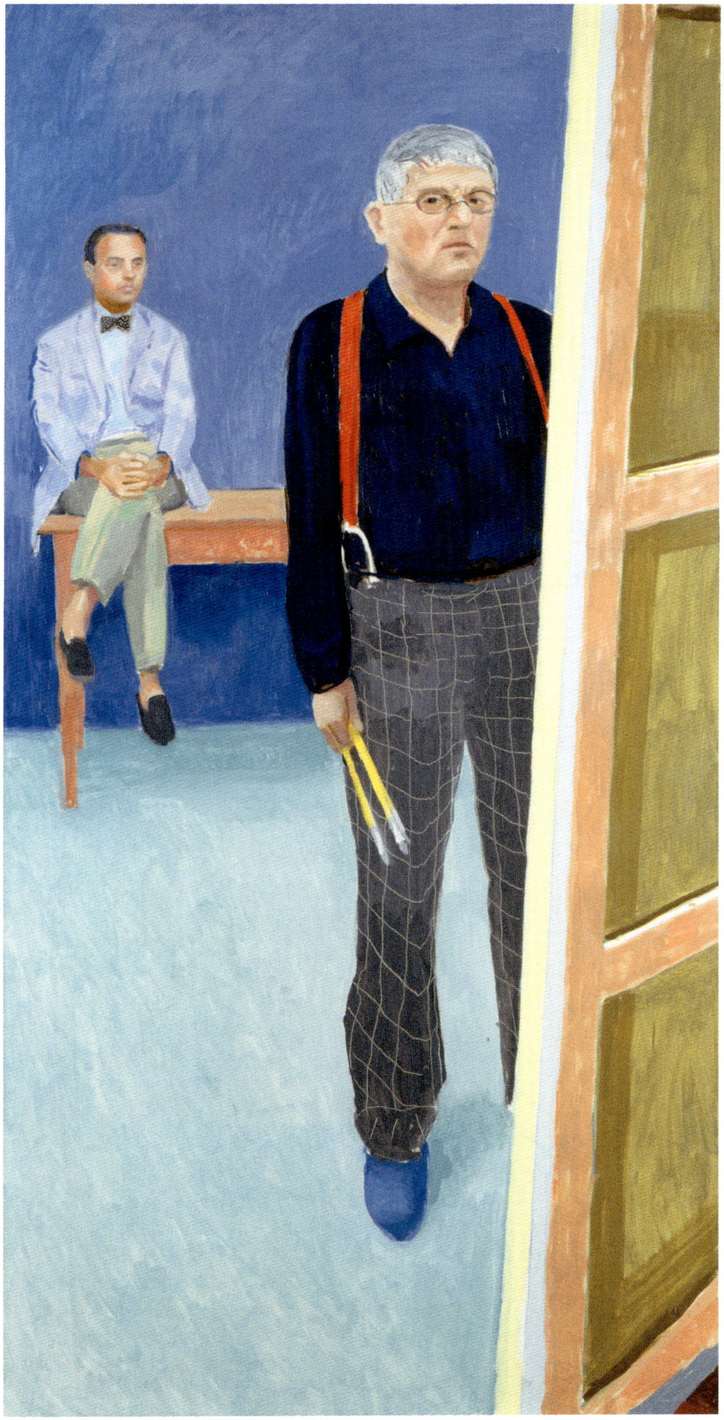

82 David Hockney (b.1937) and Charles Dare Scheips (b.1959) ('Self-Portrait with Charlie')

David Hockney, 2005

Oil on canvas, 1829 × 914mm
NPG 6819

David Hockney is one of the most celebrated British contemporary artists, whose work embraces drawing, painting, printmaking and digital technology. Born in Bradford, he studied at the Royal College of Art (1959–62). He was a leading figure in the pop art movement, before moving in late 1963 to California, where he found fresh inspiration, the swimming pool becoming a motif. In the 1970s Hockney also designed for the stage, his productions, including *The Rake's Progress* (1975) and *The Magic Flute* (1978), being performed at Glyndebourne and the New York Metropolitan Opera House.
In the late 1990s he began researching artists' use of mirrors and lenses through the centuries, publishing his discoveries in *Secret Knowledge* (2001). A series of portraits made with the aid of the camera lucida followed. His portrait drawings were the subject of the exhibition *David Hockney: Drawing from Life*, held at the National Portrait Gallery, London, in 2020.

Self-portraiture is an essential thread in Hockney's oeuvre. In periods of intense self-reflection, he has challenged himself to draw a self-portrait a day, sometimes over a number of months, from his candid charcoal drawings produced during the AIDS crisis in the 1980s to his iPad self-portraits exploring character types after Rembrandt. The self-portrait here is one of a series of almost life-size figure paintings made in Hockney's Hollywood Hills studio in 2005, all completed from life in just a few sittings. He worked directly onto the canvas in oils, without photographic reference or preparatory drawings. In the portrait, Hockney explores his fascination with mirrors and the theme of the artist and model. The work sets up a triangular exchange of gazes between the viewer, the artist and the seated figure, Hockney's friend and former studio manager Charlie Scheips, a New York-based curator.

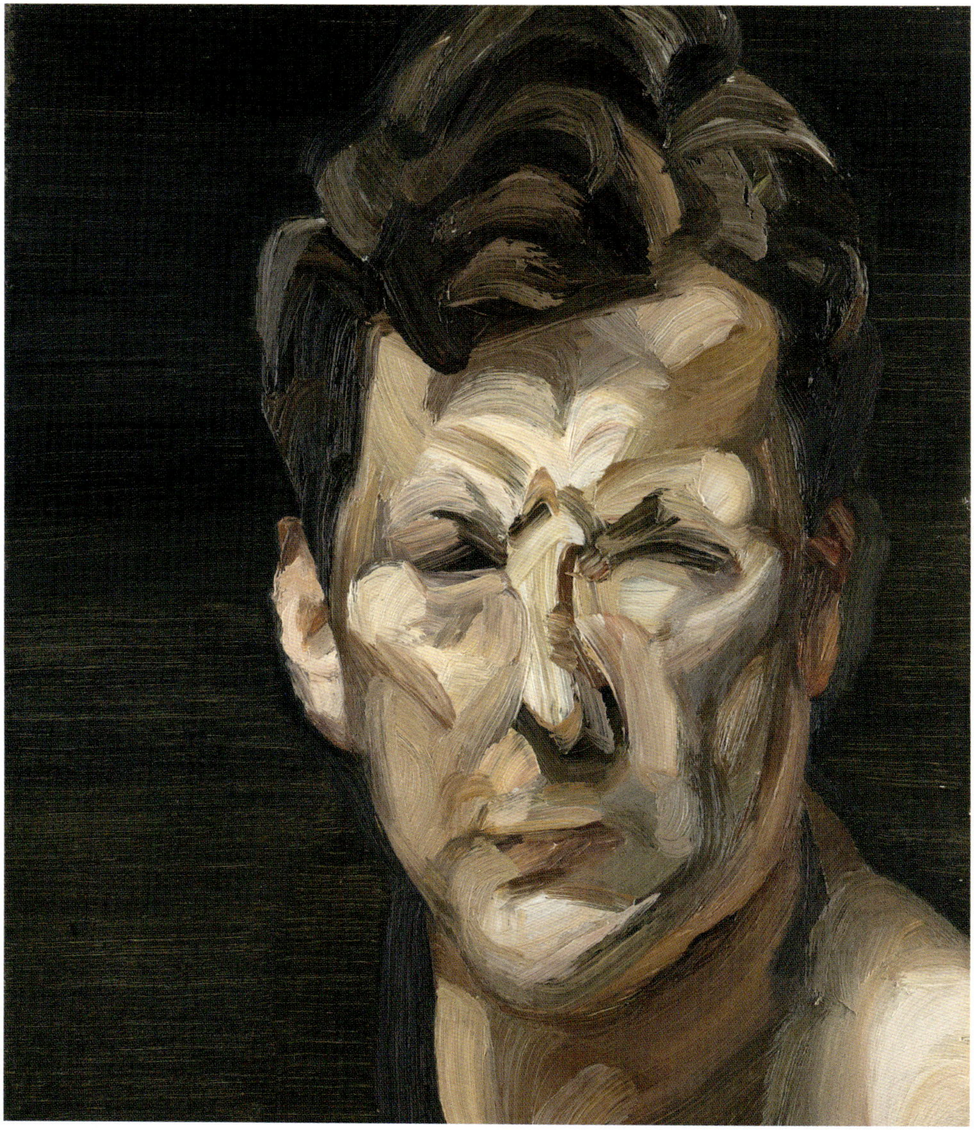

83 **Lucian Freud** (1922–2011)

Self-portrait, 1963

Oil on canvas, 305 × 251mm
NPG 5205

The artist Lucian Freud, grandson of Sigmund Freud, was born in Berlin and emigrated to England with his family in 1933. He briefly attended the Central School of Arts and Crafts in London and was also taught for a period by Cedric Morris, who influenced Freud's early precise style of painting. In the late 1950s, Freud began to adopt a looser, more expressive style, using hog's hair brushes to build a heavily impastoed surface. The result of many hours spent with sitters, his closely observed figurative works have been described as 'excessively' realist. The subjects are often naked and the scrutiny with which Freud consistently portrayed the human body distinguished him amongst fellow artists in the twentieth century.

In this painting, one of several self-portraits, Freud turned his uncompromising gaze upon himself. Yet the presence of the artist is implicit throughout his body of work, which includes portraits of lovers, children and friends, all of whom sat for him at his studios. As Freud himself has stated, 'My work is purely autobiographical ... it is about myself and my surroundings ... I work from people that interest me and that I care about.'

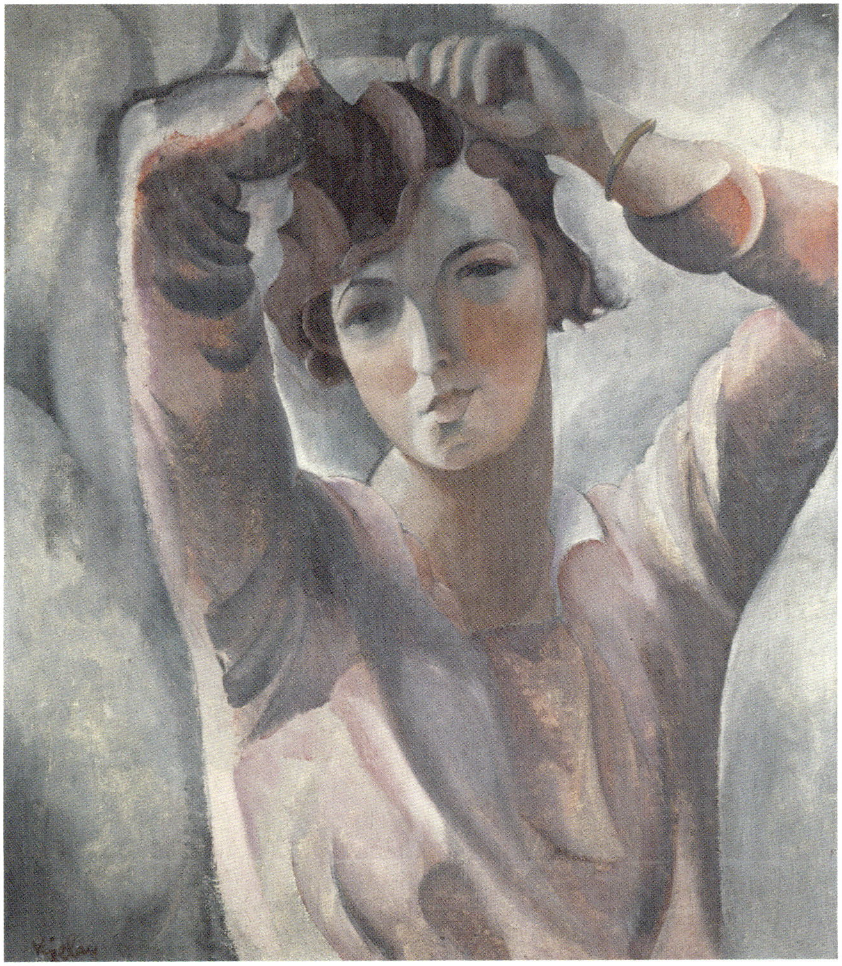

84 **Paule Vézelay** (1892–1984) **('Harmony')**

Self-portrait, *c*.1927–9

Oil on canvas, 651 × 543mm
NPG 6003

The painter, etcher, sculptor and textile designer Paule Vézelay was a pioneer of twentieth-century abstract art. Born in Bristol, she studied art there and, from 1912, joined the Slade School of Fine Art in London for a short time before leaving to study at the London School of Art under the cartoonist George Belcher. Her first solo exhibition took place in London in 1921, and several followed thereafter in Paris, Brussels and London throughout the 1920s and 1930s. 'English art then bored me to tears,' she declared in a 1984 BBC interview with the feminist writer Germaine Greer. Attracted by the avant-garde artistic developments then unfolding in Paris and also by contact with Henri Matisse, Joan Miró, Wassily Kandinsky, Juan Gris and other leading artists, she began exhibiting at the Salon des Surindépendants. Vézelay's entry into this alternative artistic world was a decisive influence, both personally and in terms of her development as an artist.

She settled in Paris in 1926 and changed her name from Marjorie Watson-Williams to Paule Vézelay, and her work became increasingly abstract. In 1934, she became a member of Abstraction-Création (an association of abstract artists), and this self-portrait reflects the pioneering abstract style that Vézelay developed in the group. Its bold, simplified forms manifest a transition from her earlier, impressionistic style towards more experimental work involving surrealist imagery and abstract shapes. A friend of the artistic couple Hans Arp and Sophie Taeuber-Arp, she exhibited with Arp, Wassily Kandinsky and Kurt Seligmann in Milan in 1938. Vézelay became one of the first British artists to abandon figuration entirely, but her contribution to the development of abstract art was largely overlooked until the 1980s.

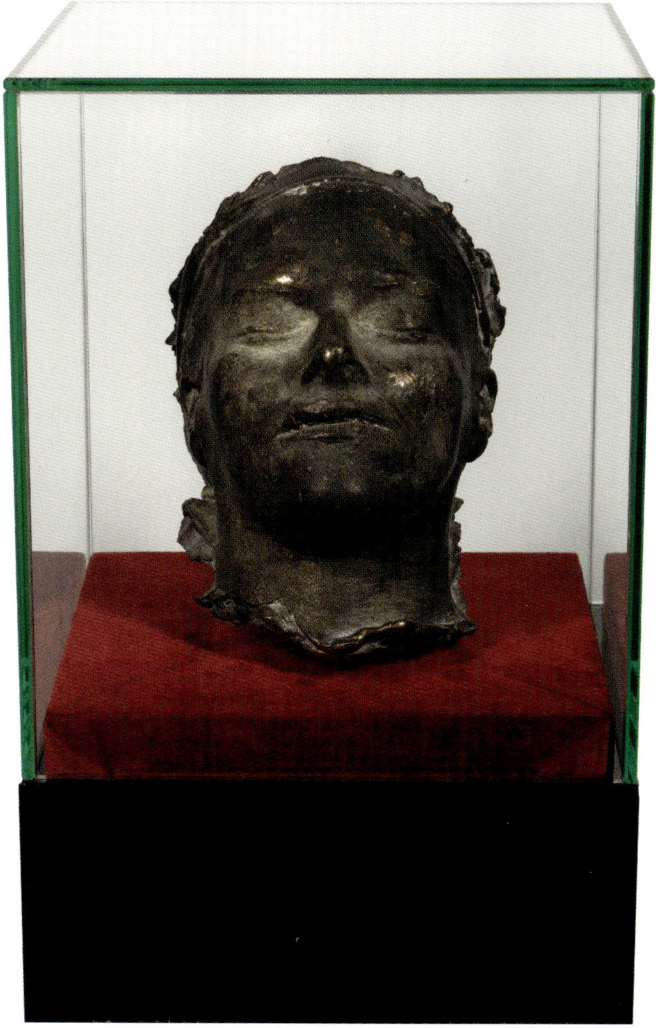

85 Tracey Emin (b.1963)
('Death Mask')
Self-portrait, 2002

Distressed bronze cast with gold plating, 195 × 175mm
NPG 7034

Tracey Emin grew up in Margate, Kent, studying at Maidstone College of Art (1986–8) and the Royal College of Art (1987–9). Thinking it would be her first and last, she titled her solo exhibition at the White Cube, London, *My Major Retrospective* (1993). Emin's confrontational and provocative work discloses the intimate details of her life across a range of media. Notable works include *Everyone I Have Ever Slept With 1963–1995* (1995), shown at Saatchi's *Sensation* exhibition (Royal Academy, 1997), and *My Bed* (1998), exhibited at the Tate Gallery for the Turner Prize shortlist in 1999. Emin represented Britain at the Venice Biennale in 2007, and was elected a Royal Academician in the same year. She was awarded a CBE in 2012.

Death Mask is Emin's first sculptural work in bronze. In an ironic reference to the autobiographical nature of her work, she cast her own 'death mask' during her lifetime. It is situated at the heart of her preoccupation with self-disclosure, and her constant engagement with and exploration of her own life and body. Emin has commented that in this work she offers herself in perpetuity as an enclosed specimen or museum display, literally transforming herself into an object for the scrutiny of generations to come.

86 Grayson Perry (b.1960)
('Map of Days')
Self-portrait, 2013

Etching from four plates, artist's proof, 1111 × 1515mm
NPG 6998

Born in Chelmsford, Essex, Grayson Perry studied fine art at Portsmouth College of Art (1979–82) and undertook pottery classes at the Central Institute from 1983. He was included in *Young Contemporaries* at the ICA in 1981, exhibited *Guerrilla Tactics* at the Barbican (2002), won the 2003 Turner Prize, and was awarded an OBE in 2013. His practice involves working primarily with ceramics, but has extended to include textiles and printmaking, through which he challenges traditional notions concerning the artist's status versus that of the artisan. His work explores a variety of contemporary and historical themes, offering a direct commentary on societal injustices and hypocrisies.

Map of Days is a highly unusual self-portrait, taking the form of a map of a walled city. Areas in and around the city correspond to the life events, experiences and emotions of the artist. Perry describes the city as dependent on the landscape in which it sits: 'I absorb the influences and the ideas of the landscape I find myself in.' This portrait was loosely inspired by a map depicting John Bunyan's 1678 allegory, *The Pilgrim's Progress*.

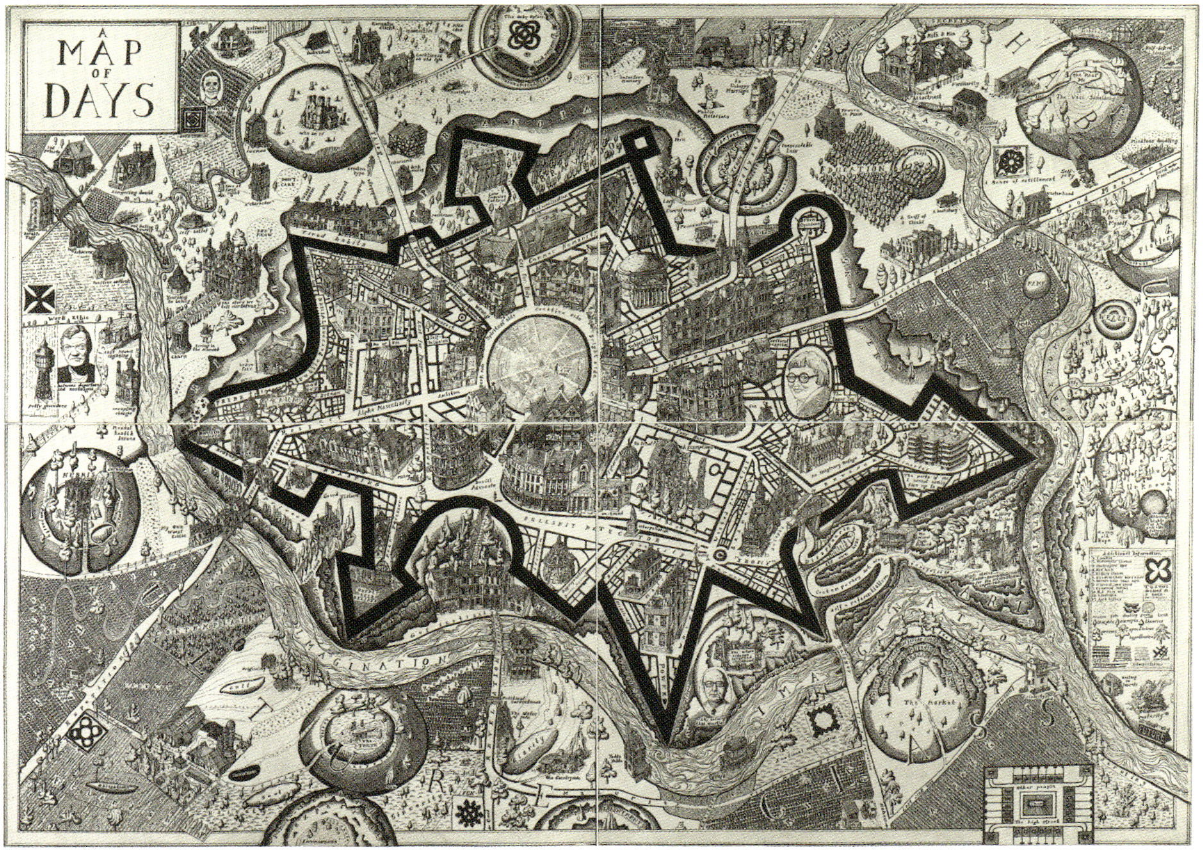

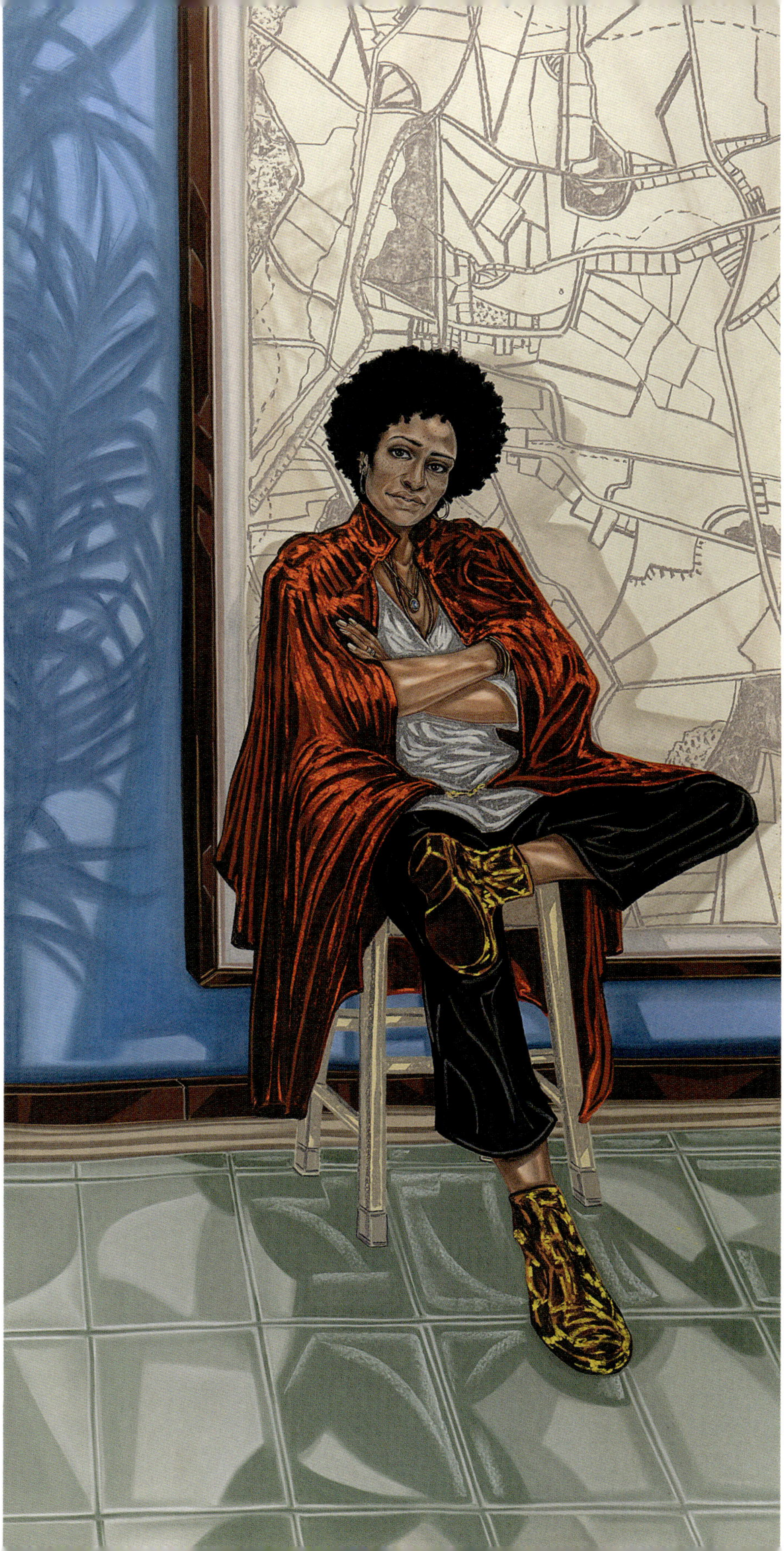

Zadie Smith (b.1975) ('Sadie')
Toyin Ojih Odutola, 2018–19
Pastel, charcoal, pencil and graphite on paper,
2235 × 1066mm overall
NPG 7105

Acquisitions Timeline by Tanya Bentley

The National Portrait Gallery was founded in 1856 to collect portraits of individuals who have made significant contributions to British history and culture, and continues to add to its Collections by purchase, gift, bequest and, since 1980, by commissioning portraits. Acquisitions are subject to the approval of the Board of Trustees and are guided by a formal collecting policy. 'Authentic likenesses of celebrated individuals' – as suggested in 1856 by Sir Charles Eastlake in a letter to the Gallery's first chairman, Lord Stanhope – continue to be prime considerations, even if the meanings of authenticity and celebrity have changed. The significance of the sitter has always been prioritised over the artistic quality of the portrait, and sittings that take place from life are also still preferred. The concept of a Primary Collection of portraits and a Reference Collection, or a study collection of prints, was established immediately after the Gallery's foundation. These Collections were extended in the 1960s to include photographs and, since 2017, popular, or ephemeral, portraits.

1856 The 'Chandos' portrait of William Shakespeare (see p.24) is the Gallery's first acquisition.

1857 William Wilberforce by Thomas Lawrence (see p.51) is the first portrait acquired by bequest, and Sir Walter Ralegh (see p.66) is the first portrait acquired by purchase.

A painting of the seventeenth-century courtier Elizabeth Hamilton, Countess of Gramont (NPG 20) is the first portrait of a woman to enter the Collection.

1861 Print collector and extra-illustrator Henry Witte Martin gifts a large collection of prints to the Reference Collection.

1871 A portrait of politician John Bright by Rupert Potter (NPG x4319) is the first photograph to be officially acquired by the Gallery.

1897 William Morris by George Frederic Watts (see p.29), acquired a year after Morris's death, eschews the usual ten-year rule regarding the acceptance of deceased sitters into the Collection.

1901 A photograph of Queen Victoria and her attendant Sheikh Chidda at Frogmore House (NPG P51) enters the Collection.

1904 The Gallery purchases twelve Camille Silvy daybooks containing around 17,000 carte-sized prints, including portraits of Sarah Forbes Bonetta (NPG Ax61384) and Adelina Patti (NPG Ax59127), taken in his London studio in the 1860s.

1914 The Gallery acquires the only surviving group portrait of the Brontë sisters, Charlotte, Emily and Anne, painted by their brother Branwell (see pp.94–5).

1917 The National Photographic Record is set up with the aid of photographer Walter Stoneman to record eminent living British figures, most of them men.

1921 The Gallery commissions group portraits of leading statesmen, and naval and army officers – including paintings by Sir James Guthrie (NPG 2463), Sir Arthur Stockdale Cope (NPG 1913) and John Singer Sargent (NPG 1954) – to commemorate the First World War.

1932 A portrait of Isabella Beeton, who wrote books on household management and cookery, by Maull & Polyblank (NPG P3) is the first photograph acquired for the Primary Collection under exceptional circumstances, as no painted portrait is known to exist. It was originally not deemed a 'real portrait', reflecting contemporary perceptions of the secondary status of photography.

1945 The Gallery reopens after the Second World War with a display of newly acquired Kit-Cat Club portraits, including poet and politician Joseph Addison (NPG 3193) by Sir Godfrey Kneller.

1968 Thomas Hudson's painting of composer George Frideric Handel (NPG 3970) becomes the first portrait purchased by a public fundraising appeal.

1969 Rules governing the acquisition of portraits change to admit living sitters to the Collection, demonstrating a move towards collecting contemporary representations of portraiture.

1970 The National Photographic Record closes in order to focus on the acquisition of portraits from a range of contemporary photographers.

1972–3 The Primary Collection of Photographs and Department of Film and Photography is established as photography is recognised as a major function of the Gallery. Numerous photographs are transferred to the Primary Collection, including portraits by Julia Margaret Cameron, and significant purchases are made, including the Hill and Adamson mammoth albums and Lewis Carroll negatives and prints.

1980 The annual Portrait Award is inaugurated for painters, and the contemporary commissioning programme is launched with a new portrait of Prince Charles by Bryan Organ (NPG 5365).

1984 A portrait of Samuel Coleridge-Taylor as a child is acquired, which is the first painted portrait of an identified black sitter purchased because of the sitter's own merits.

1994 Peter Gidal's 16mm film *Heads* (NPG 6827), showing influential art figures of the 1960s, is the first analogue film to enter the Reference Collection (later transferred to the Primary Collection in 2007).

2001 Marc Quinn's DNA portrait of geneticist Sir John Sulston (NPG 6591) is commissioned.

2006 A public appeal raises £1.6 million for the acquisition of a portrait of the poet John Donne (NPG 6790).

As part of its 150th anniversary celebrations, the Gallery stages the exhibition *David Hockney Portraits,* and acquires Hockney's *Self-Portrait with Charlie* (see p.127).

2008 A portrait of Mary Seacole by Albert Charles Challen (see p.32), discovered in a car boot sale in 2004, is acquired with support from the Heritage Lottery Fund.

2009 Tim Noble and Sue Webster's unusual silhouette portrait of Isabella Blow (NPG 6872), made up of fifteen taxidermy animals as well as Blow's lipstick and shoes, is acquired.

2012 The Gallery acquires a portrait of the Chevalier d'Éon by Thomas Stewart (see p.82), the earliest representation in the Collection of a person who is known to have presented as a man and as a woman in public life.

A posthumous painting of Amy Winehouse by Marlene Dumas (see p.76), sourced from media images, enters the Collection, marking a rare acquisition of a portrait not painted from life.

2014 The Sir Anthony van Dyck self-portrait (see p.118–19) is acquired by public appeal and with support from the Heritage Lottery Fund, the Art Fund, the Portrait Fund, the Monument Trust, the Garfield Weston Foundation, and numerous other trusts and foundations, major individual donors and members of the public.

2015 The Lucian Freud Archive is given to the Gallery through the Arts Council England's Acceptance in Lieu scheme.

Aspiration to ensure that 'social and cultural diversity' and 'a broad range of fields of endeavours' are considered when acquiring works for the Gallery is formalised in the Collections Policy.

2017 Pauline Boty's work (NPG 7030) represents the first stained-glass portrait in the Collection.

Following a major fundraising appeal, Sir Thomas Lawrence's unfinished portrait of the Duke of Wellington (NPG 7032) was purchased with support from the Art Fund (with a contribution from The Wolfson Foundation), the G and K Boyes Charitable Trust, the National Heritage Memorial Fund, Deborah Loeb Brice Foundation, the Portrait Fund, and many contributions from the public.

Forty photographs by Simon Frederick – including a portrait of Archbishop of York John Sentamu (NPG P2071) – are acquired for the Primary Collection, recognising the profound impact of black individuals on British culture.

The Gallery begins collecting 'popular portraits' with funding from the Art Fund New Collecting Award.

2018 A portrait of Dylan Thomas by Augustus John (see p.25), originally on a twenty-year loan to the Gallery, is purchased with support from the Art Fund (with a contribution from the Wolfson Foundation), the National Heritage Memorial Fund and The Thompson Family Charitable Trust.

Under-represented groups, including women and sitters from minority social, cultural and ethnic backgrounds, are listed as a key focus for acquisitions in the Gallery's Collections Policy.

2018–19 The Gallery partners with the Outset Contemporary Art Fund to commission portraits of Malala Yousafzai by Shirin Neshat (see p.62) and Jonathan Ive by Andreas Gursky (NPG P2081).

2020 A commissioned portrait of the writer Zadie Smith by Toyin Ojih Odutola (see p.132) enters the Collection, representing a step towards the Gallery's commitment to increase the representation of women and black sitters and artists within the Collection.

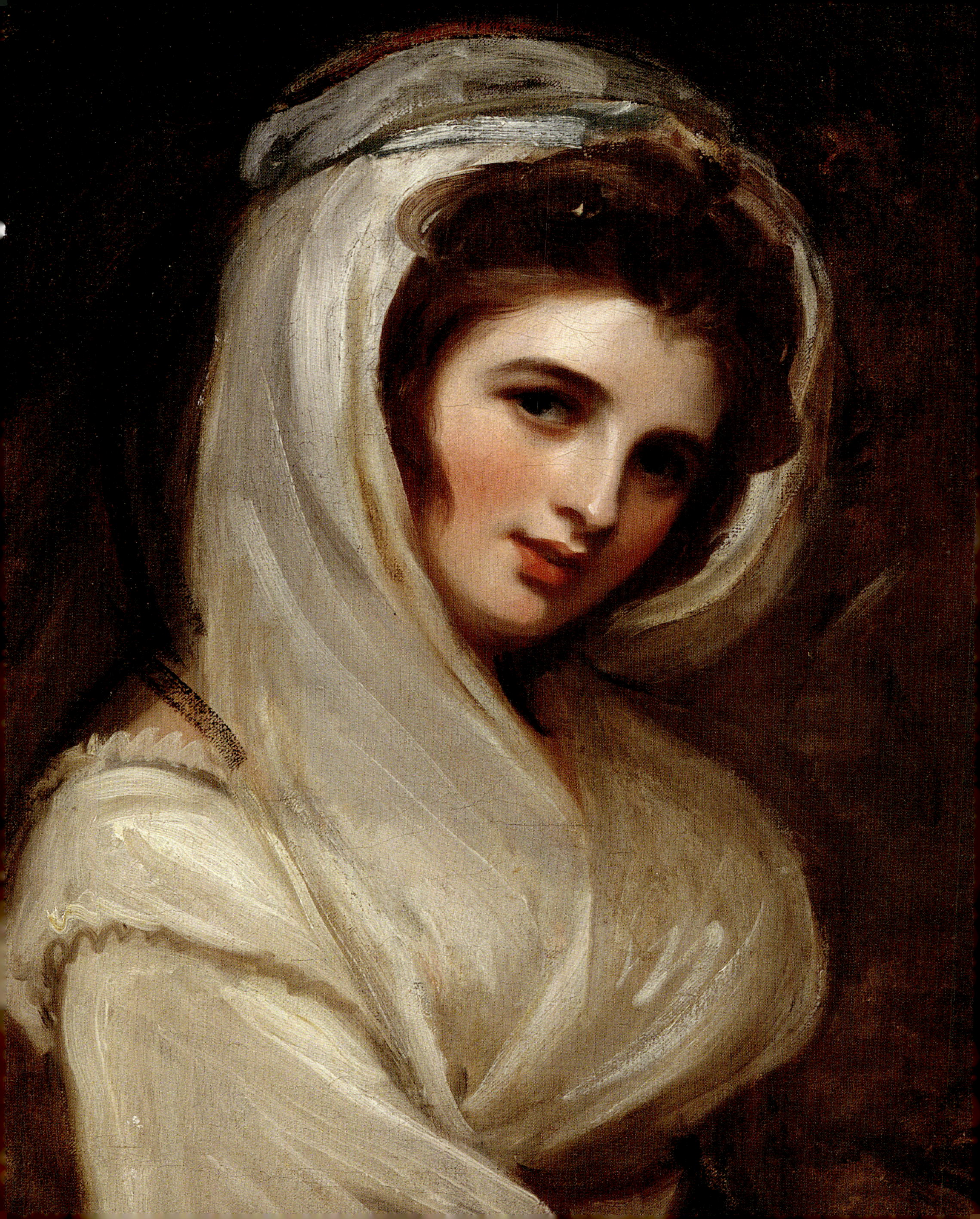

Select Bibliography

Barthes, Roland, *Camera Lucida* (London, 1993)
Brilliant, Richard, *Portraiture* (London, 1991)
Campbell, Lorne, *Renaissance Portraits* (New Haven and London, 1990)
Cannadine, David, *National Portrait Gallery: A Brief History* (London, 2007)
Cooper, Tarnya, ed., *National Portrait Gallery: a Portrait of Britain* (London, 2014)
Pointon, Marcia, *Hanging the Head: Portraiture and Social Formation in Eighteenth-Century England* (New Haven and London, 1993)
Rideal, Liz, *Self-portraits* (London, 2005)
Schneider, Norbert, *The Art of the Portrait* (Cologne, 1994)
Solkin, David H., *Art in Britain 1660–1850* (New Haven and London, 2015)
Strong, Roy, ed. *The British Portrait 1660–1960* (Woodbridge, 1991)
West, Shearer, *Portraiture* (Oxford, 2004)
Woodall, Joanna, ed., *Portraiture: Facing the Subject* (Manchester, 1997)

The captions accompanying the images draw on material from a range of National Portrait Gallery publications, and these sources are listed below with the page numbers of the relevant captions. These were compiled and edited by Tanya Bentley, Charlotte Dunbar and Rab MacGibbon, who also authored the six section openers.

100 Fashion Icons (2019): 58
100 Photographs (2017): 56, 76, 97, 108
100 Pioneering Women (2017): 26, 38, 75, 112, 129
100 Portraits (2016): 94
Anarchy & Beauty: William Morris and His Legacy 1860–1960 (2014): 29
Audrey Hepburn: Portraits of an Icon (2015): 108
Cecil Beaton's Bright Young Things (2020): 93
A Guide to Contemporary Portraits (2009): 105, 112
A Guide to Victorian and Edwardian Portraits (2011): 52
Mirror Mirror: Self-portraits by Women Artists (2001): 123, 125
The National Portrait Gallery (1997): 67
npg.org.uk: 31, 34, 36, 42, 46, 55–7, 67, 76, 78, 87, 89, 91–4, 97, 101–2, 113, 121, 124, 127
A Portrait of Britain (2014): 26–9, 49–51, 53, 57–8, 63, 66, 70, 72, 83, 85–6, 89, 96, 103–4, 110–11, 114, 118, 120, 122, 127–9
A Portrait of Fashion: Six Centuries of Dress at the National Portrait Gallery (2015): 55, 83, 121, 126
Thomas Lawrence Portraits (2010): 102
Tudor & Jacobean Portraits (2018): 24, 46–7, 84, 100
Tudors to Windsors: British Royal Portraits (2018): 46–8, 72–3
Van Dyck: The Last Self Portrait (2014): 118
Victorian Giants: The Birth of Art Photography (2018): 107
Vogue 100: A Century of Style (2016): 39

DETAIL **Emma Hamilton, c.1785**

Notes to pages 9–20:

1 Thomas Carlyle quoted by Lord Stanhope, Parl. Debs. (series 3), vol.140, col.1772 (4 March 1856).
2 Resolutions by the second meeting of the National Portrait Gallery Board of Trustees, 16 February 1857.

Acknowledgements

The National Portrait Gallery, London

This book was inspired by the Gallery's international touring exhibition *Icons and Identities*. We are most grateful to its curators, Rab MacGibbon and Tanya Bentley, for their roles in creating, authoring and editing the book and the exhibition. We are also deeply grateful to all the Gallery's curators for their contributions and expertise, including Charlotte Bolland, Rosie Broadley, Clare Freestone, Sarah Howgate, Magda Keaney, Catharine MacLeod, Sarah Moulden and Lucy Peltz. We particularly wish to thank Alison Smith, Chief Curator, for her guidance, support and tireless championing of the project.

In addition to thanking our partner venues, we are also grateful to Qatar Museums for their generous loan of the portrait of Ayuba Suleiman Diallo to the exhibition.

At the National Portrait Gallery, our thanks also go to Sarah Tinsley, Executive Director of Programmes and Partnerships; Melanie Pilbrow, Head of International Programmes; Imogen Haines, International Projects Manager; Ted McDonald-Toone, International Partnerships Manager; Richard Hallas, Senior Conservation Manager; Stuart Ager, Frames Conservation Manager; Karl Lydon, Art Handling Manager; and all their teams. Thanks are also due to Tijana Todorinovic for her expert guidance in project-editing the book, as well as to Anna Starling, Kara Green and Mark Lynch for their work on this publication, and all the staff who have contributed to realising the exhibition and the present volume.

Nicholas Cullinan
Director, National Portrait Gallery, London

Fries Museum, Leeuwarden

The Fries Museum is one of the Netherlands' leading museums on portraiture and identity. In recent years, it has developed its international profile with award-winning exhibitions on famous Frisians such as Sir Lawrence Alma-Tadema, Mata Hari, M.C. Escher, and Rembrandt and his Frisian bride Saskia. Connecting our story to that of the National Portrait Gallery was a logical step along that path.

We are most grateful to the National Portrait Gallery and the National Museum of Korea for their dynamic collaboration during challenging COVID-19 times. Bringing the exhibition to the Netherlands was only possible through the support of our partners: the Province of Friesland; the Municipality of Leeuwarden; the Ministry of Education, Culture & Science; and the BankGiro Lottery. Our thanks also go to all the museum colleagues and collaborators who made the exhibition and this accompanying publication possible.

Kris Callens
Director, Fries Museum, Leeuwarden

Index of Sitters and Artists

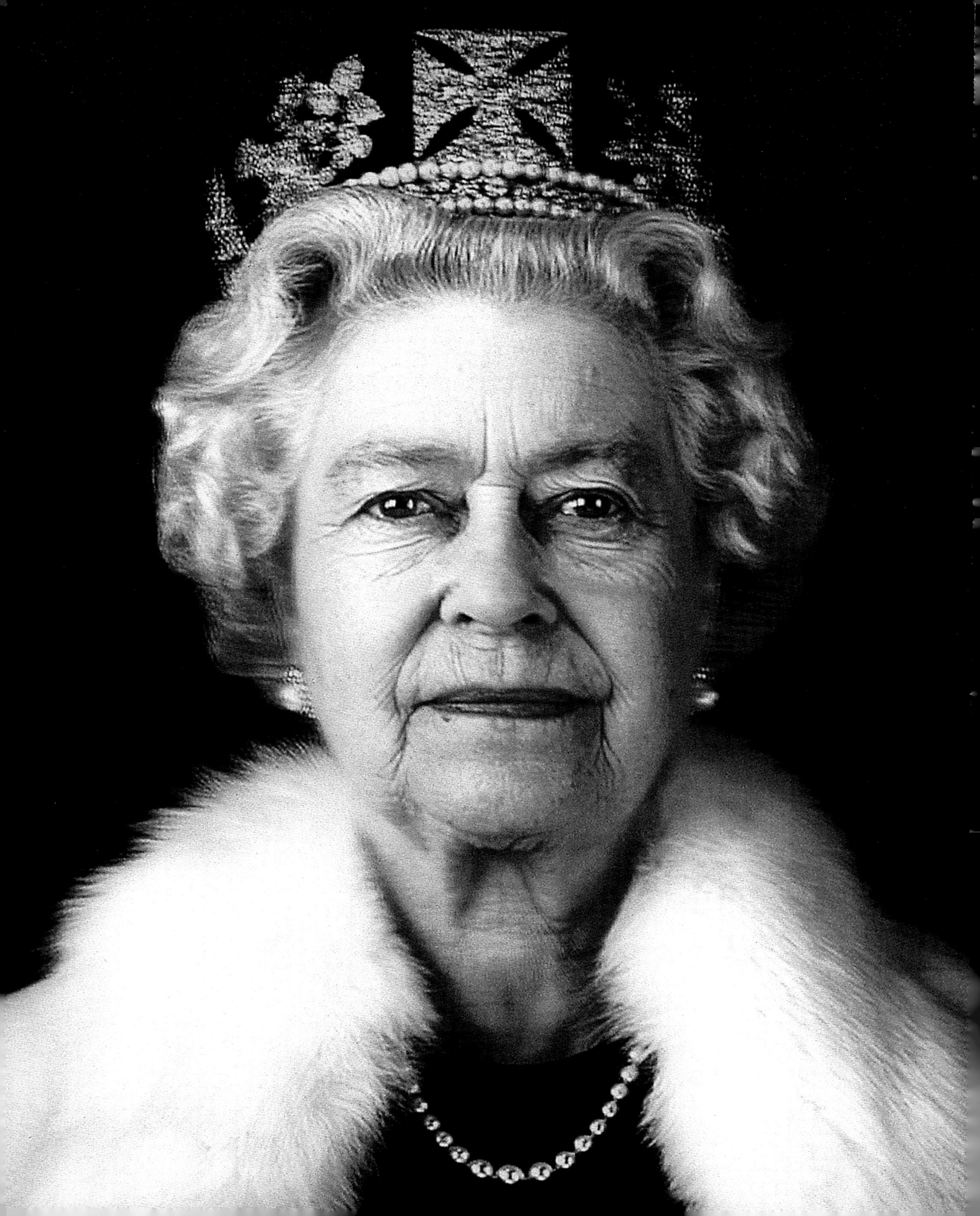

Picture Credits

The National Portrait Gallery would like to thank the copyright holders for granting permission to reproduce works illustrated in this book. Every effort has been made to contact the holders of copyright material, and any omissions will be corrected in future editions if the publisher is notified in writing.

All works are © National Portrait Gallery, London, unless otherwise noted.

pp.2–3, pp.58–9 © Alex Katz/VAGA at ARS, NY and DACS, London 2021. Purchased with help from the Art Fund, 2010; p.4, p.126 © estate of Doris Clare Zinkeisen. Purchased, 1999; p.7, p.24 Given by Francis Egerton, 1st Earl of Ellesmere, 1856; p.8, p.120 Purchased, 1876; p.11 Purchased, 1876; p.13 Rijksmuseum Amsterdam; p.14 Courtesy of Luke Walsh. Purchased, 1992; p.15 Bequeathed by Harold Lee-Dillon, 17th Viscount Dillon, 1932; p.16 Accepted in lieu of tax by H.M. Government and allocated to the Gallery, 1975; p.17 Purchased with help from the Art Fund, 1987; pp.18–19 © Stephen Willats. Purchased, 2004; p.20 Given by Cordelia Curle (née Fisher), 1959; p.21 © Marc Quinn. Photo: Marc Quinn studio. Courtesy: Marc Quinn studio. Purchased with help from the Art Fund, the Henry Moore Foundation, Terry and Jean de Gunzburg and ProjectB Contemporary Art, 2009; p.22, p.42–3 © Lorenzo Agius. Purchased, 2000; p.25 © The Estate of Augustus John/Bridgeman Images. Purchased with support from the Art Fund (with a contribution from the Wolfson Foundation), the National Heritage Memorial Fund and The Thompson Family Charitable Trust, 2018; p.26 Bequeathed by John Neale, 1931; p.27 Transferred from Tate Gallery, 2015; p.28 Given by the sitter's son, William Erasmus Darwin, 1896; p.29 Given by George Frederic Watts, 1897; p.30 © Colin Davidson. Purchased, 2017; p.31 Given by Mrs D.E. Knollys, 1934; p.32 Purchased with help from the National Lottery Heritage Fund and Gallery supporters, 2008; p.33 Purchased with help from the Art Fund, 1936; p.34 Photograph by Karsh, Camera Press, London. Given by the photographer, Yousuf Karsh, 1991; p.35 Snowdon/Vogue 1981 © Condé Nast Publications Ltd. Given by Vogue on behalf of Antony Charles Robert Armstrong-Jones, 1st Earl of Snowdon, 1982; pp.36–7 © Norman Parkinson Archive/Iconic Images; p.38 © Mario Testino. Purchased, 2003; p.39 Patrick Demarchelier/Vogue © The Condé Nast Publications Ltd. Given by Condé Nast, 2016; p. 40 © Don McCullin (Contact Press Images). Purchased, 1983; p.41 © David Bailey. Purchased, 2001; p.44, p.57 Photograph by Jillian Edelstein, Camera Press, London. Purchased, 2006; p.46 Purchased, 1974; p.47 Purchased with help from the Art Fund, 1965; p.48 Purchased with help from the Art Fund, 1965; p.49 Transferred from British Museum, 1879; p.50 Purchased, 1982; p.51 Given by the executors of Sir Robert Harry Inglis, 2nd Bt, 1857; p.52–3 Purchased, 1933; p.54 Given by William Henry Smith, 3rd Viscount Hambleden, 1938; p.55 © Norman Parkinson Archive/Iconic Images. Given by the photographer, Norman Parkinson, 1981; p.56 Commissioned; made possible by J.P. Morgan through the Fund for New Commissions, 2014; p.60 © Martin Parr/Magnum Photos. Given by Martin Parr, 2020; p.62 Commissioned by the NPG, 2018 with support from Scott Collins and Lotta Ashdown, in partnership with Outset Contemporary Art Fund; p.63 Purchased with help from the Art Fund and the National Lottery Heritage Fund, 2002; p.64, p.76 © Marlene Dumas; courtesy of the artist and Frith Street Gallery, London. Purchased with help from the Art Fund, 2012; p.66 Purchased, 1857; p.67 Purchased with help from the National Heritage Memorial Fund and the Art Fund, 1987; p.68–9 © Cecil Beaton Studio Archive. Accepted in lieu of tax by H.M. Government and allocated to the Gallery, 1991; p.70–1 Purchased with help from the Art Fund, 1970; p.72 Purchased, 1991; p.73 Purchased, 1976; p.74 Purchased with help from the National Heritage Memorial Fund, 1985; p.75, p.136 Purchased with help from the Art Fund, 1965; p.77 © Lee Miller Archives, England 2021. All rights reserved. leemiller.co.uk. Purchased, 2004; p.79 © Mario Sorrenti/Art Partner. Purchased with help from the proceeds of the 150th anniversary gala, 2007; p.80, p.93 © William Hustler and Georgina Hustler/National Portrait Gallery, London. Given by the photographer's sister, Susan Morton, 1976; p.82 Purchased, 2012; p.83 Bequeathed by Una Elena Vincenzo (née Taylor), Lady Troubridge, 1963; p.84 Given by Harold Lee-Dillon, 17th Viscount Dillon, 1925; p.85 OM.762. Orientalist Museum, Doha. Lent by Qatar Museums Authority: Doha: Qatar, 2010; p.86 Purchased with help from the National Heritage Memorial Fund, the Art Fund and the Pilgrim Trust, 1986; p.87 Purchased with help from the National Heritage Memorial Fund, 1987; p.88 © Richard Avedon Foundation. Given by the photographer, Richard Avedon, 1995; p.89 Given by Robert R. Steele, 1939; p.90 Given by the Art Fund, 1965; p.91 Given by Delmar Banner, 1948; p.92 Given by the photographer's sister, Susan Morton, 1976; p.95 Purchased, 1914; p.96 Photo Duffy © Duffy Archive & The David Bowie Archive™. Purchased, 2013; p.97 © Snowdon. Given by Antony Charles Robert Armstrong-Jones, 1st Earl of Snowdon, 2013; p.98, 109 © reserved; collection National Portrait Gallery, London. Purchased, 2007; p.100 Purchased with help from the National Heritage Memorial Fund, the Art Fund, the Portrait Fund, L.L. Brownrigg, John Morton Morris, Paul Dacre, and many other donations, 2008; p.101 Purchased, 1929; p.102 Purchased with help from the Art Fund and the National Heritage Memorial Fund, 1992; p.103 Bequeathed by Henry James, 1916; p.104 Given by the sitter's widow, Mrs Anna Henley, 1913; p.105 Purchased, 1995; p.106 Purchased, 2017; p.110 Purchased, 1994; p.111 © The Estate of Patrick Heron. All rights reserved, DACS 2021. Purchased with help from the Contemporary Art Society, 1965; p.112 Commissioned; made possible by J.P. Morgan through the Fund for New Commissions, 2018; p.113 © 2020 The Andy Warhol Foundation for the Visual Arts, Inc./Licensed by DACS, London. 2021. Purchased, 1994; p.115, p.142 © Chris Levine. Given by The People of Jersey, 2012; p.116, p.128 © The Lucian Freud Archive/Bridgeman Images. Purchased, 1978; p.119 Purchased with support from the National Lottery Heritage Fund, the Art Fund in honour of David Verey, CBE (Chairman of the Art Fund 2004–14), the Portrait Fund, The Monument Trust, the Garfield Weston Foundation, the Aldama Foundation, the Deborah Loeb Brice Foundation, Sir Harry Djanogly, CBE, Mr and Mrs Michael Farmer. Matthew Freud, Catherine Green, Dr Bendor Grosvenor, Alexander Kahane, the Catherine Lewis Foundation, the Material World Foundation, The Sir Denis Mahon Charitable Trust, Cynthia Lovelace Sears, two major supporters who wish to remain anonymous, and many contributions from the public following a joint appeal by the National Portrait Gallery and the Art Fund, 2014; p.121 Purchased, 1892; p.122 Purchased, 1858; p.123 © Bowness. Bequeathed by Dr Priaulx Rainier, 1987; p.125 Given by the sitter and artist, Gluck (Hannah Gluckstein), 1973; p.127 © David Hockney, Collection National Portrait Gallery, London. Purchased with help from the proceeds of the 150th anniversary gala and Gift Aid visitor ticket donations, 2007; p.129 Purchased, 1988; p.130 © Tracey Emin. All rights reserved, DACS 2021. Purchased with support of the Art Fund, White Cube and the Artist, 2017; p.131 © Grayson Perry and Paragon | Contemporary Editions Ltd. Purchased with support of the Art Fund, White Cube and the Artist, 2017; p.132 © Toyin Ojih Odutola. Courtesy of the artist and Jack Shainman Gallery, New York. Purchased with support from Zekiye Cingillioglu, 2020.

DETAIL **Queen Elizabeth II, 2012**

Published in Great Britain by National Portrait Gallery Publications
National Portrait Gallery
St Martin's Place
London WC2H 0HE

Published to accompany the exhibition: *Icons and Identities*
This exhibition is organised by the National Portrait Gallery, London, and will tour to the National Museum of Korea and the Fries Museum in The Netherlands.

Every purchase supports the National Portrait Gallery, London.
For a complete catalogue of current publications, please visit our website at www.npg.org/publications

Cover: Malala Yousafzai, 2018 (detail). © National Portrait Gallery, London. Commissioned by the NPG, 2018 with support from Scott Collins and Lotta Ashdown, in partnership with Outset Contemporary Art Fund.
pp.2–3: Dame Anna Wintour, 2009 (detail)
p.5: Doris Zinkeisen, exhibited 1929 (detail)
p.6: William Shakespeare, *c.*1600–10 (detail)

ISBN 978-1-85514-718-8

A catalogue record for this book is available from the British Library.

10 9 8 7 6 5 4 3 2 1

Director of Commercial: Anna Starling
Publishing Manager: Kara Green
Project Editor: Tijana Todorinovic
Picture Researcher: Mark Lynch
Proofreader: Patricia Burgess
Design: Raymonde Watkins

Printed in Italy by Printer Trento
Origination by DL Imaging

FSC www.fsc.org MIX Paper from responsible sources FSC® C015829